How to Write

Powerful

Fund Raising Letters

Other books by Herschell Gordon Lewis:

Direct Mail Copy That Sells
How to Make Your Advertising Twice as Successful at Half the Cost
How to Handle Your Own Public Relations
The Businessman's Guide to Advertising and Sales Promotion
More Than You Ever Wanted to Know About Mail Order Advertising
Herschell Gordon Lewis on the Art of Writing Copy
Open Me Now!

As co-author:

Spirit of America: Norman Rockwell
Everybody's Guide to Plate Collecting

How to Write *Powerful* Fund Raising Letters

Herschell Gordon Lewis

Bonus Books, Inc., Chicago

Except for appropriate use in critical reviews or works of scholarship, the reproduction or use of this work in any form or by any electronic, mechanical or other means now known or hereafter invented, including photocopying and recording, and in any information storage and retrieval system is forbidden without the written permission of the publisher.

Library of Congress Catalog Card Number: 88-64123

International Standard Book Number: 0-944496-05-9

Bonus Books, Inc.
160 East Illinois Street
Chicago, IL 60611

99   98   97   96   95   6   5   4   3   2

Composition by Point West Inc., Carol Stream, IL

Printed in the United States of America

Contents

Acknowledgments

I am deeply indebted to Ms. Rita Smith of the National Taxpayers Union and Mr. Joseph Kachorek of St. Jude Children's Research Hospital. These two fund raising experts graciously shared with me the results of several test mailings and allowed me to share them with you in turn. The tests form the basis of Chapter 5.

My favorite proofreader, Ruth Moffett, did her usual superlative job of finding mistakes in typesetting I had missed.

Prime mover in this project has been my full-time partner, professionally and personally. . . my wife Margo. I'm completely dependent on her help, advice, and creative suggestions, and this book reflects her organizational and creative abilities as much as my own.

—Herschell Gordon Lewis
Plantation, Florida, 1989

CHAPTER *1*

"Our Organization Is Different"

"We need your help."

Cancer-fighting organizations say it. Hospitals say it. Homes for wayward children say it. Colleges and universities say it. Museums say it. Libraries say it. Symphony societies say it. Funds for threatened wildlife species say it. Public television stations say it.

And that's exactly what's wrong with it.

The Advantage of Creative Scar-Tissue

I've written as much fund raising copy as anybody in this business.

(I use the term "business" advisedly, because any fund raiser with stars in front of his or her eyeballs is going to waste a lot of money pleading for dollars that don't come, before losing the job or scuttling the organization altogether.)

Over the years I've had a lot of winners, *plus* enough losers to give me scar-tissue where those stars once might have been. If you're in this business for keeps, writing an occasional loser doesn't make you gun-shy; rather, it sharpens the sights on your rhetorical rifle. You know what *not* to do next time.

Don't Be Cowed by Tradition

Somebody once said, "The only thing we learn from history is that we don't learn from history."

If you're reading this book you're a fund raising professional. You aren't looking for entertainment. You're looking for solid ways to boost response to your direct mail.

Unless you're an inflexible tyrant running a fund raising oligarchy, you *know*: The deadliest sentence in fund raising is...

"We always do it this way."

The guy who *should* be a donor but who has resisted your last eight "We need your help!" cries isn't going to cave in because you plead, "We need your help!" a ninth time. He's stoically resistant, unmotivated by the human reality of your cause.

"We always do it this way" generates that wasted ninth letter. "Let's try this on him" might be a waste, too. . . or it might bring his first contribution.

Who could have dreamed, ten years ago, how many fund raising giants would stoop to sweepstakes? Here we have hypocrisy from both fund raiser and fund giver. But it works—for some. If it works, philosophy quickly changes from "It isn't dignified" to "It works." That's how organizations stay alive.

"Why Should I Give to YOU?"

A sweepstakes, with its headaches and gigantic annoyances, is one solution to the gray sameness of appeals. But, thank the good Lord, it isn't the only way to add octane to your mailings. Here's a *partial* list of tests any fund raiser can try:

> —Letter length.
> —"You" versus "we."
> —Letter from a victim.
> —Tear-jerking episode.
> —"Thank God."
> —"You made it possible."
> —Personal thanks from an individual who was helped.

—Mechanical tricks (see section in chapter 4).
—Demand for a yes/no answer.
—Multiple computer personalizations.
—Laser-printed "handwritten" greeting.
—Powerful p.s.
—Two separate letters.

Bear in mind, please: I warned you, it's a *partial* list. Variety is limited only by your imagination. But CAUTION: Limit your imagination with good business sense.

What We Aren't Covering

This book is about fund raising letters.

Obviously the letter is only one possible component. Many mailings have a separate response device (often stupidly complex, to confound the donor at the moment of truth). Many have a descriptive brochure. Some have exotic enclosures, such as the venerable Foote System mini-notebook of donor names, a wonderful guilt-generator if you don't return it. Some have another guilt-generator, the giveaway—such as a pencil, a sheet of stamps, a coin, a scratch-off card, or a certificate.

To prevent this book from being unwieldy, the publisher has limited it to letters. Letters. It's a logical move, because if you can write effective fund raising letters, components other than a response device become either easy to do or unnecessary.

How to Test

In five words: Test in and test out.

Here's what this means: Suppose you have a mailing which pulls just enough to pay for itself. It isn't a big winner but it isn't a loser.

That becomes the "control."

Don't try a 50–50 test of your brilliant new idea against the control. That's the short road to more scar-tissue. Instead, mail 70 percent to 80 percent of your next mailing with the control letter and 20 percent to 30 percent with your "challenger."

Let's then suppose the challenger wins. *It* becomes the control. The next brilliant idea tests in against it, again on a 20 percent to 30 percent basis. This is the road to success in testing. The road to perdition is paved with brilliant new ideas which totally replaced the old workhorse letter, without testing.

Now, what if you *don't* have a successful mailing? Everything you've tried has been a loser.

Then reverse the numbers. Mail 70 percent to 80 percent of the new concept. After all, you have little to lose.

The reason you're mailing 20 percent to 30 percent of the best-pulling letter you've had so far is to enable you to keep score. Without a yardstick, you can't determine the actual effectiveness of your mailing. It might have succeeded because of national news or because nobody else was mailing. It might have flopped because of national news or because many others dropped their mail at the same time. You need the comparison.

Oh, yes, one more point: Keep testing. Somewhere, out there in limbo, is the approach that will double your response. Never quit looking for it, because while you're looking you'll chance upon two or three approaches that add five percent to 10 percent.

Add enough five percents and you're a sure winner.

CHAPTER 2

"They," Please . . . Not "I"

I suppose there's a place for arrogance in fund raising—if you're Lee Iacocca and your project is the Statue of Liberty.

But what if you're Sophie Glutz and your project is a new roof for the local gymnasium?

Then you'd better hit the "search" key and change some of those "I"-references to "You"-references. And if you're sending a letter to the local Coca-Cola bottler, you'd better be sure he 1) knows what you're talking about and 2) sees some benefit to the community *and* himself.

Why? Because every goat goes to the same pond to drink. We aren't the only ones clamoring for eleemosynary dollars. Self-importance isn't much of a sales argument to somebody who doesn't know you or your cause, however worthy either of you might be.

Put Some Schmaltz in the Letter

My wife is on the board of an organization which supports the local symphony orchestra. She came home from a meet-

ing, fuming: "Look what they expect us to mail to business leaders."
This is the letter she's supposed to mail:

"Break The Ice" Letter To Make an Appointment

(DATE)
Mr. John Doe

Dear Mr. Doe:

Enclosed please find information on the new Performing Arts Center being built in Broward County. As a member of one of the Performing Arts Centers major support groups, I would like to make an appointment with you to discuss some of our projects and how you, as a business leader, can get involved.

This $42 million dollar Performing Arts Center will have a positive economic impact on our South Florida area. I will call you within (five days or other time) to make an appointment regarding this major project.

In advance, I want to thank you for your time and commitment to bettering our community. I am looking forward to working with you.

Sincerely,

Now, suppose you were teaching a fifth grade class in letter-writing and a student handed in this exercise. What grade would you put on it?

If grammar is a factor I wouldn't grade it at all. I'd hand it back for rewrite, pointing out the need for an apostrophe in "Performing Arts Centers major support groups" and the redundancy of "$42 million dollar."

But grammar is a symptom here, not the ailment. May I suggest: If you don't see anything wrong with *Enclosed please find,* take another look at your own letters for pomposity and non-communication.

Let's dig a little deeper into this proposed letter. Direct response fund raising doesn't differ all that much from the world of commerce, which means we can apply the Specifics Superiority Principle:

> ## Specifics outsell generalities.

So when we write, "I would like to make an appointment with you to discuss *some of our projects,"* we've lapsed into generalization. What projects? Why not *the* project? Why have we put this cart—what *we* care about—before the horse—what the *message-recipient* cares about?

Why, too, do we emphasize the $42 million? This means we've set our goals and budgets without consulting the business leaders we now ask to back those goals and budgets.

And "I'm looking forward to working with you"? Okay if the person we're writing to has asked us to be general contractor on a tunnel; not okay if we're thoughtlessly suggesting he has to roll up his sleeves while we natter illiterately at his side.

Too Brutal a Judgment?

Am I being too harsh? I don't think so.

Why? Because this is the opening gun. It may be, in fact, our only shot. The letter is neither businesslike nor personal, wavering in limbo somewhere between those logical poles. And it's typed flush-right, adding a touch of uncalled-for formality that rivals "Enclosed please find."

A Ridiculously Easy Rule— And Three Sub-Rules

A ridiculously easy rule can make a surprising difference in the pulling-power of fund raising mailings to cold lists. I call this the Anti-Hair-Spray Copy Rule:

> ## A neatness complex will cost you.

Three Sub-Rules help explain the Anti-Hair-Spray Copy Rule.
Sub-Rule 1:
Use a typewriter face for a fund raising letter.
Why? Because fascination with laser-printers has made a lot of fund

raisers gadget-happy. We see letters typeset in Times Roman because Times Roman is one of the printer fonts. Times Roman has about as much personalization as gray paint.

Sub-Rule 2:

Ragged right is more readable and more personal than flush-right.

Readership study after study backs up this point. Since we have evidence, why not profit from it?

Sub-Rule 3:

Indent the first line of paragraphs, to enhance personalization.

Don't you, in personal letter-writing, indent paragraphs? This is a personal letter, isn't it?

The Anti-Hair-Spray Copy Rule and its sub-rules are true because of a broader psychological truism:

Emotion outsells intellect.

Typesetting is intellectual. Typewriting is more emotional. Handwriting is the most emotional of all, but it's textually inconvenient and hard to read in large blocks.

Neatly engineered paragraphs maintain an arm's-length relationship with the message-recipient. This is the exact reverse of what we want our fund raising letters to accomplish.

So What Should We Say?

Let's take the John Doe letter and re-structure it, bearing the Anti-Hair-Spray Rule in mind. We'd come up with something like this:

Dear Mr. Doe,

    I'd like you, as a business leader in our community, to consider taking an active role in making Broward County's new Performing Arts Center a reality.

    Aside from its positive economic impact on our area, the Center will bring prestige and leading cultural activities—sorely overdue, I think you'll agree—to Broward.

On behalf of a support group formed
solely to make the Performing Arts Center a
reality, I can tell you frankly: It can't happen
without the support of those who have the
power and know-how to inspire—movers and
shakers such as you.

Of course I'm aware of the many
demands on your time. Can you spare me a few
minutes so I can explain the vital (but not
time-consuming) role we'd like you to play? I'll
call you in a few days to find out.

Thanks for your attention . . . and
your help.

Sincerely,

What's missing from this second version? "Enclosed please find" has gone to its well-deserved limbo. "A support group" replaces the phrase "one of the major support groups," which emphasized the existence of many such organizations (both references weaken the value of *our* group, but we can't claim exclusivity unless we have it). Importance without a major time commitment on the part of the message-recipient is keyed, and a little warmth replaces the overall brassiness of the original letter.

Take Off the Spats and Monocle

If your fund raising letters aren't pulling the way they used to, take a look at their structure. Are they formal? Are they peppered with "we shall" instead of "we'll," "you are" instead of "you're," "I have" instead of "I've"? Are they neat blocks of copy with all paragraphs the same approximate length?

Consider taking the spats and monocle off your copy. Fund raisers are communicators. If we send out a stiffly formal communication we deserve a stiffly formal reply.

CHAPTER 3

The Three Monumental Commands

You can be the brightest, most clever fund raiser yet born.

You can be a mathematical wizard, a master of database analysis.

You can be a top executive whose crisp decisions enable the work-flow to channel perfectly.

What have these attributes to do with writing effective fund raising letters?

Nothing.

Correction: Less than nothing. They're a *minus* attribute for force-communication.

If you ignore the three monumental commandments, your mailings will die. No amount of cleverness, database juggling, or executive ability can save them.

In my opinion very close to 100 percent of failed fund raising mailings shoot themselves in the foot, either because the writer didn't know these commandments or because arrogance overrode them.

Natural arrogance is the enemy of force-communication in any form. In fund raising, it's the most common way to build a gap between you and prospective donors or, worse, to irritate them.

The First Commandment

The first commandment is the Clarity Commandment.

Whatever you're writing...whoever your target is...however worthy your cause...if you ignore this commandment, you're slashing the guts out of your appeal.

The Clarity Commandment is simple enough:

> *Clarity is paramount over any other ingredient of your mailing. Without clarity, you've transmitted no message. Without a message, the target-individual can't respond.*

The chief enemy of clarity is "in-talk." BEWARE of acronyms, of governmentalese, of initials instead of words. Within the office, you and your associates may refer to the ABP all day every day and know it's the *A*utomatic *B*lood *P*ump. But how about those people out there?

Sure, you've spelled out automatic blood pump four paragraphs back. Now you revert to your in-talk, and it's ABP. Asks your target: "ABP? Is that American Beet Producers? Associated Banking Partners?" Not privy to the automatic interchange of letters for phrases, the reader feels left out. Omission = apathy.

Using big words is another enemy of clarity. A sophisticated fund raiser, in copy on the outer envelope of a mailing, referred to industrial ne'er-do-wells dumping "a plethora of chemicals" into the rivers. Okay, you and I know *plethora* doesn't mean "fresh fish." But how about those people out there? Why show off your massive vocabulary, risking obfuscation? (Which is what this last sentence just did.)

A subrule helps:

Write inside the experiential background of the typical donor. Forget your own.

Who is our typical donor? If we don't know, safety lies in clarity. Highly educated individuals know the less-formidable words as well as the obscure ones.

Clarity means using short sentences. It means having no paragraphs longer than seven lines and occasional paragraphs of one line or even a few words.

THE MOST SERIOUS LACK OF CLARITY: Not telling the reader what you want him or her to do.

The Second Commandment

The second Commandment is the Emotion-Over-Intellect Commandment.

The Emotion-Over-Intellect Commandment, like the Clarity Commandment, is simple enough:

An emotional appeal will outpull an intellectual appeal.

Academicians are notoriously poor communicators, because they feel appealing to human emotions is somehow an admission of a less-than-supreme position. Their textbooks reflect this contempt for person-to-person communication.

Take a look at a mailing whose appeal was logical rather than emotional. Snip off the spats and throw away the monocle. Peel off the layer of rhetorical insulation holding dynamite out of the communication.

Logic has its place in a debate...but we aren't debating with prospective donors, we're asking them for money. We're competitive not only with parallel eleemosynary organizations but with every other nonprofit institution.

If the reader's vocabulary can't connect with your rhetoric, you're costing yourself both rapport and contributions. I mentioned Greenpeace using the word *plethora* on an envelope. How many recipients—including some highly-educated ones—tossed the envelope into the waste-basket because they didn't know the word?

(This parallels the old vaudeville joke: The lifeguard says, "Sir, I just resuscitated your daughter." The farmer yells, "Then, by God, you'll marry her!")

Some of the examples we'll dissect in future chapters suffer from Debater Syndrome. They reflect an anachronism, an era before the Age of Skepticism and the "Me" Generation dawned. In those golden times, it was possible for a fund raiser to squeeze dollars out of the populace, who hadn't yet turned to stone.

No more. Oh, it's possible the person who hasn't given you money before just didn't know where to send a check. But it's hundreds of times more likely that person doesn't recognize your need as *his* need or *her* need. What chance do you have if you don't tell that target-individual, "It's up to you"?

Effective commercial direct response appeals to one of four great motivators—Fear, Exclusivity, Guilt, and Greed. Fund raisers have an extra weapon: Anger.

Anger applies primarily to either an extremist position or an attack on an extremist position. "Stand up and be counted!" won't sell merchandise, but it *will* raise funds.

If you accept the logic of these five motivators, you'll quit writing analytical appeals, appeals for equipment and buildings, and explanatory appeals. You'll switch to a motivational appeal.

And every one of the five great motivators is *emotional.*

Fear is the most powerful of the five, but for that very reason it's the most difficult to control. Fear can turn on its creator, a golem or Frankenstein's monster, by generating anger or resentment instead of fear.

Exclusivity is the easiest of the five to mount. Advisory boards, boards of trustees, charter memberships, Committees of 100—these are built on exclusivity.

Greed is the basis for the sweepstakes and scratch-off craze. Today's society is increasingly greed-oriented. As dispassionate commentators we can criticize the state of our world; as fund raisers we can use our knowledge to make greed work for us.

Guilt can bring money from individuals who never had any intention of supporting our cause. The ability to induce guilt is in direct ratio to our knowledge of *who* is reading the message. That's why guilt is an excellent re-animator of dormant donors. "How did we fail you? Where did we go wrong? Don't you still care?" These work when "Johnny is dying" or "The Russians are coming!" doesn't work.

And anger? A letter beginning, "I'm sick and tired of..." or "I'm fed up with..." can bring blood out of a stone if the pace holds up and the writer carefully ties "you" to "me."

The Third Commandment

The third Commandment:

Milk your donors.

If you've been a fund raiser for more than two hours, you know it's almost impossible to overcircularize your bank of existing contributors. They not only are seven times more likely to respond to an appeal than a cold list name; they're your family, and you can go back to your family time and time again. The saturation factor is far down the line, if it exists at all.

Think of the family as a single unit. What affects one affects all. That's why hospitals can circularize former patients, schools can circularize alumni, save-the-animals groups can circularize travelers to wildlife areas, save-the-environment societies can circularize scuba divers, and save-our-parks clubs can circularize tennis players and golfers.

Really, it's no different from a neighborhood, threatened by a land developer, calling on homeowners. It's the *In-Group Assumption.*

CAUTION: If you want your targets to *feel* like an in-group, treat them as family. Give them certificates and membership cards (gold ones for regular donors, "Advisory Board" membership for heaviest donors). Your family deserves no less.

A "Bonus" Suggestion

What's wrong with this appeal, from the Ellis Island Foundation?

"Donations are desperately needed."

Right. Two problems here. First, the Foundation doesn't give us a clue about exact use of the donations. Sure, money will rebuild Ellis Island. Sure, many of our grandparents came through Ellis Island. But this loose cry of "Help!" doesn't grab us.

Second—and a worse error—the statement is *passive,* not *active.* Passive voice not only is less emotional than active voice; it has a graver problem: Both organization and prospective donors are *outside* the orbit, not inside it.

An absolute rule: Active voice will bring in more contributions than passive voice. And while you're at it, stay out of the subjunctive. "Could" and "would" have fractional power compared with "is" and "will."

Implementing one of these changes might mean a $1/10$ percent improvement. So why not do it?

CHAPTER 4

Today's Fund Raising Letter-Writing "Marketplace"

No question about it: Fund raising has problems today it never faced before, say, 1987.

First of all, scandals have rocked the fund raising world. Much of this concerns religious broadcasters, but we all know how we're tarred with the evangelical brush.

Tax deduction tightening, stringent postal regulations, Internal Revenue Service scrutiny, and above all public skepticism have made us bums before we can even claim to be heroes.

Overuse of celebrities damages the effectiveness of *any* celebrity use because the public thinks they're watching a commercial. Sports heroes mumble unconvincingly about one cause or another in dully-produced television spots, then get arrested for cocaine use, sabotaging every fund raiser's use of professional baseball, football, or hockey players.

So what's the mailing weather forecast for the 1990s?

Sweepstakes, Scratch-Offs, and Such

We look back at 1987 as the Year of the Sweepstakes. We look back at 1988 as the Year of the Scratch-off. We look at 1989 as the Year of the Premium. We look to the 1990s as Years of Increasingly Competitive Attention-Getters.

What's wrong with that?

Really, nothing. Realists among fund raisers, who know the value of new-name recruitment and the difficulty (and almost impossible cost) of acquiring a new donor without making *a competitive offer,* don't feel it's hypocritical to make an offer the recipient can't refuse. Certainly this approach is more logical than turning on the tear-ducts, wildly hoping the reader will synchronize.

Yes, you bet this is a hard-boiled approach. What matters is survival, and altruism isn't a universal-enough motivator for a fund raiser to use with any effectiveness.

Tell you what: You appeal to the reader's sense of decency. I'll appeal to one of the five great motivators—fear, exclusivity, guilt, greed, and anger. I'll match your response dollar for dollar with one keyboard-hand tied behind my back.

"But Is It Legitimate?"

Fund raisers see giant sweepstakes operators such as Publishers Clearing House accomplish a lovely masquerade: The reader enters a sweepstakes and may subscribe to one or more publications as he or she does.

Certainly the same mailing, offering the same groups of magazines but lacking the sweepstakes incentive, would fail. Certainly the sweepstakes concept is one of the most powerful fund raising techniques we have available to us today.

And certainly mailing a sweepstakes offer is one of the most complex and sophisticated undertakings a fund raiser can undertake. Where unwary fund raisers can run into grief is ignoring the word "may" which precedes the word "subscribe"—and also precedes the word "contribute." Technically, offering a sweepstakes and insisting on a contribution to qualify is illegal.

I heard this point discussed by the staff of a regional nonprofit organization. The (astonishing to me) conclusion: "Enough local officials are on our board to keep the post office from bothering us."

My opinion: Stay away from any promotion which gives grist to *any* critic. One of the direct marketing publications reported a fund raising sweepstakes offer that tried to mask the mandatory "no contribution necessary to enter" in tiny type set solid on the backside of the entry form and that required a personal check marked "Void" to enter, if the individual didn't actually contribute. Clever? Yes. Dangerous? Yes.

The law on premiums is equally clear. You mail an *unsolicited* premium—a necktie, or a solar calculator, or a notebook, or a pen, or, most commonly, seals and/or stamps—and expect a contribution in return. Leaning heavily on *guilt* is an accepted and sometimes admirably professional fund raising practice. Failing to clarify that the recipient is under no obligation to contribute is a flat violation of the law.

Remember, in considering borderline ethics: You're damaging the entire cause of fund raising by mail. Copy accompanying your holiday seals should be potent enough to generate contributions without resorting to marginal tricks with disaster-potential.

And How Much Does It Cost You?

Masking imaginative sterility by spending more money on your mailing can be self-defeating.

Does computer-personalization outpull non-personalized appeals? Usually. Does it outpull by enough margin to justify the extra cost? *Sometimes.* That's one reason we test. (See previous chapter.)

In my opinion the most commanding weapon we have is a convincing, earnest, apparently heartfelt letter that reaches the reader within his or her own experiential background. If that works, *then* start experimenting with adjuncts.

(A variation: "Apparent value." Nonprofit organizations such as Consumers Union don't say, "We need help"; they say, *"You* need help." Delivering apparent value for the dollar separates this genre from conventional fund raisers, philosophically—which dictates copy-thrust. This book includes samples.)

Frequency, Timing, and "Who?"

How often can you mail?
No answer exists. A general rule might be:

> *You can't overcircularize donors who have contributed more than once within a calendar year.*

> **Mail to existing once-a-year donors four times a year.**
> **Mail to lists whose demographics indicate a matchup twice a year. Assume each "speculative" mailing is a one-shot, but be ready to move new donors into their properly upgraded categories.**

Does each mailing have to pay for itself? The answer lies in your organization's resources and long-range goals. A donor name has value. If you regularly mail and produce results just a little below the break-even point, keep going. Adding new names to your donor list will pay off.

And how much lead-time do you need? Most of the sophisticated fund raising mailers I know plan their schedules a year ahead. They don't schedule actual copywriting until about three months before mailing, to avoid running afoul of political or economic changes which can cause a letter written too early to obsolesce.

The "Who?" question can affect lead-time. An unfortunate circumstance seems to be: The less-experienced the organization, the greater the number of people involved in approving a piece of copy.

Committees can't write effective copy. One paragraph goes hopelessly out of key with another, and steam can't build up because of seepage between elements.

If you're cursed with committee approval, give your mailings a better chance of success by designating one individual to give final approval.

This contact person deals with the writer, either showing samples of acceptable previous mailings or giving the writer a typed-out sheet of guidelines. When the letter comes in, the contact person circularizes copies among committee members. Based on their comments—and committee members do comment, whether they have anything to say or not—the contact person goes back to the writer with final suggestions, if any.

If you have this cumbersome superstructure, include an absolute deadline for committee comments. Once the deadline is imposed, enforce it. Otherwise your mailings haven't a prayer of going out on time.

Follow the Yellow Brick Road

People will send money to causes they think affect them. That's a genuine challenge if your cause is unrelated to the experiential background of the recipient, who sees no personal affinity to your cause. And that challenge is a primary reason for the existence of this book.

So the trick is telling the reader, "YOU can make a difference. One day YOU or YOUR family might be better off because YOU had compassion and foresight. And you'd better make your commitment and your positive move right now."

Getting the commitment...holding the donor...and upgrading, upgrading, upgrading...these are the components of successful fund raising letter writing in the 1990s.

CHAPTER 5

The Advantage of Letter Tests

Two of the most astute mailers in the world of fund raising are the National Taxpayers Union, Washington, DC; and St. Jude Children's Research Hospital, Memphis, Tennessee.

An indication of the statesmanship of these two organizations is their willingness to share information from the many tests they continually run. Some of these tests are more highly sophisticated than the average mailer would ever mount.

With deep gratitude to Ms. Rita Smith of the National Taxpayers Union and Mr. Joseph P. Kachorek of St. Jude Children's Research Hospital, we reprint one letter test from each organization.

The National Taxpayers Union Letter Test

Which letter pulled best? Read all three, then decide—before looking at the actual results, page 37.

(Actually, this was a "package" test as much as a letter test, because envelope treatment differed. For that reason we're reproducing the envelopes as well as the letters.)

Package No. 1

Jack Warren Wade, Jr.
Washington, D.C.

Dear Taxpayer,

Please. . . for your own good, take every word in the enclosed letter very seriously.

As a former IRS agent, I can assure you that innocent taxpayers are harrassed by the IRS on a regular basis.

And believe me, nothing is worse than to see a hard-working American financially destroyed at the hands of the IRS. . . when it turns out he owed them NOTHING.

Please get involved. . . Help Jim Davidson from the National Taxpayers Union get the TAXPAYERS BILL OF RIGHTS PASSED through Congress as soon as possible.

If you know what's good for you, I advise you to do everything in your power to help.

I know I will because even I fear the power of the IRS and their abusive practices.

Sincerely,

Jack Warren Wade, Jr.
Former IRS Revenue Officer

24

NATIONAL TAXPAYERS UNION
325 Pennsylvania Avenue S.E.
Washington, D.C. 20003 • (202) 543-1300

Dear Concerned Taxpayer:

I need your help now to stop the IRS.

We must stop the IRS from trampling on the rights of thousands of law-abiding citizens.

No other agency of the government, <u>none</u>, has the power of the IRS. In the name of tax collecting they can take your house, almost all of your wages, your bank account, and almost any personal possession you own.

And they can do it, even if you're not guilty, or don't owe any taxes.

You see, the IRS acts as if you are "guilty until proven innocent."

That's what I want to stop.

If the IRS even thinks that you're guilty of tax evasion, tax fraud, or delinquency, <u>just thinks it</u>, they can come after you, ruthlessly.

That's wrong.

That's why I need your help in getting the Taxpayers' Bill of Rights passed in Congress.

The Taxpayers' Bill of Rights will protect you and all Americans from the abuse of power by

Over, Please

Page 2

the IRS.

It was introduced because of the horror stories told to Congress by American citizens.

- Americans like the Olivers of Fairbanks, Alaska who were sitting in their car when IRS agents broke the windows, dragged them out of the car, and then took the car to satisfy claims of back taxes.

- Americans like several parents who said their children were held captive in a back room of their local day care center by IRS agents who wouldn't release them until an agreement had been reached with the school to pay back taxes.

- Americans like Pennsylvania businessman Thomas Treadway who was left flat broke after the IRS incorrectly said he owed $247,000 in back taxes, interest, and penalties. The IRS started seizing everything in sight — including $22,000 from his girlfriend's bank account. He actually owed only $11,000. After five years, and $75,000 in legal bills, a federal court ruled that the IRS was wrong. By then Thomas Treadway was broke. Treadway says he felt as if he had been living in an invisible prison for five years. The IRS employee responsible for this fiasco got a raise and a promotion.

- Americans like Joseph B. Smith, Jr., a

Next Page, Please

senior IRS revenue officer and manager for 18
years, now retired, who revealed a Nevada dis-
trict office memorandum that instructed revenue
officers to seize property "as soon as possible"
and to put "as little space between the
(taxpayer's) back and the wall as possible."

- Americans like a Colorado woman who owed
just $1,725 in taxes. The IRS took her $50,000
home and sold it — for $1,725.

<u>You may not be safe from the IRS — even if
you owe them nothing!</u>

I'm not trying to scare you.

But, until there are more controls put on the
IRS, no one, not you or anyone else, is safe from
their abuse.

Right now there is not enough protection
against the IRS improperly seizing your money,
your house, your wages, or almost anything you
own.

More frightening is the fact that IRS employee promotions are often based on their col-
lections — correct or incorrect.

The burden of proof is on you to prove your
innocence — not the IRS' to prove your guilt.

Right now, the National Taxpayers Union is
Over, Please

leading the way in pressing Congress to enact S.
604 in the Senate and H.R. 1313 in the House, the
Taxpayers' Bill of Rights.

For the first time in decades, maybe ever,
there is a good chance to put a leash on the IRS.

The Taxpayers' Bill of Rights (S. 604) is a
bill that will protect you. It will:

- Establish an ombudsman with the power to
STOP or RELEASE unfair or illegal IRS seizures;

- Shift the burden of proof from you to the
IRS;

- Stop the IRS from promoting or grading its
employees based on the money they collect or the
property they seize from the taxpayers, innocent
or guilty;

- Establish a watchdog who will closely
monitor IRS actions and protect the taxpayer from
abuses;

- Stop the IRS from singling out certain
groups or individuals for "special attention"
because of their beliefs or associations;

- Require the IRS to stick to an installment
plan it agrees to, rather than change its mind

Next Page, Please

Page 5

and suddenly seize your property, and;

   - Require the IRS to advise taxpayers of
their rights before being subjected to an audit
interview.

   The time has come to stop IRS abuse.

   And the Taxpayers' Bill of Rights is a critical step.

   Hearings have been held, and NTU was just one
of the first witnesses testifying on the critical
need for a Taxpayers' Bill of Rights.

   This legislation has strong support.

   Senator David Pryor, the chairman of the U.S.
Senate Finance Subcommittee on IRS Oversight is
the chief sponsor of the Taxpayers' Bill of
Rights. He will fight — and fight hard — for
passage of this essential legislation.

   Believe me, this time there is a real chance
of putting some real control on the overzealous
IRS.

   Here's how I plan to do it:

   1) We must pay the expenses of abused taxpayers who are broke — like Thomas Treadway — to
come to Washington and testify about their horrible treatment from the IRS before the appropri-

                                 Over, Please

Page 6

ate congressional committees.

   2) We must lobby members of Congress to sign
on as sponsors of this important legislation.
Right now there are 43 cosponsors. More are
needed.

   3) We must be prepared to challenge any IRS
resistance. We must retain expert advisors to
refute IRS arguments against this bill.

   4) We must generate a nationwide avalanche
of support for the Taxpayers' Bill of Rights
through mass mailings.

   5) We must see that this issue gets maximum
media coverage.

   The National Taxpayers Union has been serving
the American Taxpayer for over 19 years.

   We've saved you and other taxpayers billions
of dollars by stopping government waste and over-
spending by blocking outrageous tax increase
schemes.

   Now we need your help.

   Our annual dues are only $15. Not only will
your dues help us mount our nationwide campaign
to pass the Taxpayers Bill of Rights, but with
your dues you will receive our eye-opening news-

                              Next Page, Please

letter, <u>Dollars and Sense</u>. It will bring you our annual Congressional Spending Study, our Taxpayers Action Guide, and discounts on publications and conferences.

We can't afford to let time slip away. We must keep the pressure on Congress to pass this bill soon, before they lose interest.

I want the Congress to know that this bill has the support of the American people. Please join NTU <u>and</u> tell your representative and your two senators that you support the Taxpayers' Bill of Rights.

I can assure you, if enough pressure is put on the Congress, it will pass the bill, soon.

<u>Help me stop the IRS from ruining the lives of innocent people.</u> Please send a check to NTU today so we can mount a nationwide tidal wave of support for this bill.

Your donation will be used to put pressure on Congress to pass the Taxpayers' Bill of Rights.

If this bill is passed you and your family will be protected from IRS persecution.

And, to get it passed, you need to do your

Over, Please

part.

After all, you're really protecting yourself from what is now an uncontrolled government agency.

Don't delay. This could easily be the most important contribution you've ever made.

You're really helping protect yourself.

What better reason could you have?

Sincerely,

Jim Davidson
Chairman

P.S. Truly this bill, the Taxpayers' Bill of Rights, will protect every innocent American from the heavy-handed abuses of the IRS. Remember, today you have few rights when you're dealing with the IRS. With the passage of the Taxpayers' Bill of Rights, you'll have the power to stop unfair IRS tactics. Don't delay — get back to me today with a generous contribution. Thank you.

Package No. 2

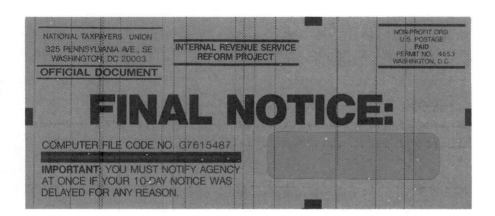

Internal Revenue Service Reform Project
A project of the National Taxpayers Union
325 Pennsylvania Avenue, S.E.
Washington, D.C. 20003

☆☆

I hope this envelope didn't scare you -- but citizens all around us are getting NOTICE and DEMAND letters from the IRS and you need to be prepared. Sometimes these Demand Notices are for several thousand dollars; sometimes for less -- and sometimes for much more.

 But often nothing is actually owed -- the NOTICE was simply produced as the result of a computer error. When this happens, the real human beings in the IRS offices are often powerless to do anything -- once the computer has triggered the automatic tax collecting procedures.

You can be given 10 days to pay up -- or the IRS can take your bank account, seize your car -- and even sell your house -- often without further warning. To make matters even worse, the IRS sometimes seizes property without taxpayers even getting the Final Demand notice.

The result can be sheer horror for the innocent victim.

You could be next . . . unless you take action!

☆☆

Fellow Taxpayer:

Will you take the 30 seconds required for this action now?

Will you take 30 seconds to demand of Congress: **Pass the Taxpayers Bill of Rights?**

Unless you take this 30 seconds now, you could be the next law abiding citizen casualty of an IRS computer error -- IRS employees could confiscate your bank accounts, seize your car, put a lien on your house -- or worse -- all by mistake and without a court order!

For your sake -- for the sake of your family -- please take 30 seconds now to demand of Congress: Pass the Taxpayers Bill of Rights! Do this by marking YES on the enclosed ballot and return it in the enclosed postage-paid envelope.

Your ballot is part of the Official National Election commissioned for the Congress of the United States by the National Taxpayers Union.

Why do we need a Taxpayers Bill of Rights? **So the kind of horror inflicted on our fellow taxpayers already caught by IRS mistakes and computer errors won't ever happen to you and your family.** Put yourself in the place of -- say, Tom Treadway.

Mr. Treadway testified to the Senate Committee on IRS oversight that the IRS totally destroyed him and his business. They presented him with an assessment for $247,000. He testified: "They stripped me of everything and even seized $22,000 out of my girlfriend's bank account for my alleged tax liability." Treadway's girlfriend was not involved and owed nothing.

Later, the entire assessment was thrown out on appeal. But Treadway and his girlfriend spent a life savings of $75,000 in legal fees fighting IRS injustice. They were left with nothing and the IRS employee responsible for this taxpayer tragedy got a promotion and a raise!

Tom Treadway said in his testimony: "I used to pray that what happened to me would happen to every American because only then would the system change." We taxpayers must learn from what has happened to others and change the system NOW!

Senator David Pryor, chairman of the Senate Committee responsible for oversight over the IRS is doing everything in his power to get the Taxpayers Bill of Rights passed -- but he must have your help!

SEIZURE FEVER -- CATCH IT! ...
... so reads a sign in the Los Angeles IRS office

IRS managers often make promotions on the basis of the number of seizures of taxpayers' property they make! Agents <u>are not</u> penalized when they or their computers make mistakes -- or go around the law in making seizures.

The IRS annually seizes approximately 1,600,000 bank accounts or paychecks and some 22,000 homes, cars, or other personal possessions <u>Many of these seizures are by mistake -- and you could be their next prey!</u>

Even our children have been IRS targets. But they hit a nerve when they seized the total savings: $10.85, of a 12-year old boy in Chesapeake, Virginia. This youth was so incensed he fired off an angry letter to President Reagan warning that "there is once again trouble in the colonies. <u>This time it does not involve a tax on tea.</u>" <u>The IRS revised its policy:</u>

A child's bank account can no longer be seized for payment of taxes allegedly owed by the parents -- unless the bank account contains at least $100!

But abusive and arrogant treatment of American citizens by IRS agents -- using Gestapo tactics continues.

- A Colorado woman owed just $1,725 in taxes. The IRS took her $50,000 home and sold it for $1,725.

- Henry James of Charlotte, North Carolina received a notice demanding $7,799.01 <u>in taxes he did not owe.</u> The IRS then slapped a lien on his property, jeopardizing his credit rating.

- The Oliver family of Fairbanks, Alaska was sitting in their car when IRS agents broke the windows, dragged them out of their car, and then took their car to satisfy claims of back taxes.

<u>Horror stories involving thousands of law abiding citizens were revealed during Senate Committee hearings on the IRS.</u>

"The hearings sort of opened our eyes. Many of us (in the Congress) probably know more about the (Soviet) KGB than we do about the IRS."

– United States Senator David Pryor

The faceless bureaucrats who work for the KGB or who delivered for Hitler's Gestapo executed such tactics of trembling fear. Only one thing can stand between these outrageous attacks on innocent law abiding citizens and these IRS zealots . . . passage of the Taxpayers Bill of Rights -- bill numbers: HR 3470 in the House and S 1774 in the Senate. Its key provisions are printed on <u>your</u> National Election Ballot and include:

<u>Your right</u> to fair treatment by the IRS; <u>your right</u> to have your home, your car and other possessions safeguarded from arbitrary IRS seizure, protection by a government paid ombudsman working on your behalf with power to stop unfair or illegal IRS seizures; and holding the IRS liable for damages for wrong-doing it commits in the cause of collecting revenue.

You see, when our Founding Fathers wrote our Constitution in 1787, there was no IRS. The income tax itself was unconstitutional -- until the 16th Amendment authorizing a personal income tax on the people was passed in 1913.

Congress has passed complicated tax laws -- and allowed the IRS to enforce the tax code in practically any way it sees fit. IRS field managers require <u>their</u> revenue officers to follow <u>their</u> policy, <u>their</u> philosophy of collection, and <u>their</u> whims and moods. This may be the way things are done in a dictatorship -- but this is America!

<u>Your immediate help is absolutely essential!</u>

Please mark your ballot <u>YES</u> for the Taxpayers Bill of Rights right now, before you do another thing -- and mail it back to me in the postage-paid envelope. This is the best way we taxpayers can stop this outlaw federal agency -- the IRS -- from harassing us and unfairly seizing our property without benefit of a trial.

No sane individual would dare to take on the IRS alone -- only with massive grassroots pressure will we succeed. This is why the Special Election on whether Congress should pass the Taxpayers Bill of Rights has been commissioned. Congress must see a tidal wave of support if our Taxpayers Bill of Rights is to pass. I figure it will take at least one million YES ballots -- maybe more to force Congress to act.

This special Taxpayers Election must be financed entirely with private contributions -- and that's why I must ask you to make an emergency donation to the National Taxpayers Union. <u>Your contribution of just $20 will bring this critical message and Taxpayers Bill of Rights ballot to more than 80 of your fellow citizens.</u>

– 4 –

And this is why it's so critical you make your contribution now! Our only source of money to complete this massive election and referendum on this critical taxpayer protection bill is from patriotic and concerned taxpayers like you.

So along with returning your ballot, please enclose your contribution of $100, $50, $25 or $15 so we can get this critical information about the IRS and millions of ballots to our fellow taxpayers – and help organize the massive grassroots lobby effort essential to passing our Taxpayers Bill of Rights.

We've already won in the Senate Finance Committee. Total taxpayer victory over the IRS is within our grasp -- but we must have your help now. I'm afraid we won't succeed unless you help us right now!

If we fail, you and I -- and our children, and their children -- will continue to live under the shadow of a "KGB" like IRS. **Please!** It's absolutely essential you do your part. **My only fear is if people don't think their vote counts. I hope you don't feel that way!**

With your contribution of $15 or more you automatically become eligible for membership in the National Taxpayers Union. Your membership benefits are fully explained in the enclosed Membership Benefits Memo -- including your NTU newspaper, Dollars & Sense, and your free copy of Tax Savings Report, written by former IRS insiders and national tax experts.

Aside from IRS' sheer panic that taxpayers will force Congress to pass the Taxpayers Bill of Rights, their next greatest fear is that taxpayers by the thousands will discover the big "little loopholes" disclosed in NTU's newsletter, Tax Savings Report. Articles in this newsletter could save you thousands of dollars in taxes!

But what's important is for you to return your ballot and vote YES for the Taxpayers Bill of Rights. **Please do these two things now, before you forget:**

1. Vote for the Taxpayers Bill of Rights and return your ballot in the postage-paid envelope within the next 48 hours.

2. Enclose your check to NTU for $15, $25, $50, $100 or as much as you can provide to help us distribute this kit to other taxpayers.

I'm urgently awaiting your reply. You and I simply must return our country to the point where law abiding citizens can go to bed at night without fear our homes will be threatened by IRS agents using Gestapo-like tactics.

Sincerely,

James Dale Davidson
James Dale Davidson
Chairman

P.S. Passage of the Taxpayers Bill of Rights may be the most important act to prevent IRS abuses since the personal income tax was adopted 75 years ago. So please return your ballot today -- and if you only make one major contribution this year, please make it now!

31

Package No. 3

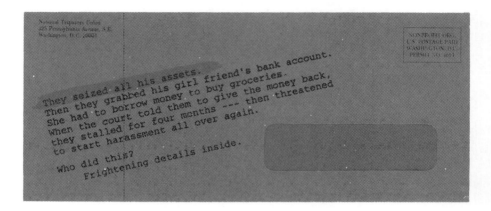

NATIONAL TAXPAYERS UNION
325 Pennsylvania Avenue S.E.
Washington, D.C. 20003 • (202) 543-1300

Dear Taxpayer,

Your HOME, INCOME, AND PERSONAL PROPERTY could be in jeopardy.

In fact, the INTERNAL REVENUE SERVICE, (IRS), could take practically everything you own . . . even though you don't owe them a penny.

Worse yet, the IRS can flagrantly VIOLATE your basic human rights with total immunity.

Meanwhile, you could be forced into financial ruin, fighting to get your property back after being left with thousands of dollars in legal bills . . .

All this because you tried to protect yourself against the ABUSIVE AND UNFAIR tax-collecting powers of the IRS.

Hardworking, honest taxpayers everywhere — just like you — are alarmed and frightened.

Just ask Tom Treadway . . .

Tom's an honest, taxpaying citizen who lives in Pipersville, Pennsylvania. A hard worker, Tom built a successful business and was looking forward to a comfortable retirement.

And then it happened . . .

Over, please

Page 2

<u>THE IRS SENT TOM A BILL FOR $247,000.</u>

What seemed like nothing more than an oversight or mistake on the part of the IRS soon mushroomed into a nightmare that drained this man of every ounce of energy and dollar he had to his name.

Two years later, Tom finally proved his <u>innocence,</u> and the IRS agreed that he didn't owe the 247,000 in the first place.

But, by that time, his life was totally destroyed. . .

Tom had lost his house, his business, . . . EVERYTHING . . . he was forced into bankruptcy and even had to fight the IRS to get back the $22,000 <u>they seized from his girlfriend's bank account</u> under the "trumped-up" charge that she was concealing his assets.

And on top of all this, . . . Tom Treadway is now faced with trying to pay off over $75,000 in legal and accounting bills that piled up in his efforts to defend himself.

This isn't just one horror story, either . . .

According to Joseph P. Smith, a former IRS employee who testified before a Congressional Committee, "there are a lot of Tom Treadway's in the United States."

In fact, experts believe that between 50,000 and 150,000 taxpayers are either mistreated or totally devastated <u>EACH AND EVERY YEAR BY THE IRS. . .</u>

And remember, to be a victim of the IRS, you don't

Next page, please

Page 3

have to owe them one red cent . . .

That means it IT CAN HAPPEN TO YOU.

Here's how . . .

As outrageous as it sounds, THERE ARE NO <u>CHECKS AND BALANCES</u> built into the IRS's collection process.

So when they come after you, anything is possible.

And it boils down to this . . .

YOU'RE GUILTY UNTIL PROVEN INNOCENT because right now there are <u>NO SAFEGUARDS TO PROTECT YOUR BASIC RIGHTS.</u>

You see, the IRS has powers <u>no other agency of the Federal Government has . . .</u>

. . . With little or no warning, the IRS can clean out your savings and checking accounts, levy almost all of your paycheck and even confiscate money and property that belongs to a friend or relative if they even <u>suspect</u> you are trying to hide assets.

Even your home, car or other personal belongings might not be safe.

But there's more to worry about . . .

It's a known fact that over-zealous and mean-spirited IRS tax collectors actually LIE TO AND DECEIVE innocent taxpayers <u>ON A ROUTINE BASIS.</u>

It's absolutely chilling . . .

33

Over, please

No one should have to put up with treatment like this.

. . . Especially when everything you own — your entire financial well-being — could be in jeopardy.

It's any wonder that to thousands of taxpayers, the IRS looks more like some Nazi-run bureaucracy than a so-called "service" agency of the U.S. Government.

Unfortunately, you and I have <u>every</u> reason to fear the iceberg.

But I think you can see why it's so important — in fact URGENT — that something is done right away to curb these abusive IRS practices.

Without taking up anymore of your time, let me get down to the bottom line. . .

The Congress of the United States recently held hearings on legislation known as the TAXPAYERS BILL OF RIGHTS.

This bill — if passed into law — will protect you and me and other innocent taxpayers against UNFAIR, ILLEGAL AND ABUSIVE treatment at the hands of the IRS.

For example . . .

    **The IRS would be <u>required</u> to notify you by certified mail <u>before</u> seizing your personal property.

    **If you owed the IRS money but couldn't pay it all back immediately, the IRS would have to honor its installment plan with you as long as you make the payments on time.

    **If the IRS causes you to suffer needless finan-

Next page, please

cial loss because of unjustified actions they took that violate the law, the IRS would have to pay you for the damages.

    **If it were discovered that you did owe the IRS money, the IRS would not be allowed to deprive you of your right to be self-supporting and thus take care of your family.

Sounds fair enough, right . . . ?

And yet, if the TAXPAYERS BILL OF RIGHTS doesn't get passed into law, the IRS has no obligation WHATSOEVER to do any of the things I just told you about.

That's why we've got to make this bill the law of the land . . .

. . . And our chances of doing just that are very good.

The TAXPAYERS BILL OF RIGHTS has been introduced as HR 3470 in the House of Representatives and <u>over 180 representatives support it.</u>

In the Senate, it's known as S1774 and <u>over 64 U.S. Senators are co-sponsors.</u>

Too, the bill has <u>ALREADY</u> passed the Senate Finance Committee.

Now, here's where you come in . . .

I've enclosed an <u>OFFICIAL CONGRESSIONAL PETITION.</u>

I need you to sign and return it as soon as possible.

This petition will be turned over to the Congress of

Over, please

Page 6

the United States so they know without a doubt that you
WANT the TAXPAYERS BILL OF RIGHTS passed immediately.

If you don't return this petition, let me tell your
what's going to happen. . .

Every IRS bureaucrat, tax collector, and special interest group who benefits financially from your personal
tragedy with the IRS will flood the Congress with dis-
torted information that will — with certainty — lead to
the defeat of this historic bill.

With the TAXPAYERS BILL OF RIGHTS defeated, the IRS
will then be encouraged to continue their ruthless and
abusive tactics which have ruined the lives of thousands
of honest Americans.

Please, don't let this happen . . .

After all, you might be protecting yourself.

Act now . . . Do the responsible thing by filling out
and returning your OFFICAL CONGRESSIONAL PETITION immediately.

I'll take care of everything else. I'll personally
hand deliver your petition to the Congress at precisely
the moment when it will have the most impact.

One last thing . . .

It's very important that the Congress receives thousands of these OFFICIAL CONGRESSIONAL PETITIONS from taxpayers all across the country.

And since the National Taxpayers Union is the only nationwide organization conduction this petition drive, we

Next page, please

Page 7

have the responsibility of mailing out several million petitions immediately.

This is a costly campaign . . .

Will you help me reach and alert the other taxpayers I
must send petitions to by enclosing a contribution of $15,
$20 or $25?

$15 will make it possible for us to reach 60 taxpay-
ers. With your help of $25, we'll be able to alert 100
people and get their voices heard.

NTU has been serving the American Taxpayer for over 19
years.

Literally, we've saved you and other taxpayers billions of dollars by stopping government waste and over-
spending by blocking outrageous tax increase schemes.

So by sending in your OFFICAL CONGRESSIONAL PETITION
now and enclosing $15, $20 or $25, you'll not only be pro-
tecting yourself against IRS abuses, you'll also receive a
membership in this nation's leading tax-fighting citizens'
lobby.

. . . And, as a member of NTU, you'll receive — if you
act now — our award-winning publication, DOLLARS AND
SENSE.

Additionally, you'll get valuable tax-saving information, discounted books, bi-monthly updates and much, much
more.

So please . . . protect yourself by helping me now.

Fill out and return your OFFICIAL CONGRESSIONAL PETI-

Over, please

35

```
Page 8

TION today.

     Secondly, help me alert other taxpayers by sending
$15, $20 or $25 along with your petition.

     Remember, it's really an important OBLIGATION. It'll
protect you, your family and your property.

     Return your OFFICIAL CONGRESSIONAL PETITION along with
your check for $15, $20 or $25 as soon as possible.

     Thank you . . .
                              Sincerely,


                              Jim Davidson
                              Chairman
                              NATIONAL TAXPAYERS UNION

P.S. The IRS can literally destroy you . . .

     Here's your chance to protect yourself and your fam-
ily.

     Don't hesitate another minute. Sign your OFFICIAL CON-
GRESSIONAL PETITION immediately and return it to me.

     And please . . . do your utmost to enclose at least
$15, $20 or $25 with your petition.
```

What's Your Guess?

The value of testing is obvious to anybody who has been raising funds through the mails for more than five minutes. We know *The Law of Preconceived Fund Raising Mailing Opinion:*

> *Preconceived opinions mean absolutely nothing.*

Had I not been involved in creating and tabulating part of this test, I'd have picked number three—in the "They seized all his assets" envelope—as the winner.

My rationale: Envelope copy is credible and provocative, not gim-micky. The letter, although not a direct carry-through of the envelope copy (a tactical mistake, in my opinion), is straightforward and convincing.

The first letter, in the "Official Business" envelope, is nondescript. It has no specifics on the first page, a deadly error in fund raising. It generates little empathy.

The second letter, in the "Final Notice" envelope, is gimmicky. It violates a cardinal rule in not using a typewriter face. It aims its thrust far below the intellectual level of the typical recipient.

Here are the actual results:

The winner, in terms of number of people responding, was number two.

Taking response to number two as 100, number one pulled 79 percent. Number three pulled 60 percent.

The winner, in terms of dollar-per-donor, was number three.

Number two brought almost as high an average gift, 99 percent. Number one brought an average gift 84 percent as high as number three.

With *all* factors considered—total response weighted by amount of gift—the winner was number two. Second was number one. Third was number three.

Did your guess match the results? If so, you're either prescient or lucky, because no one associated with the test could predict in advance which would outpull the others.

St. Jude Hospital—A Startling Test

This test by St. Jude Children's Research Hospital is both easier and more predictable.

As you can see, the letters are short. They also are identical, with one exception: The second letter has a p.s.

Danny Thomas, Founder
ST. JUDE CHILDREN'S RESEARCH HOSPITAL

ALSAC   505 N. Parkway,   Memphis, TN 38103

October 5,

Capt Randy Hudon
PO Bx 37712
Raleigh, NC. 27627

Dear Capt Hudon,

   It's too early for Jimmy to say hello to God,
Capt Hudon.

   He has leukemia.

   Jimmy loves God, but we don't want God to take him
now. He's only nine. We're fighting to save him ... to
save his family's fragile hopes and dreams.

   And do you know what? We're winning. I must tell
you, ten years ago Jimmy's chances for lasting a year
wouldn't have been good at all. That's how far science
has come in so short a time.

   There's a point to this: I need help from you. It
takes money for us to help Jimmy and all the other
children at St. Jude, Capt Hudon.

                                    over, please

   Please, my friend, right now, while you're reading
this, write your check to St. Jude Children's Research
Hospital. It's tax deductible, and it could make the
difference between life and death for the next Jimmy
whose parents, trying to hold back tears of hoplessness,
bring him through our always-open doors.

                     Bless you for caring,

                     Danny Thomas

Danny Thomas, Founder

**ST. JUDE CHILDREN'S
RESEARCH HOSPITAL**

ALSAC   505 N. Parkway,   Memphis, TN 38103

October 5, ____

Ms. Myrtle Mitchell
1533 Whitemore
Modesto, CA. 95351

Dear Ms. Mitchell,

It's too early for Jimmy to say hello to God, Ms. Mitchell.

He has leukemia.

Jimmy loves God, but we don't want God to take him now. He's only nine. We're fighting to save him ... to save his family's fragile hopes and dreams.

And do you know what? We're winning. I must tell you, ten years ago Jimmy's chances for lasting a year wouldn't have been good at all. That's how far science has come in so short a time.

There's a point to this: I need help from you. It takes money for us to help Jimmy and all the other children at St. Jude, Ms. Mitchell.

over, please

Please, my friend, right now, while you're reading this, write your check to St. Jude Children's Research Hospital. It's tax deductible, and it could make the difference between life and death for the next Jimmy whose parents, trying to hold back tears of hoplessness, bring him through our always-open doors.

Bless you for caring,

Danny Thomas

P.S. I hope that your own family never suffers the tragedy of losing a child to an incurable disease. At St. Jude, we're fighting to conquer these killers, and one day someone in your own family may live because we succeeded.

39

What's Your Guess?

You probably guessed the letter with the p.s. pulled better. If so, you're right.

In today's marketplace, a p.s. seems to add a final kick in the head. But how much improvement can one expect from this simple addition? (Or how much response-deterioration from its omission?)

In this case, the letter with the p.s. outpulled the letter without the p.s. by 19 percent. That's a big number!

(One warning: If you put together a mailing which has two letters, put a p.s. on only one of them to prevent a self-cancelling effect resulting from weakening of centralized emphasis.)

In the next chapters let's take a critical look at some of the letters others (or maybe you) put into the mails. How did they fare? They didn't tell us, so comments in these pages are limited by happy ignorance of which ones succeeded and which ones failed.

The purpose of this book isn't to generate brilliant copy; rather, the purpose is to generate workmanlike copy. Comments on the letters may give you copy-models making possible workmanlike copy for every letter you write.

CHAPTER *6*

Arts and Education Letters

Dear Viewer,

Who determines the topnotch quality of programs you see on WPBT2?

You do.

Because when I sit down with other people here at WPBT2 to plan what programs you'll see in the seasons ahead, one rule guides our decisions: "Nothing but the best for our viewers."

We want to keep it that way. But we need your cooperation.

Consider this proposal:

We promise to do everything in our power to keep bringing you television's finest hours on WPBT2. In exchange, we ask you to take one simple step to help make these programs possible.

That step is to change your status from that of a WPBT2 viewer to that of a WPBT2 Member.

WPBT2 Members are responsible people in this community who are proud to support the programs they see on this station. Our Members are people who care about South Florida and who take great satisfaction in knowing that their tax-deductible financial support enables WPBT2 to produce and purchase the very best programs on television.

They're your friends and neighbors. They're younger families just getting started who want nothing but the best for themselves and their kids. They're families with youngsters in high school or college who look to WPBT2 for continued enlightenment, as well as enjoyment. They're

(over, please)

older folks who are thankful that WPBT2 programs allow them
to keep up with a fast-changing world.

These people recognize their responsibility to keep
WPBT2 going. Because, as you well know, WPBT2 is a <u>public</u>
broadcasting station. That means that what you enjoy on
this station is not constantly interrupted by commercials
to pay for the cost of producing or purchasing the programs.
That means we have to rely on the public to keep us going.
That means <u>you</u>.

Research has revealed that an overwhelming number of
viewers who enjoy WPBT2's programs would like to become
Members -- but they just never get around to it. Well,
here's your opportunity to join right now. We've made it
as easy as can be.

The enclosed Membership Form already has your name and
address on it. All you need to do is slip it into the reply
envelope, along with your check or charge instructions, and
mail it back to me.

This is an especially important time for you to join
WPBT2. Quality programming is very expensive. And the
costs of bringing you these programs have seriously
escalated ... So we need additional public support -- <u>your</u>
support -- now more than ever.

Your reply today will help assure that you <u>continue</u> to
enjoy the first-rate television you're used to on WPBT2. For
just a moment, I ask you to think about these extraordinary
programs.

Programs like:

> <u>Masterpiece Theatre</u> has presented some of
> television's most memorable productions in
> favorites like <u>Upstairs, Downstairs, The
> Jewel in the Crown</u> and <u>Poldark.</u>

> <u>NOVA</u> is the longest-running, most successful,
> most watched science documentary series in the
> history of television.

> <u>Nature</u> has transported you to the four corners
> of the globe to observe close-up some of the
> joys and mysteries of nature in one of the most
> beautifully photographed programs ever seen on
> television.

> <u>Live from Lincoln Center</u> has brought you the
> world's most renowned conductors, singers and
> dancers in unforgettable concerts and ballets.

(next page, please)

> <u>Live from the Met</u> has brought you Luciano
> Pavarotti, Joan Sutherland, Placido Domingo,
> Marilyn Horne and other superb singers of our
> time in outstanding productions of the world's
> greatest operas.

> <u>Great Performances</u> has brought you everything
> from the musical genius of Leonard Bernstein and
> Zubin Mehta to the theatrical genius of Lawrence
> Olivier and Julie Harris.

> The <u>Nightly Business Report</u> has brought you the
> latest in business news, and it's produced right
> here at WPBT2!

I could go on and on, filling page after page with the
names and descriptions of all the programs you view on
WPBT2 -- shows that are praised by critics and the public
alike as television's finest hours.

In effect, what you get on WPBT2 is a year-long
festival of music, theater, politics, humor, dance, nature
and science, news, movies, current affairs, wonderful
children's programs, and much, much more.

These programs are for you ... <u>and</u> for those you love.
For the children in your life who laugh and learn on WPBT2.
For the older people in your life -- parents and grandparents
-- whose lives are enriched by WPBT2.

How many WPBT2 programs have you and your family enjoyed
in the past year? Two or three? Ten or eleven? Forty or
Fifty? Even more?

How much is all this worth to you? Surely, it's worth
just 13 cents a day. And miraculously, that's all membership in a WPBT2 Family Membership costs.

If you visited New York with your family to go to the
theater, a concert and an opera, it would cost you a hefty
sum to enjoy all this. Theater tickets go for $50 apiece or
more. Opera seats can cost even more. For a family of three
to go to one play, one opera and one concert, you'd have to
dole out close to $400. Close to $400!

But you get the best seats in the house for that play,
opera and concert -- and for <u>dozens</u> of other plays, operas
and concerts -- without leaving South Florida ... without
even leaving the comfort of your home. Because you get
them on WPBT2 ... commercial-free.

Our Members -- all 55,000 of them -- are our "silent
sponsors." They are people who appreciate what they see
on WPBT2 and who want to say "Thank You."

(over,please)

4.

Please join them. Please do your share in supporting one of our community's most important assets. And please respond at this particularly important time, when the rising cost of putting these programs on the air has put a strain on our budget.

As a Member, you can take pride in knowing that every time you hear our announcer say that a program has been made possible by the generous support of WPBT2 Members, he's talking about you.

First-rate television stations don't just happen. People make them happen -- exceptional, caring people who recognize their responsibility and want to do their share. Too often, too many take too much for granted. Fortunately, there are the good people of South Florida who don't take our commercial-free programming for granted and who do their share to make it happen by becoming WPBT2 Members.

South Florida means a lot to us here at WPBT2. And I know that MemberVision means a lot to the people of our community. We want to keep bringing you a feast of exceptional television viewing ... an endless variety of programs for every member of your family. With your help, we will.

So how about it? How about saying, "Yes, I will become a WPBT2 Member". Not someday. But today.

We're counting on you. It's time you got into the WPBT2 picture.

Sincerely,

George Dooley
President

P.S. When you send in your membership contribution, think of the pleasure you'll be giving people you love -- children, grandchildren, nieces, nephews, parents, grandparents. And for them, perhaps you can send a few dollars more. Those few dollars more will do a lot to bring them a lot more pleasure on WPBT2 in the year ahead. Keep in mind that your membership contribution is tax-deductible ... and that you may charge your contribution to your VISA, MasterCard or American Express.

Exhibit 6-1: WPBT2

Comment:

Would you respond to this letter?

The "Johnson Box" at the top tries to strike a bargain with the reader, and in doing so unmasks the pitch—too early, in my opinion.

The letter opens without excitement. The first statement is untrue. Viewers know they don't determine the programming, and the lack of one-on-one sincerity results in a "boiler plate" approach to fund raising letter writing.

Having an extra flap with photographs is an excellent attention holder, but most of the photographs are posed headshots.

The p.s. is too long and without impact.

Herschell/Margo Lewis
9748 Cedar Villas Blvd.
Plantation FL 33324

Dear Herschell/Margo Lewis:

I'm pleased to announce a new giving opportunity of special
interest to you. On May 1, 19__, WPBT introduced the Leadership
Circle.

The Leadership Circle is designed to give you the credit you
deserve for your loyal support. Because of your faithful service
as a WPBT2 member, I'm inviting you to join the Leadership Circle
which gives you more frequent and more prestigious on-air
acknowledgment of your support and aids us in fulfilling our
year-end obligations.

I want to include your name among those who have already joined
the Leadership Circle. Your dedication and leadership should be
recognized by all those who enjoy public television.

Please consider moving into this prestigious new program with an
additional $500 contribution and join those who are empowering
further the vision of WPBT2. Thank you for your continued support.

I look forward to hearing from you soon.

Sincerely,

George Dooley
President

P.S. Our new $1500 and above Leadership Circle is a part of
      our new emphasis to recognize the important role you play
      in keeping public television alive in our community.

Exhibit 6-2: WPBT2

Comment:

Exclusivity and recognition are forceful motivators in the world of fund raising. Those in the "Leadership Circle" apparently have their names scrolled on the screen at various times. Opinion: The letter should emphasize this recognition more strongly.

Confusion attends the dollar numbers. The letter asks for "an additional $500 contribution"; the p.s. points out qualification for the Leadership Circle: "$1500 and above."

Fund raising letters invariably pull less response than they might when they violate *The Clarity Commandment:*

> *In any force-communication letter,*
> *clarity is paramount. Don't let any*
> *other component of the communications*
> *mix interfere with it.*

	POWELL SYMPHONY HALL
Saint Louis Symphony Orchestra	718 NORTH GRAND BOULEVARD, ST. LOUIS, MISSOURI 63103
	PHONE: (314) 533-2500
	TELEX: 434450 STLSYMORCH STL

Leonard Slatkin, Music Director and Conductor
David Hyslop, Executive Director

The Saint Louis Symphony Society
Operating The Saint Louis Symphony Orchestra,
The Saint Louis Symphony Chorus
& Powell Symphony Hall.

Dear Friends:

Enclosed please find the travel details for the St. Louis Symphony September Music Festival at Sea in the Mediterranean, August 28–September 16, 1988. You are warmly invited to join this unique music/travel experience that has come to be called, "An experience of a lifetime."

Where else would you expect to hear such great artists as Mstislav Rostropovich, Salvatore Accardo, Vladimir Spivakov, Bruno Canino, Michel Dalberto, Ruggero Raimoundi and many many more—except on the St. Louis Symphony Music Festival at Sea in the Mediterranean?

As both performers and passengers will be traveling on board together, the cruise is all inclusive. Performances, lectures, all sightseeing trips ashore, an open bar throughout and vintage wines with meals are all included. For the St. Louis Symphony the trip is inclusive of air transportation from New York and includes a tax deductible donation to the St. Louis Symphony of $250.00 per person. Accommodations on board ship vary in price. Complete deck plans and rates are described in the brochure. A color coded deck plan is available from our travel agents, The Leonard Haertter Travel Co.

Here is the ideal trip for those who like music and prefer the timing and advantages of a September Mediterranean cruise. It is an ideal trip of unequalled musical performances, superb food, sun, relaxation and good company.

We hope that you will be able to join us. Convenient air transportation is available from most major cities. Full details are available from our travel agents.

Travel Agents:
The Leonard Haertter Travel Co.
7922 Bonhomme Avenue
St. Louis, MO 63105
Telephone 314/721-6200
Nationwide Toll Free 800/942-6666

Most sincerely,

Patricia E. Essen

Chairman Symphony Trips

Exhibit 6-3: St. Louis Symphony

Comment:

This letter is the top inside panel of a five-panel fold-down. Each panel is 6⅞″ deep, making the total piece more than 34″ long.

"Dear Friends" violates a principal rule of letter writing: *No plural targets.* "Enclosed please find" is an antiquated arms-length opening.

The sentence, "As both performers and passengers will be traveling on board together, the cruise is all inclusive," is a weak way of projecting what could be a dynamic sales point.

The only dollar number mentioned in the letter is $250, the portion of the cost which will be a donation to the St. Louis Symphony. Elsewhere in the literature, the cost of the trip appears: $7,360 to $25,755 per person.

The prosecution rests.

Union Development Trust
P.O. Box 102
Graaff-Reinet, 6280
Inquiries: The Co-ordinator
Tel.: (0491) 23848 a.m. 22488 p.m.

THIS IS NOT JUNK MAIL
DON'T THROW AWAY

Dear Friend

This is a sincere appeal and attempt to further uplift educational standards. You are part of a selected market which we believe is concerned about your own children and South Africa's future.

We could give you a long sales-talk about why you should take part in our fund-raising effort. We don't think that's necessary.

As a person in a leadership position you know what it's all about — providing improved education to ensure a better South Africa's for all ... after all, education is what it's all about.

All we can ask is consider the fund-raising campaign favourably... and if you don't want to take part, pass our leaflet on to a friend or friends who will ... because if you throw our leaflet away, that's the end of our cause.

Finally, if you participate, we hope you will win, not only because you stand to gain substantially, but mainly because you care.

Thank you.

W. J. Chambers.

DES CHAMBERS
(Fund-raising Co-ordinator)

Exhibit 6-4: Union Development Trust

Comment:

The imperative at upper right reads:

THIS IS NOT JUNK MAIL
DON'T THROW AWAY

—an excellent de-fanger of implicit skepticism.

"Union Development Trust" in the United States would seem to be a financial institution. In South Africa, where the letter was mailed, the organization is eleemosynary, dedicated to education.

The next-to-last paragraph is as polished a piece of fund raising writing as you'll see in this book.

(Accompanying the letter: a sweepstakes drawing and a response device.)

Exhibit 6-5: West Broward Philharmonic Guild

Comment:

Invariably, use of passive voice ("...it was decided...") instead of active voice ("...we decided...") is less effective in generating acceptance of a concept. Why? Because the writer removes herself from the arena, retreating behind a faceless organizational front.

Statements such as "You are not only in an important position in our family life" puzzle the reader and create unease; phrases such as "purveyor of classical music" seem poorly chosen and deliberately obscure.

The handwritten greeting is superior to a typed greeting. This one obviously was done by hand; contemporary computer-addressing programs have made it possible to use this technique on mass mailings as well.

CHAPTER 7

"Diseases" Letters

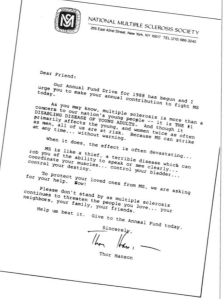

Multiple Sclerosis: A Threat To Us All

Facts about MS...

- *MS strikes in the prime of life.* Just when you think you have everything going for you, multiple sclerosis can turn your world inside out.
- *There is no way to guard against MS.* It comes unexpectedly and without warning.
- *Like polio, MS can be beaten!* With your help research is an ongoing commitment.
- *It is possible to have multiple sclerosis and still be a winner.*
- *Your support holds the key!* 95% of *all* our funding comes from concerned people like you!

The fact is, without your help, we can't fund the research that is searching for a cure for MS...we can't protect your loved ones...we can't offer hope to the 250,000 Americans who struggle to cope with this disease.

Give to the Annual Fund TODAY!

NATIONAL MULTIPLE SCLEROSIS SOCIETY
205 East 42nd Street, New York, NY 10017 TEL (212) 986-3240

Dear Friend:

Our Annual Fund Drive for 1988 has begun and I urge you to make your annual contribution to fight MS today.

As you may know, multiple sclerosis is more than a concern to our nation's young people -- it is THE #1 DISABLING DISEASE OF YOUNG ADULTS. And though it primarily affects the young, and women twice as often as men, all of us are at risk. Because MS can strike at any time... without warning.

When it does, the effect is often devastating...

MS is like a thief, a terrible disease which can rob you of the ability to speak or see clearly... coordinate your muscles... control your bladder... control your destiny.

To protect your loved ones from MS, we are asking for your help. Now!

Please don't stand by as multiple sclerosis continues to threaten the people you love... your neighbors, your family, your friends.

Help us beat it. Give to the Annual Fund today.

Sincerely,

Thor Hanson

Exhibit 7-1: National Multiple Sclerosis Society

Comment:

This letter is printed within a three-panel self-mailer, half of which is a response device with glued carrier envelope.

Letters such as this point up motivational differences separating prior donors from cold list names. As written, the letter has more impact among prior donors—although "Dear Friend" suggests a cold list mailing.

To those unfamiliar with the organization, this letter is rhetoric, nothing more. It lacks emotion and impetus. The devastating effects of multiple sclerosis aren't dramatized. A better opening: "If somebody asked you which is the *number one* disabling disease of young adults, would you know the answer?"

(A parenthetical point: "Number one" or "#1" usually has a *positive* overtone. Look for a more negative phrase when referring to a devastating disease.)

FACTS ABOUT MS

- **It strikes in the prime of life**
- **There is no way to guard against it... no known cure**
- **Like polio, MS can be beaten**
- **Your support holds the key!**

AN IMPORTANT HEALTH ALERT...

Dear Friend:

Our Annual Fund Drive for 1988 has begun and I urge you to make your annual contribution against MS now.

As you may know, multiple sclerosis is more than a concern to our nation's young people; it's *THE* #1 crippling disease of young adults. When it strikes, its effect is devastating.

MS is like a thief, a terrible disease which can rob you of the ability to speak or see clearly... coordinate your muscles... control your bladder ... control your destiny.

To protect your loved ones from MS, we ask for your help. Now!

Please, don't sit by as multiple sclerosis continues to strike those you love. Help us fight it. Help us beat it. Aren't your loved ones worth it?

Sincerely,

Thor Hanson
Vice Admiral, U.S. Navy (Ret.)
President & C.E.O.

Exhibit 7-2: National Multiple Sclerosis Society

Comment:

This two-sided slip (the other side is the personalized fund request) is printed rather than typewritten. It has strength the letter in exhibit 1 has lost, because it deals in specifics; but the format itself is cold-blooded.

Opinion: a worthwhile test—this inexpensive mailing against the more expensive letter/lift note mailing.

September 19, 19??

Mr. Herschell G. Lewis
9748 Cedar Villas Dr
Plantation, FL 33324-2315

Dear Mr. Lewis:

You may never need us...but right now we
need you!

Of course, none of us likes to think about
cancer. But the sad fact is, cancer still
strikes two out of every three American
families.

In fact, last year alone, over 470,000 men,
women and children died from some form of this
disease in the United States.

This is why all of us, physicians, researchers, and staff here at Memorial
Sloan-Kettering Cancer Center are working so
hard day and night to find a way to control and
cure cancer.

I'm writing to ask for your help.

Memorial Sloan-Kettering is the world's
largest non-profit cancer research center. We
must depend on private support from friends like
you if our vital cancer research is to
continue...if we are going to discover new and
more effective ways to control this disease.

Today new techniques are being used for
improved patient care and treatment, and exciting
new developments are occurring in cancer research,
developments that give us tremendous hope for the
future.

And the results of research done here at
Memorial Sloan-Kettering are felt beneficially
throughout the country. For example, over 3,000

- 2 -

doctors have been trained at Memorial Sloan-
Kettering who are applying their knowledge and
abilities to cancer research and care across
this country.

Because of such efforts in cancer research,
we have seen real progress against cancer. More
than 50% of those who will be treated at Memorial
Sloan-Kettering in 1988 may expect to have
their cancer controlled or cured.

The results of our research are used in the
clinical treatment of cancer throughout the world.
Your gift of $25, $50, $100, $500 or more to
support our research effort will help bring us
closer to the cure of cancer.

Please understand that any gift you can
send will be greatly appreciated and put to
effective use.

Right now, Memorial Sloan-Kettering Cancer
Center needs you.

Sincerely,

Mortimer H. Chute, Jr.
Vice President for Development

P.S. Memorial Sloan-Kettering Cancer Center
also needs friends who can give major
tax-deductible gifts of $1,000, $5,000
or even more, on an annual basis. Every
gift is important!

52

Jay Weinberg

You don't know me, but if you would take a few minutes to read this, I would like to tell you about my experiences at Memorial Sloan-Kettering Cancer Center.

It was lucky that my malignant melanoma (a deadly form of skin cancer) was discovered early and that my wife had the courage to take me out of a small general hospital less than an hour before I was to be operated on and to take me to MSK. It's probably the top cancer research center in this country. And the treatment I received for my type of cancer just wasn't available very many places back in 1974.

Soon I shall celebrate my 70th birthday, and recently I participated in an Outward Bound four-day wilderness experience. I went with a group of recovered cancer patients. All of us are volunteers at MSK in a program called "Patient to Patient," designed to help newly diagnosed cancer patients with their questions and anxieties.

But I know that the fact I'm alive and walking around today is more than just luck. In a large part it's because of the research being done at MSK and because of the commitment and dedication of the doctors and staff there.

And I know that if anyone in my family needs any cancer care in the future, I would make sure that it was done at MSK, which offers the best possible surgical care and research.

Thanks for taking the time to read this.

Jay M. Weinberg

Exhibit 7-3: Memorial Sloan-Kettering Cancer Institute

Comment:

First, the letter. The opening is flat.

This letter would have been stronger if it opened with the fifth paragraph. Statistics such as "470,000 men, women and children..." aren't motivators. "Two out of every three families" is far weaker than the point deserves. (A stronger way: "Think about your home and the homes on either side of you. Chances are someone in *two* of these homes will be stricken with cancer.")

Generalizations such as "...new techniques are being used..."

and "exciting new developments are occurring..." have impact only if *specifics* follow the generalizations. What new techniques? Which developments?

The p.s. may turn away as many potential donors as it attracts. Mixing major and minor donor-appeals is dangerous.

Still, this organization has remailed this appeal a number of times. Criticism becomes valid only when it matches results, or lack of results. (The critic's inevitable position: "Yes, but what if they'd...")

Consider the "lift" letter. First impression is one of overlong paragraphs.

As often happens in lift letters, the first paragraph has no pace. The note parallels an old-fashioned steam locomotive, rods thrashing and wheels spinning until the ungainly machine lurches into motion. The note succeeds better *without* the first sentence.

Episode is always a formidable weapon in fund raising, and once this story gets under way it's interesting reading.

Opinion: Injecting a single "you" reference would give this letter the wallop it deserves.

FLORIDA DIVISION, INC.

Dear Mr. Lewis:

Last year 965,000 Americans were diagnosed as having cancer; 483,000 died of it. Cancer can affect any of us, and the fight against it is far from over.

But you can help us beat this dread disease, by contributing to the nation's oldest and largest cancer control organization.

We put your cancer-fighting dollars to work where it counts, right here in Florida:

* <u>In research</u> - to find better ways to identify, treat and control cancer.

* <u>In education</u> - more than 2.1 million Floridians received life saving information about cancer last year, through our public education programs.

* <u>In service and rehabilitation</u> - we provide many free benefits - such as sickroom equipment, transportation, counseling, and emotional support - to cancer patients and their families.

Many organizations are competing for your support, but there is only one American Cancer Society.

We need your contributions now more than ever. Please give what you can to help us win the fight against cancer.

Sincerely,

Wallace D. Hunter, Ph.D.
Chairman of the Board
Florida Division, Inc.

American Cancer Society, Florida Division • 1001 S. MacDill Avenue, Tampa, Florida 33629
please detach and return in enclosed envelope

Exhibit 7-4: American Cancer Society

Comment:

The relationship between 965,000 and 438,000 is unclear. To the typical recipient, "Fewer than half died...but that still isn't good enough..." might appear more germane.

Localizing the use of funds is an excellent hook. All in all, this is a concise and workmanlike letter.

AMERICAN CANCER SOCIETY FLORIDA DIVISION, INC., WEST BROWARD UNIT

May 5, 1988

Everyone loves bargains! And, this time, through the courtesy of Smart Shoppers, The American Cancer Society is able to offer the Smart Shoppers Directory.

What is the Smart Shoppers Directory? It is a discount directory with a one year membership card designed to help the consumer get the most from their shopping dollars. The Annual membership is valid through May, 1989.

The Smart Shoppers Directory consists of some of the finest restaurants, clothing stores, gift shops and services available exclusively in the West Broward area.

Local merchants in the Plantation, Sunrise, Tamarac and Coral Springs areas want your business and offer you savings as a Smart Shopper. Membership entitles you to the following discounts:

Coupons ranging from 50% - 100% off (2 for 1).

Permanent discounts to be used each and every time you shop, ranging from 10-50%, just by showing your Smart Shoppers Card to the participating merchants listed in this directory.

Using your Smart Shoppers membership on just one occasion, more than pays for the initial cost of purchasing this directory---and you will be donating some of your dollars to help a worthwhile cause---The American Cancer Society. Savings are unlimited.

Simply tear off the coupon below, make your check payable to: Smart Shoppers, and return to The American Cancer Society, in the envelope enclosed. Your Smart Shoppers Directory and Membership Card will be mailed directly to you.

The cost of the directory with a one year membership card is $10.00. Help eradicate cancer in our lifetime---and NEVER PAY RETAIL PRICES AGAIN.

- -

Please send me_____directory/directorie(s) @ $10.00 each (membership card to be included.)

NAME_____

ADDRESS_____

CITY, STATE & ZIP_____

MAKE CHECKS PAYABLE TO - SMART SHOPPERS---RETURN TO AMERICAN CANCER SOCIETY OFFICE.

4977 N. UNIVERSITY DRIVE, LAUDERHILL, FLORIDA 33351 305/742-2201

Exhibit 7-5: American Cancer Society

Comment:

I prefer a handwritten or rubber stamp overline, proclaiming the "Discount Coupon Book" theme so the recipient won't assume this is a standard fund raiser.

Still, it's hard to quarrel with this example of contemporary fund raising—"painless" fund raising in which the message-recipient senses an equivalence of value. In today's "Me!"-emphasizing society, offering "Twofer" books will bring $10 from those who never would respond to a standard appeal.

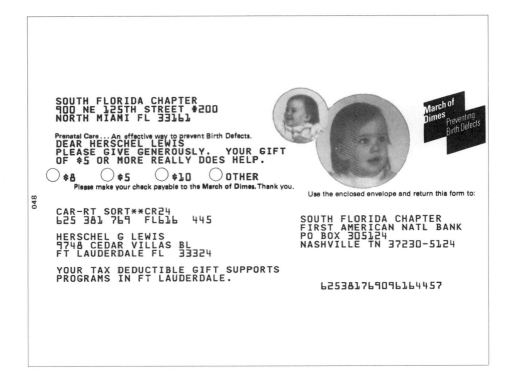

Exhibit 7-6: March of Dimes

Comment:

Muscular Dystrophy was one of the first organizations to use this type of short form. Although it's about as personal as a mortgage payment notice, the low cost means a fund raiser can mail many more pieces for the same amount of money—which may be more than an equalizer.

Testing this format is logical, especially if conventional mailings have begun to flag and aren't pulling the way you think they should.

I'd like to tell you about a
little deaf boy who learned
to 'talk', with the help
of someone just like you.

22 April 19..

Dear Friend

For a child who is born deaf - like little Fransie - the
frustrations and the heartbreak are two-fold.

Because, not only can they not hear - they can't speak
either.   They don't even know what words are.

So they sit in dreadful isolation - big eyes blank and
uncomprehending - completely cut off from everyone around
them.

This time last year, Fransie was like that.

Then a kind lady who'd never even met him
--- but who'd heard about our work with
the deaf --- sent us a cheque for R40. And
she asked us to use the money to help teach
a deaf child to communicate.

So we did. And Fransie was the lucky little boy who got
some very special teaching aids, including his own sign
language dictionary. He still has it, in fact. Now, the pages
are grubby and worn - but Fransie's a completely different
child.

Thanks to professional training methods and audio visual
aids, his wonderful book, and the love and encouragement of
his family, he's become a confident and sociable little
person.

It's always a wonderful, throat-catching
moment - the first time a child like Fransie
realises that each object, each emotion,
has a special word to describe it. And
that he can share that word with you ...
and you will understand.

It's as if a new light comes into their eyes. Suddenly

over please ...

- 2 -

they're not cut off from the rest of the world anymore.
They're part of it - as they're meant to be; able to tell
you what they want, how they feel, things that have happened.

And you can put that brightness in a child's
eyes ... those magical words at his fingertips.

With a gift of R40, you can provide a sign-language
dictionary or a video tape of signs that will put 2 000 essential
words in front of a deaf child.

This is a gift that will never lie unused or unread
inside a dusty cupboard! For a child who cannot hear,
struggling to make contact - it's a lifeline. Something he'll
use again and again.

And this wonderful gift of yours will last a lifetime.
Because once he's mastered the communication skills and learned
the words - no one can ever take them away from him.

If you can't manage R40 right away, please
try and send R20 - and I will find another
person to share the cost of the dictionary
or visual aid with you. Even if you can
only spare R10, it will be a start
towards one more thankful child.

You see, our dream is to put language into the hands of
every deaf child in South Africa. But only you can make that
dream come true.

So please, will you use the donation form and envelope
I've enclosed to help a deaf child today?

Yours sincerely

DR J H HAMILTON
Chairman

P.S. Every dictionary you sponsor carries your name on a
special label on the inside cover. So the child you've
helped will never forget your generosity.

Please let me hear from you soon. The new school term
is already underway --- and so many deaf students are
counting on us for the help they need to communicate
with their teachers and each other.

58

S.A. National Council
for the Deaf

P/Bag X4, Westhoven, 2142
Phone: (011) 27-5368

25 September 1 .

I'd like to tell you about a
little deaf boy who learned
to 'talk', with the help
of someone just like you.

Dear Friend

For a child who is born deaf - like little Jamie - the
frustrations and the heartbreak are two-fold.

Because, not only can they not hear - they can't speak
either. They don't even know what words are.

So they sit in dreadful isolation - big eyes blank and
uncomprehending - completely cut off from everyone around
them.

This time last year, Jamie was like that.

Then a kind lady who'd never even met him
--- but who'd heard about our work with
the deaf --- sent us a cheque for R40. And
she asked us to use the money to help teach
a deaf child to communicate.

So we did. And Jamie was the lucky little boy who got
some very special teaching aids, including his own sign
language dictionary. He still has it, in fact. Now, the pages
are grubby and worn - but Jamie's a completely different child.

Thanks to professional training methods and audio visual
aids, his wonderful book, and the love and encouragement of
his family, he's become a confident and sociable little
person.

It's always a wonderful, throat-catching
moment - the first time a child like Jamie
realises that each object, each emotion,
has a special word to describe it. And
that he can share that word with you ...
and you will understand.

It's as if a new light comes into their eyes. Suddenly

over please ...

Exhibit 7-7: S.A. National Council for the Deaf

Comment:

This may have been a test, but it's a strange one. The only change is the name of the victim, from "Fransie" to "Jamie."

Victim letters are "grabbers," relatively easy to write and comparatively easy to read.

This letter sparkles with bright writing—phrases such as *the pages are grubby and worn* and *throat-catching moment* and *inside a dusty cupboard.* The p.s. is relevant to the donor, which may capture the wavering contributor.

GUIDELINES TO HELP PREVENT HEART DISEASE
1. Eat a variety of foods
2. Maintain ideal weight
3. Avoid too much fat, saturated fat and cholesterol
4. Eat foods with adequate starch and fiber
5. Avoid too much sugar
6. Avoid too much sodium
7. If you drink alcohol, do so in moderation

BONANZA HOTLINE
801-392-9422

AMERICAN HEART DISEASE PREVENTION
F O U N D A T I O N
42B1M

★ ★ ★

M. E. Lewist
9748 Cedar Villas Dr.
Fort Lauderdale, FL 33324

2 002 6557300225

Dear M. E. Lewist:

This letter will serve as your legal notification that the three individuals named in the Cash Disbursement Box below are Grand Finalists in the $5000.00 Cash Bonanza Sweepstakes.

One of the individuals named below is the Third Round Grand Finalist and is a guaranteed winner of a $1000.00 certified bank check.

The other two individuals are guaranteed 4th Round Grand Finalists and their prize checks will be mailed to them on or about March 1, 1989.

CASH DISBURSEMENT BOX ★ ★ ★ UK

Paul S. Hughes

M. E. Lewist

Rosa M. Griffin

2 002 6557300225

If your name does not appear in the Cash Disbursement Box above, please disregard this Notice.

over, please

If your name does appear in the Cash Disbursement Box, you must return the Official Cash Claim Voucher below in the enclosed pre-addressed envelope along with your check for $7 to help in our fight against heart disease OR a blank check with the word VOID written across it.

Follow these instructions and on or about March 1, 1989 a bank check will be drafted and sent to you by return mail. Remember, you must send a check to claim your prize.

This massive $5,000.00 Cash Bonanza Giveaway is sponsored by American Heart Disease Prevention Foundation(AHDPF). As I write to you today, 43 million Americans are suffering from heart disease and over half will eventually die from heart disease. Through this give-away we are hoping to raise desperately needed funds to help in the fight against heart disease.

Already, AHDPF has been able to let millions of Americans know about nutritional prevention methods - methods that have the potential to save thousands of lives.

But to continue this important work we need your help and the help of our other friends.

So, please send your check for $7 or more today.

Remember, to claim the cash prize you have already won you must send us your check either made out for $7 or more or your blank check with the word "VOID" written across it.

Either way, on or about March 1, 1989 a bank check will be mailed to you.

Sincerely,

Marvin Bierenbaum, M.D.
Executive Director

P.S. If this letter is addressed to you and your name appears in the Cash Disbursement Box, PLEASE NOTE, your Cash Claim Coupon has a certified cash value.

This means if you do not return the Coupon before the deadline date, you forfeit the certified cash value associated with your name. So we recommend you mail your Coupon back to our Redemption Office as soon as possible.

Exhibit 7-8: American Heart Disease Prevention Foundation

Comment:

This mailer uses the sweepstakes approach to induce recipients to send a check for $7 (or more). Options are two: A check for $7 or more; or a check with the word "Void" written across it. Effective primitive psychology is at work here.

The question many fund raisers ask is whether the bother of running a sweepstakes and the possible difficulty of getting a second donation from entrants is worth the game. Only tabulation of a direct comparison, *carried through the second year,* can answer that question.

Almost no copy refers to the American Heart Disease Prevention Foundation, and *no* copy tells us what the Foundation does. If the words "Non-Profit Organization" weren't on the postal indicia, we'd wonder whether this might be a commercial enterprise.

I hope these foldover notes brighten
your day and that, when you use them,
they will brighten someone else's, too!

Dear Fellow American:

They really are lovely, aren't they? I
hope you'll enjoy them.

I'm sending them to you today, however, to
call your attention to something that's
anything but lovely --

-- Alzheimer's disease!

Our organization, Alzheimer's Disease
Research, is dedicated to the goal of finding a
cure for this mind-destroying malady!

Even if you've had no first-hand
experience with the disease (and I sincerely
hope you haven't), I'm sure you're familiar
with some of the heart-breaking stories about
those afflicted with Alzheimer's.

It seems so new, yet it was first
diagnosed in 1907. Today, it ranks as the
fourth leading cause of death among older
Americans, with official estimates of at least
two million Alzheimer's sufferers -- and a
strong possibility that the actual number may
be twice that high.

Alzheimer's kills. Slowly, relentlessly,
and without exception.

Usually, its destruction of the brain
takes six or seven years before it ends in
death. On the other hand, it can kill in half

(over, please)

Better Health Through Research

15825 Shady Grove Road, Suite 140, Rockville, Maryland 20850 / 1-800-227-7998

---

that time...or stretch out the agony for 20
long years!

We tend to think of it as a disease that
attacks older people, yet victims as young as
28 have been reported!

And there's nothing we can do about it!

What causes it? How can we cure it? What
can we do to prevent it?

WE JUST DON'T KNOW!

But we do know that the incidence of
Alzheimer's, and the incalculable misery and
pain it causes, are likely to reach epidemic
proportions in the very near future -- unless
we make an all-out effort to stop it now!

So I'm writing to you in the sincere hope
that you'll help us find the answers to
Alzheimer's disease in our lifetime...

...hopefully before you or I or
one of our loved ones becomes the
next victim!

And only if we fight this merciless
killer together can we avoid this
terrible tragedy!

Alzheimer's Disease Research is currently
sponsoring 10 pioneering research efforts at
some of the most prestigious medical
institutions in the nation.

But since there's no way of knowing which
approach may yield the answer we so desperately
need, we must do everything in our power to
expand the scope of this crucial scientific
quest.

And that costs money! Lots of it!

Obviously, we can't turn to the federal
government for help -- their preoccupation with
budget cuts makes that impossible.

So it's up to us -- to you and me and
other concerned Americans -- to cover the cost

62

of this all-important research.

Because if we don't do it, <u>no one else will</u>!

By using the enclosed notes, you'll give pleasure to a few others. But your financial assistance, will give the even greater gift of <u>hope</u> to two million Alzheimer's victims!

Your contribution of $25, $50, $15, or as much as you can possibly afford, may well be the gift that launches a very special research project --

-- <u>the one that finds a way to cure and prevent Alzheimer's</u>!

Until that happens, none of us is safe from this affliction -- a disease that's so terrible, its victims often beg for death...and their loving families can't help but wonder if that wouldn't be a blessing!

Let's end this agony. <u>Now</u>! <u>Together</u>!

Please be as generous as you can. Thank you.

Sincerely,

Eugene H. Michaels
President

EHM/pn

P.S. Please send the most generous gift you can manage right away. Remember, precious human lives are hanging in the balance. We don't have a moment to spare!

Exhibit 7-9: Alzheimer's Disease Research

Comment:

The five major motivators are fear, exclusivity, greed, guilt, and anger.

This mailing leans heavily on *guilt* by enclosing some "foldover notes." Although the letter says, on page 2, "And there's nothing we can do about it!" this organization tells us its research goes in many directions.

Oddly, this is a three-page letter. Many letter-writers (including me) feel having a blank page is a waste. One way to tell, for your organization: Test.

Opinion: This letter would have been stronger had it isolated a victim of Alzheimer's and recounted the tortured tale of gradual deterioration.

MIAMI
CHILDREN'S
HOSPITAL
THE MARY ANN KNIGHT INTERNATIONAL INSTITUTE OF PEDIATRICS
FOUNDED AS VARIETY CHILDREN'S HOSPITAL

Dear Friend:

Miami Children's Hospital is one of the world's
leading pediatric medical centers. And South
Florida children are fortunate to have such
reliable quality care only a few minutes away
from their home.

As the largest free-standing pediatric teaching
hospital in the Southeast United States, Miami
Children's treats over 100,000 youngsters from
birth to age 21 every year.

Be it a severely injured child flown via helicop-
ter for life-saving care, infants with congenital
conditions requiring specialized surgery, or any
commonplace pediatric ailment, Miami Children's
offers a complete patient care package to insure
a healthy start in life.

Our state-of-the-art facilities include the
nation's largest neurological center for children
with brain disorders, a new heart center headed
by one of the world's top cardiovascular pediatric
surgeons, and scores of other specialized areas.

But Miami Children's is not just "high tech," it
is also "high touch." As children experts, the
staff is aware that children have a special need
for sensitive, caring attention. This hospital
provides just that.

The children of South Florida have the very best
that modern medicine can provide thanks to the
support of a caring community. Please, won't
you help too by sending a generous gift?

Sincerely,

Peter L. Bermont
Chairman of the Board   PLB:B

6125 S.W. 31st Street, Miami, FL 33155 / USA / (305) 666-6511

Exhibit 7-10: Miami Children's Hospital

Comment:

This letter overdoes its chest-thumping. The danger of a "We're the greatest!" letter is the possibility of having the reader ask, "Then why do they need me?"

Opinion: The letter would be more successful if it leaned on what the hospital wants to accomplish and how many children aren't able to benefit from treatment because the facilities are stretched wire-thin, instead of suggesting to the reader that success has been achieved without him. "There's so much more to do" involves the reader; "Our state-of-the-art facilities" leaves the reader where he began, as an outsider.

CHAPTER 8

"Domestic Animals" Letters

65

Exhibit 8-1: Humane Society

Comment:

The enclosures within this mailing were two—this "Report" and a response device.

Opinion, not fact: Impact would be increased if a letter-plea, in typewriter-face, occupied part of the first page. The Report is professional, eye-catching, and easy to read; but relevance to the reader is a question.

I've never heard of Dick Garden's "Wonder Zoo" and wonder if the society is using an elephant gun to knock down pygmies. If I didn't live in Florida, the rabies-control story would have little meaning for me.

For newsletters, a logical suggestion is to assure reader-involvement in the lead stories. Otherwise, the tenuous emotional connection leading to a contribution is too easily brushed away.

Dear Member,

This membership packet has a special meaning for both of us.

First, it helps to identify you as a loyal member of the Humane Society of the United States and signifies that you agree that protecting all living things is important.

Second, it confirms for us your active participation in the largest animal protection organization in the nation (with over 500,000 constituents), as we work to end all forms of animal suffering and abuse.

Throughout the year you will continue to receive our magazine, Humane Society News, our newsletter, Close-up Report, and our periodic special notices, Action Alert.

Through these publications you will learn more about the programs and activities of the Humane Society of the United States, especially as they relate to: companion animals; laboratory animals; farm animals; marine mammals; and wildlife.

I encourage you to read about our programs and activities

(over, please)

Humane Society of the United States

2100 L Street, NW
Washington, D.C. 20037
(202) 452-1100

The Helping Hands for Animals

and to continue to spread the word about the importance of protecting all animals.

As you know, the work of the Humane Society of the United States is entirely dependent upon the generosity of our members and donors, so I hope you will continue to support our important work.

Tax-deductible contributions of any amount are always welcome and are put to immediate use in working to eliminate all forms of animal cruelty and abuse.

Again, thank you for your past support and I look forward to your continued participation in the work of the Humane Society of the United States.

Sincerely,

John A. Hoyt
President

Dear Member,

I am pleased to enclose your 19__ Membership card and window decal in recognition of your loyal support of The Humane Society of the United States. Please display them proudly as a symbol of your thoughtful generosity in working to protect all animals.

Sincerely,

John A. Hoyt
President

Humane Society of
the United States
The Helping Hands for Animals

MS MARGO E LEWIS
MEMBER NUMBER 8497113

Humane Society of the United States
Contribution Reply Form

☐ **YES,** I support the important programs of The Humane Society of the United States in working to protect all animals. Here is my donation of:

☐ $_____ (other)   ☐ $50   ☐ $15
☐ $100   ☐ $25   ☐ $10

☐ check enclosed (Payable to: Humane Society of the United States)

☐ Please charge my: VISA MasterCard (circle one)

Card no. _ _ _ _ _ _ _ _ _ _ _ _ _ _ _

Exp. Date _____

Signature X_____

8497113 HE4 0127211
MS MARGO E LEWIS
9746 CEDAR VILLAS BOULVARD
PLANTATION, FL 33324

Humane Society of the United States
2100 L Street, NW, Washington, D.C. 20037

Exhibit 8-2: Humane Society

Comment:

Ostensibly a single-purpose mailing (delivery of the membership card), this is a "Thank you, please" communication.

The letter is standard boiler-plate copy, thin in impact because it generalizes. A second note, just above the glued-on card, says as much as the letter.

Is the letter necessary at all? Yes, if one believes (as I do) the best potential donor is the recent donor. No, if the letter has as little impact as this one does.

How would you have handled this? Mightn't you have put a more powerful message adjacent to the response device?

Dear HSUS Member:

The Marine Mammal Protection Act (MMPA) is up for re-authorization this year and Congress has already devoted a good deal of time to the issues involved. It is vital to the interests of dolphins who are drowned by the thousands in tuna nets in the eastern Pacific that you let your legislators know where you stand on this matter.

More than 300 dolphins will continue to die every day until the U.S. government acts to stop the slaughter. The dolphins urgently need your voice.

Please write to your representative and two senators as soon as possible and urge them to support a rewrite of the MMPA that includes the following protections for dolphins:

The United States must *immediately embargo* tuna imports from all countries killing dolphins until such countries can prove compliance with U.S. marine mammal protection laws.

The 20,500 U.S. annual dolphin-kill quota must be *reduced immediately* to reflect the original intent of the MMPA of 1972; "...that the incidental kill or serious injury of marine mammals permitted in the course of commercial fishing operations be reduced to insignificant levels approaching *zero* mortality and serious injury rate."

The United States must require *government observers* aboard *100 percent* of all U.S. and foreign tuna purse seine vessels.

The United States must begin an intensive search for yellowfin tuna-catching technology that does not involve the chasing, harassment, and catching of dolphins or other marine mammals. *This has been a requirement of the MMPA since 1981 but has never been carried out.*

Lastly, one of the most important aspects of the MMPA is the additional protection it provides to depleted species, including some species of dolphins and many other kinds of marine mammals, such as northern fur seals, Steller sea lions, and whales. Yet, elements of the fishing industry are lobbying hard to be permitted unimpeded intentional killing of these animals. This cannot be allowed. *Please help all the marine mammals by asking your legislators to support full and necessary protection for depleted species.*

Please send a copy of one of your letters to U.S. Secretary of Commerce C. William Verity, who can order an embargo of tuna from nations not complying with U.S. laws regarding dolphins. Write to: Hon. C. William Verity, Secretary of Commerce, U.S. Department of Commerce, Washington, DC 20230.

By working together we can stop the suffering and slaughter of dolphins and all marine mammals.

ACTION ALERT•ACTION ALERT•ACTION ALERT•ACTION ALERT•ACTION ALERT

Exhibit 8-3: Humane Society

Comment:

The format damages this message. Size, typesetting, and lack of any sort of personalization give the "Action Alert" a commercial look.

Opinion: The second paragraph has far more impact than the first. Switching paragraphs might improve readership.

If I were writing an "Action Alert" I wouldn't give it this slick, carefully prepared look. I'd have the impression of haste, of urgency. "Action Alert" would be a rubber stamp.

As it stands, this communication has little verisimilitude.

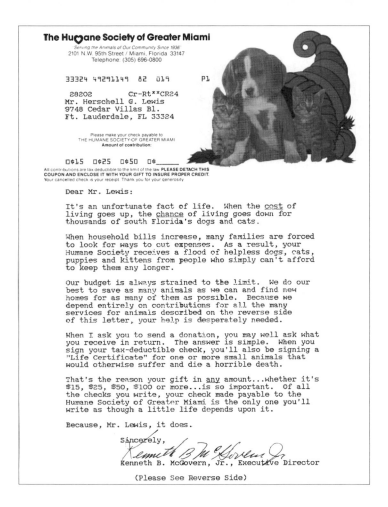

Dear Mr. Lewis:

It's an unfortunate fact of life. When the cost of
living goes up, the chance of living goes down for
thousands of south Florida's dogs and cats.

When household bills increase, many families are forced
to look for ways to cut expenses. As a result, your
Humane Society receives a flood of helpless dogs, cats,
puppies and kittens from people who simply can't afford
to keep them any longer.

Our budget is always strained to the limit. We do our
best to save as many animals as we can and find new
homes for as many of them as possible. Because we
depend entirely on contributions for all the many
services for animals described on the reverse side
of this letter, your help is desperately needed.

When I ask you to send a donation, you may well ask what
you receive in return. The answer is simple. When you
sign your tax-deductible check, you'll also be signing a
"Life Certificate" for one or more small animals that
would otherwise suffer and die a horrible death.

That's the reason your gift in any amount...whether it's
$15, $25, $50, $100 or more...is so important. Of all
the checks you write, your check made payable to the
Humane Society of Greater Miami is the only one you'll
write as though a little life depends upon it.

Because, Mr. Lewis, it does.

Sincerely,

Kenneth B. McGovern, Jr., Executive Director

(Please See Reverse Side)

Exhibit 8-4: Humane Society of Greater Miami

Comment:

This is another letter which might have been stronger if the writer
had started with the second paragraph.

The first paragraph is on the tricky side, and cleverness *always* interferes with an emotional reaction.

For some reason I react negatively to sentences such as, "Our
budget is always strained to the limit." It may be the overtone of inability to operate inside a budget; it may be the suggestion that no amount
of money ever will be enough.

This suggests a warning to all fund raising letter writers: Be certain
every paragraph makes you either a hero or a martyr.

The "Life Certificate" idea is a good one, and if I were advisor to
this organization I'd suggest it test this avenue more aggressively. But
the passive word "receive" saps another few percentage points of
force from this letter.

John F. Kullberg
President

ASPCA

America's First Humane Society

Dear Friend,

Before you read my letter, will you take a moment to find two important items in this envelope?

The <u>first</u> is the reward we promised you -- a free sheet of ASPCA stamps.

The <u>second</u> is the ASPCA's "10 Most Unwanted List" -- a brief record of ten of the most cruel and inhumane practices the ASPCA is fighting to abolish.

The stamps are yours to keep. Put them on your personal mail as a way to spread our name and message around the country. By doing so, you'll help us celebrate our 122 years of protecting animals.

I know you'll like the stamps.

But the "10 Most Unwanted List" you won't like at all.

Take the so-called "Classic LD50 test," for example -- number one on our list.

"LD" stands for "lethal dose." And "50" stands for 50%.

Translated, the LD50 Test is a laboratory "experiment" in which a group of animals are force-fed massive amounts of things like drain opener fluid, floor wax, and toilet bowl cleansers until 50% of the animals die, typically in a horribly painful way.

Number two on our unwanted list is "Pound Seizure."

You always thought dogs and cats were treated humanely when you took them to an animal shelter, didn't you?

Well, think again.

As you know, ASPCA shelters will <u>never</u> surrender an animal to a laboratory, but many states and cities have "pound seizure" laws that <u>force</u> animal shelters to give stray dogs and cats to laboratories and

THE AMERICAN SOCIETY FOR THE PREVENTION OF CRUELTY TO ANIMALS
441 East 92nd Street • New York, N.Y. 10128

- 2 -

medical schools for experimentation. Such laws pervert the meaning of shelter and care.

As a result these so-called shelters become nothing more than way stations on the road to great suffering and often agonizing death.

I could go on and on.

I could tell you about "factory farming," a practice that treats animals like inventoried machines with little or no attention to their basic needs. Many veal calves, for example, spend their entire lives on factory farms, confined in darkened stalls just a few inches wider than their bodies.

I could talk about animal fighting, the mistreatment of animals used in entertainment, hot-iron face branding of cattle, and even ritual sacrifices of animals by "religious" and satanic cults -- rituals that ASPCA law enforcement officers raid frequently.

But I don't want to overwhelm you with these seemingly endless varieties of horror and abuse we daily encounter and try to stop. <u>What I want most is for you to understand that literally millions of animals need our help even as you are reading my letter -- and that we need your help to help them</u>!

How?

By joining the ASPCA, and our 122 year crusade to protect animals from cruelty.

When you become a member of this country's first humane society, The American Society for the Prevention of Cruelty to Animals, you join hands with thousands of concerned people around the country who are fighting to protect defenseless creatures from agonies like the ones I've described.

Although we are widely known for our veterinary hospitals, spay/ neuter clinics, rescue ambulances, animal shelters and law enforcement activities in New York state, <u>the ASPCA fights for the protection of animals throughout the country</u>.

Take <u>legislation</u>, for example.

The ASPCA is one of the most powerful and respected forces in Washington, D. C. when it comes to passing tough laws for animal rights.

In recent years, we've fought for laws and government regulations to:

* Improve the care and comfort and reduce the
  volume of laboratory animals;

* Find scientifically acceptable alternatives to the use of animals for experiments;

* Ban the interstate shipment of and intrastate use of steel-jaw leghold traps;

* Drastically curtail the always senseless use of the classic LD50 test;

* Protect animals used for entertainment purposes, particularly during television or movie productions.

Or take <u>public education</u>.

Through a massive media campaign, nationally-distributed publications and school presentations, the ASPCA is working independently as well as with other humane groups to put an end to the vicious cycle of pet over-population and abandonment.

By educating the American public on responsible companion animal stewardship, we're helping to stop one of the worst of all animal tragedies in this country -- the millions of unwanted dogs and cats who are abandoned and eventually die every year, all too often from disease, torture, mutilation or starvation.

<u>Will you join our 122-year-old humane crusade on behalf of these needy animals</u>?

If so, there are three things I'd like you to do.

<u>FIRST</u>, as I mentioned earlier, use your ASPCA stamps on all your personal mail. Your friends respect you and your opinions. By telling them you support the ASPCA, you'll make it easier for us to gather their support as well.

<u>SECOND</u>, give me your opinion on what you think is the most senseless of the practices on our "10 Most Unwanted List." Place an "X" by it. This will tell me which practice you think the ASPCA should focus even more attention on this year. It's a way for me to take an informal survey of our new members, and -- symbolically, at least -- a way for you to "X" out a cruelty.

<u>THIRD</u>, become a member of the ASPCA. Symbolic gestures are fine, but your $20 membership contribution will go to work in state and federal courts, in Congress, and in the streets to help protect animals.

As a member of the ASPCA, you will receive our quarterly journal, <u>The ASPCA Report</u>.

But the most important "benefit" of membership I can offer you is this:

<u>The good feeling that comes in knowing you saved an animal from needless pain and suffering</u>.

Please join our fight against the senseless suffering of animals by returning your completed survey and contribution of $20, $50, $100 or more today in the postage paid envelope I've enclosed.

Sincerely,

John F. Kullberg

John F. Kullberg
President

P.S. I don't like asking you to do this, but I think it's necessary to dramatize why I need your help.

As you read our "10 Most Unwanted List," imagine how you would feel if your own pet were subjected to such tortures. Think how your cat would feel with its paw in the steel-jaw leghold trap for days. Picture your dog in a clandestinely-held dogfight, in which the winner is the dog that is still alive, however barely, at the end.

I know it will make you want to do something about such horrors -- and <u>you can by joining us in our efforts to end such abuses</u>.

P.P.S In addition to our work in federal and state courts, in Congress, with government agencies and through national education programs, we directly and individually care for more needy animals each year than are cared for by any other humane society in America. <u>We do more and we need more</u>. <u>Please be as generous as you can</u>! <u>Thank you</u>.

JK

A financial report and specific information on ASPCA programs, activities and grants to non-affiliated organizations are available upon request from the ASPCA. A financial report is also available from the New York Department of State, Office of Charities Registration, Albany, N. Y. 12231.

ASPCA

John F. Kullberg
President

America's First Humane Society

Dear Friend,

Before you read my letter, will you take a moment to find two important items in this envelope?

The <u>first</u> is the reward we promised you -- a free decal which in case of fire will alert firefighters and police that help is needed.

The <u>second</u> is the ASPCA's "10 Most Unwanted List" -- a brief record of ten of the most cruel and inhumane practices the ASPCA is fighting to abolish.

The decal is yours to keep. Please make use of it. It could save a life.

I know you'll like the decal.

But the "10 Most Unwanted List" you won't like at all.

Take the so-called "Classic LD50 test," for example-- number one on our list.

"LD" stands for "lethal dose." And "50" stands for 50%.

Translated, the LD50 Test is a laboratory "experiment" in which a group of animals are force-fed massive amounts of things like drain opener fluid, floor wax, and toilet bowl cleansers until 50% of the animals die, typically in a horribly painful way.

Number two on our unwanted list is "Pound Seizure."

You always thought dogs and cats were treated humanely when you took them to an animal shelter, didn't you?

Well, think again.

As you know, ASPCA shelters will <u>never</u> surrender an animal to a laboratory, but many states and cities have "pound seizure" laws that <u>force</u> animal shelters to give stray dogs and cats to laboratories and medical schools for experimentation. Such laws pervert the meaning of shelter and care.

As a result these so-called shelters become nothing more than way stations on the road to great suffering and often agonizing death.

THE AMERICAN SOCIETY FOR THE PREVENTION OF CRUELTY TO ANIMALS
441 East 92nd Street • New York, N.Y. 10128 • (212) 876-7700

I could go on and on.

I could tell you about "factory farming," a practice that treats animals like inventoried machines with little or no attention to their basic needs. Many veal calves, for example, spend their entire lives on factory farms, confined in darkened stalls just a few inches wider than their bodies.

I could talk about animal fighting, the mistreatment of animals used in entertainment, hot-iron face branding of cattle, and even ritual sacrifices of animals by "religious" and satanic cults -- rituals that ASPCA law enforcement officers raid frequently.

But I don't want to overwhelm you with these seemingly endless varieties of horror and abuse we daily encounter and try to stop. <u>What I want most is for you to understand that literally millions of animals need our help even as you are reading my letter -- and that we need your help to help them</u>!

How?

By joining the ASPCA, and our 122 year crusade to protect animals from cruelty.

When you become a member of this country's first humane society, The American Society for the Prevention of Cruelty to Animals, you join hands with thousands of concerned people around the country who are fighting to protect defenseless creatures from agonies like the ones I've described.

Although we are widely known for our veterinary hospitals, spay/neuter clinics, rescue ambulances, animal shelters and law enforcement activities in New York state, <u>the ASPCA fights for the protection of animals throughout the country</u>.

Take <u>legislation</u>, for example.

The ASPCA is one of the most powerful and respected forces in Washington, D.C. when it comes to passing tough laws for animal rights.

In recent years, we've fought for laws and government regulations to:

* Improve the care and comfort and reduce the volume of laboratory animals;

* Find scientifically acceptable alternatives to the use of animals in experiments;

* Ban the interstate shipment of and intrastate use of steel-jaw leghold traps;

* Drastically curtail the always senseless use of the classic LD50 test;

* Protect animals used for entertainment purposes, particularly during television or movie productions.

Or take <u>public education</u>.

Through a massive media campaign, nationally-distributed publications and school presentations, the ASPCA is working independently as well as with other humane groups to put an end to the vicious cycle of pet over-population and abandonment.

By educating the American public on responsible companion animal stewardship, we're helping to stop one of the worst of all animal tragedies in this country -- the millions of unwanted dogs and cats who are abandoned and eventually die every year, all too often from disease, torture, mutilation or starvation.

<u>Will you join our 122-year-old humane crusade on behalf of these needy animals</u>?

If so, there are three things I'd like you to do.

<u>FIRST</u>, as I mentioned earlier, please make use of your ASPCA rescue decal. It could save lives.

<u>SECOND</u>, give me your opinion on what you think is the most senseless of the practices on our "10 Most Unwanted List." Place an "X" by it. This will tell me which practice you think ASPCA should focus even more attention on this year. It's a way for me to take an informal survey of our new members, and-- symbolically at least -- a way for you to "X" out a cruelty.

<u>THIRD</u>, become a member of the ASPCA. Symbolic gestures are fine, but your $20 membership contribution will go to work in state and federal courts, in Congress, and in the streets to help protect animals.

As a member of the ASPCA, you will receive our quarterly journal, <u>The ASPCA Report</u>.

But the most important "benefit" of membership I can offer you is this:

<u>The good feeling that comes in knowing you saved an animal from needless pain and suffering</u>.

Please join our fight against the senseless suffering of animals by returning your completed survey and contribution of $20, $50, $100 or more today in the postage paid envelope I've enclosed.

Sincerely,

John F. Kullberg
President

P.S. I don't like asking you to do this, but I think it's necessary to dramatize why I need your help.

As you read our "10 Most Unwanted List," imagine how you would feel if your own pet were subjected to such tortures. Think how your cat would feel with its paw in the steel-jaw leghold trap for days. Picture your dog in a clandestinely-held dogfight, in which the winner is the dog that is still alive, however barely, at the end.

I know it will make you want to do something about such horrors -- and <u>you can by joining us in our efforts to end such abuses</u>.

P.P.S. In addition to our work in federal and state courts, in Congress, with government agencies and through national education programs, we directly and individually care for more needy animals each year than are cared for by any other humane society in America. <u>We do more and we need more. Please be as generous as you can</u> ! <u>Thank you</u>.

A financial report and specific information on ASPCA programs, activities and grants to non-affiliated organizations are available upon request from the ASPCA. A financial report is also available from the New York Department of State, Office of Charities Registration, Albany N.Y. 12231.

73

Exhibit 8-5: ASPCA

Comment:

Were these two letters a test?

The first reaction is, "Of course." But the letters weren't mailed at the same time, and both were mailed to the same name and address.

The letters are identical, except for the free enclosure. One version has a window decal "In case of fire," so the fire department will know at once children and/or pets are inside. The other has a sheet of stamps.

Actually, the letters aren't quite parallel because the "sheet of stamps" version is spaced to prevent a paragraph from ending at the bottom of the page—good force-communication technique.

But copy is curiously intellectualized. This could stem from the overly clever, non-emotional "10 Most Unwanted List."

We have the "Classic LD50 Test," our lead item. The word "Classic" damages the effect, because most people attach a positive overtone to the word. How much more horrifying the episode would be if it began:

"A helpless puppy is strapped to a table. Hands pry open its jaws and pour in toilet bowl cleansers loaded with caustic acids, searing the throat and burning away the stomach. The puppy howls in unbearable agony, but the pain won't stop. Not until the animal is dead."

Now the second problem: The list itself. Did the writer become hung in his own device? A list of ten *anythings* will include some weak ones. One of the Great Laws of direct response is:

$E^2 = 0.$

When you emphasize everything, you emphasize nothing. Laundry lists are *dangerous*. Choose an argument and subordinate the rest.

SPCA JOHANNESBURG SOCIETY FOR THE PREVENTION OF CRUELTY TO ANIMALS

Reg. No. 05/00386/08
Fr No. 01/00018 000 5

PO BOX 38035, BOOYSENS, 2016 TEL: (011) 680-6430

22 April '96

Dear Friend

The <u>Rich Dog</u> lives with caring owners who make sure it is fed properly, kept clean and healthy and who will go to any lengths to act responsibly towards their pet. The owners need not be rich ... however, the dog <u>is</u> well off.

The <u>Poor Dog</u> is fun as a puppy but eventually, the novelty wears off and the owners lose interest. At holiday time, the owners decide that it's an unwarranted expense to pay kennel fees, (and anyway the dog has got to go), so one night they throw it over the SPCA's fence at Booysens. The owners are considerate really - they might have kicked it out on some country road. These owners are not necessarily poor ... but the dog is 'down and out'.

<u>The SPCA has thousands of dogs and cats thrown into its back yard!</u>

As well, all year round we provide rescue services, animal ambulance and protection services. Inspectors watch over commercial, domestic and rural animal welfare and we provide education and a kennels service - <u>in fact, if it's got to do with animals then we're probably involved.</u>

The authorities do not provide us with enough money to do this public work. So we exist mainly because of thousands of members of the Society and donors who believe in what we do and refuse to let the services be cut.

'Rich Dog ... Poor Dog' is a story that can be told a thousand times over. The poor ones will come to us and we'll care for them somehow. We can't budget for these new boarders, so we need your help now.

<u>Please make a donation to help these lonely animals. R25.00 is the average all inclusive cost to the SPCA for just one animal. If you can send more, we'd be grateful.</u>

And on behalf of some Poor Dog ... thank you.

Archer Wilson

ARCHER WILSON
Manager

P.S. Please rush your donation to us in the envelope provided, today.

Exhibit 8-6: SPCA, Johannesburg

Comment:

This South African mailing parallels the ASPCA mailing in intent and organization-services.

The one emotional word in this letter appears far down the page. The word: "Lonely." What a wonderful word, far more motivational than the "Rich Dog...Poor Dog" theme.

Do we really have a lot of sympathy for the poor dog? The owners didn't throw the dog onto the street; instead, they threw it over the fence into the SPCA's yard.

Why not develop this theme—a frightened little dog, limping from having hurt a leg when the insensitive owner threw it over the fence? Instead, the letter lapses into a standard "We need money" approach.

The letter isn't a bad one, but why not use ammunition readily at hand?

NATIONAL
ANTI-VIVISECTION
SOCIETY

THE CAMPAIGN FOR LIFE

The time has come...

   ...when we can make real progress in the struggle to save animals from the needless, wasteful and inhumane practice of vivisection.

   With viable alternatives now available, we ask you to join us in THE CAMPAIGN FOR LIFE, a three-step program to end animal experimentation while protecting the future health and safety of you and your family.

   1. Replace all animals used in toxicity testing with existing alternative methods.

   2. End abusive, duplicative and frivolous research on animals.

   3. Develop and apply non-animal alternatives for conducting worthwhile biomedical research.

   Given strong support, these goals can be reached. Unfortunately, the experience of past humanitarian movements tells us progress is never initiated by those who have a vested interest in the status quo. To ensure true and lasting change, the sustained pressure of public concern – your concern – will be needed.

   This could take years. And for every one of those years millions more animals will be destroyed, painfully and needlessly.

   With your help, and the help of other concerned citizens, we can turn the clock ahead. For every hour gained, a minimum of 2400 animals can be saved in the U.S. alone.

   May I welcome you as a new member of NAVS? If you are now a member we appreciate your support. If you do not wish to join, please contribute what you can. No amount is too large or too small. Even one dollar will help.

   But don't delay. With every second lost, time runs out for another innocent and helpless creature. So please act today.

                                          Thank you for caring,

                                          Mary Margaret Cunniff

                                          Mary Margaret Cunniff
                                          Executive Director

Exhibit 8-7: National Anti-Vivisection Society

Comment:

Words such as *duplicative, viable alternatives, progress is never initiated,* and *ensure* show impeccable grammar. In combination with sentence after sentence in which active voice gives way to passive, they establish an arm's-length relationship instead of rapport.

Once again, episode surely would have been more dramatic than this intellectualized approach. Who opposes vivisection? Not the intellectuals. Those who do may not be able to respond to "Toxicity testing" and "non-animal alternatives."

We have an emotional issue which demands conversational rhetoric.

If you're one of the first 50
to reply to this letter about
our homeless dogs and cats ...

... we'll send you one of these pocket-sized radios ABSOLUTELY FREE.

Dear Friend:

It seems so heartless, but thousands and thousands of homeless pets are
put to sleep every year. There is, I suppose, nobody to care for them.

> But let me tell you about the North Shore Animal League,
> which has rescued sick, hurt, and unhappy dogs and cats
> for 44 years -- a haven where we refuse to destroy help-
> less pets. (Last year we saved over 43,000 animals.)

I wish you could see our shelter. It is always crowded with dogs and
cats, with more arriving daily. And each year, more come. Each year,
more folks have pets. Each year, more pets are lost or abandoned.

Don't think the North Shore Animal League is a gloomy place. Far from
it, the shelter is bright and cheerful. Newcomers are inoculated against
disease, bathed, de-flead, and checked for injury or illness -- and any
with a problem are immediately sent to our own veterinary clinic.

> Frightened and abused dogs get extra attention. Volunteers
> spend hours daily playing with them, walking and gentling
> them. Conditioning problem dogs for good homes may take
> weeks, but we feel loving care is worth the time spent.

Anyway, what choice is there? We can't kill them. We won't kill them.

> *   *   *   *   *

There's only one thing: It costs an arm and a leg to care for our many
thousands of non-paying "boarders" that come to the shelter annually.
Costs still keep rising, and more money is constantly needed for food,
veterinarian fees, heat, light, and so on. Well, you know how it is.

So we come to people like you for help -- for money to keep the animals
alive until tomorrow or next week or next month, when some kind families

will take them from their cages and provide homes, real homes.

Happily, not much money is needed from anyone.

> If each person gives just a dollar, we can keep the shelter
> open, and continue to save pets. And when I say this, let
> me add that we're in no danger of shutting down. I know
> that won't happen. Too many people like cats and dogs, so
> I know we'll keep our doors open.

What about you? Will you help?

You needn't send money to win a prize, but your gift to keep the puppies
and kittens fed and sheltered will be welcome. All you have to do is ...

... pick prizes you prefer on the Entry Tickets, and return all six tickets

with your tax deductible contribution. A pre-addressed reply envelope is

enclosed for your convenience.

> Thank you very much,
>
> _Mrs Alex Lewyt_
>
> Mrs. Alex Lewyt, for the
> NORTH SHORE ANIMAL LEAGUE

P. S. Our shelter's model spaying program leads the fight to reduce the
number of unwanted pets. We do all such things without government
help. Not only is no tax money received, but we pay no commissions
to professional fundraisers.

Remember - if you hurry - if your reply
is one of the first 50 received - we'll
send you a new pocket-sized radio.

LTR-63A

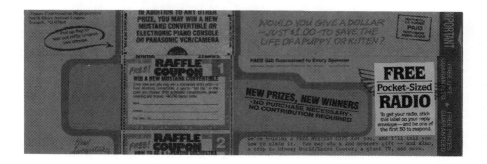

Exhibit 8-8: North Shore Animal League

Comment:

Typical of sweepstakes and giveaway mailings, this letter has two messages. One caters to the cynicism and hypocrisy typical of the last decade of the 20th century: People give in expectation of getting back more than they gave.

This is the "State Lottery Syndrome." Part of the take may help finance schools, but to the lottery player such dedication of funds is inconsequential.

Opinion: Offering the free radio to "the first 50 to respond" is neither fish nor fowl. Unquestionably some, whose response-pattern is slow, won't respond because they think the first 50 already are spoken for.

Are you jarred by the sudden swing into "It seems so heartless"? I was. I'm bothered, too, by the lack of specificity. And the word "newcomers" to describe lost or abandoned pets generates less sympathy than a more apt phrase would.

The entire envelope has a Publisher's Clearing House look, grabbing attention with prizes and free offers. The letter makes no reference to envelope copy or the other contents of the mailing until another abrupt change of pace just before the close.

Opinion: This letter tries to serve three separate masters and in doing so loses emphasis and generates confusion. A better approach might have been a hard sweepstakes letter *plus* a separate monarch-size highly emotional note.

CHAPTER 9

"Geriatric" Letters

If you want the protection provided by AARP's Group Hospital Plan but would rather have a lower monthly rate, you might want to consider our optional Plan (V-1). This Plan pays lower daily benefits at a lower monthly rate.

To take advantage of this opportunity, complete and sign the enclosed Enrollment Form - indicating the level of coverage you prefer, and whether you wish to have spouse coverage - and return it in the reply envelope provided.

Your coverage will begin on the first of the month after your Enrollment Form and first month's payment are received. So, the sooner you enroll, the sooner your protection will begin.

As with all insurance in the AARP Group Health Insurance Program, you are guaranteed the right to cancel your coverage - with no obligation - within 30 days if you are not completely satisfied.

When you consider the Plan's benefits and cost, you'll see that AARP's Group Hospital Plan gives you value other plans usually can't match.

Sincerely,

J. M. Tiede

J.M. Tiede
Product Specialist
Marketing Communications

Exhibit 9-1: AARP

Comment:

This letter from the American Association of Retired Persons begins with a masterful combination of stroking and projected benefits.

The simple technique of indenting paragraphs would give the letter a more convivial appearance. In keeping with accepted techniques for communicating with older readers, paragraphs are short.

Accompanying the letter is an "Enrollment Form" plus a computer-personalized validator, a "Benefit Qualification" card, punched to resemble an old IBM computer punch-card.

The letter doesn't "hustle" the reader. Older people are gun-shy, even of AARP. Although the letter does use phrases such as "I encourage you to. . ." it stays low-key.

In the classic tradition, the letter exhorts (mildly), leaving explanation to the other enclosures. A few specifics about the actual cost of hospital care would add the dimension of fear, which in my opinion would give the reader an absolute reason to respond, not dependent on comparative advantages of AARP's insurance plan against other sources.

JAMES ROOSEVELT
United States Congressman (Retired)
Chairman, National Committee to
Preserve Social Security and Medicare
Washington, D.C.

MARGO E LEWIS
9748 CEDAR VILLAS BOULEVA
PLANTATION, FL 33324

Enclosed find Certified Petition
Number 13352288 M--9959089
Please check your Petition to be
certain that your Certification
Number is correct.

**My father started Social Security. Now, we must
act to protect Social Security and Medicare!**

DEAR CONCERNED AMERICAN:

Will you spend 45 seconds right now, to protect Social Security and Medicare?

If your answer is "Yes" then sign and return the enclosed Certified Petition. It's addressed to your U.S. Senators and Congressman:

SENATOR LAWTON MAINOR CHILES JR.
SENATOR BOB GRAHAM
CONGRESSMAN LAWRENCE J. SMITH

Never in the 53 years since my father, Franklin Delano Roosevelt, started the Social Security system have there been such threats to our Social Security and Medicare benefits as the decade of the '80's. That's why I started the National Committee to Preserve Social Security and Medicare.

Just consider these facts:

• Last November, Administration and Congressional budget negotiators came within days of proposing to cut the cost-of-living adjustment (COLA) almost in half. That cut would have cost the average senior $2,064 over the next five years. Over the objection of major business leaders, we stopped the plan in its tracks with our hand-delivery of almost eight million Petition signatures to Members of Congress.

• In 1985, the Administration used the Social Security Trust Funds to help pay other government bills. National Committee Members wrote 75,000 letters to Congress demanding the restoration of the Trust Funds and Congress restored all assets and lost interest. But there is still no law to prevent this from happening again.

• During the last Congress, the Senate voted to delay Social Security cost-of-living adjustments and cut Medicare benefits by $2,300,000,000 (2 billion,

(please turn page)

---

(2)

300 million dollars). This action would have cost each recipient more than $1,200.00 over the next five years. National Committee Members helped defeat these ill-conceived acts, and we will continue to oppose any future attempts to cut benefits.

• Each year since 1981, Congress has debated legislation which would sharply increase the premium payments and deductibles for Medicare coverage. Over the past seven years, Congress has cut the Medicare program by $46 billion.

• In the last Congress, the National Committee worked successfully to defeat a Reagan Administration proposal which would have cut Medicare benefits by over $20 billion dollars over five years.

• Even so, the Medicare Part B Premium jumped 38.5% in January— 9 times the increase in this year's COLA — and you can bet more increases are on the way.

• Cost-of-living increases in Social Security were delayed six months in 1983, and further suspensions of badly needed cost-of-living increases have been threatened almost every year since 1981.

• Since 1984, more than five million Social Security beneficiaries have had to pay income taxes on their Social Security benefits for the first time in history. Over 100,000 owe more than $1,000.00 each year in additional taxes. This tax causes a benefit cut for millions of senior citizens — and the numbers being forced to pay this tax will continue to grow each year.

• For many of today's workers, the retirement age for receiving full Social Security benefits will increase to 67, and they will suffer significant reductions if they have to retire before age 65.

• And as a result of the outrageous inflation of hospital and doctor's fees, the average senior now pays more for health care than they did before Medicare. By 1991, elderly out-of-pocket health care spending will grow to $2,633.00 a year even without further cuts.

• Congress has unfairly cut Social Security benefits for up to 10 million Americans born in the "notch years" after 1916. And every year another 1.6 million new retirees fall into the "notch" pothole. This benefit cut averages almost $660.00 per year and could be costing you or a loved one up to $2,500.00 each year depending on the year you were born and the year you retired.

We, as a nation, have a solemn commitment to the tens of millions of our people who have paid into Social Security and Medicare over their long working years. These Americans are counting on Social Security and Medicare, and they must have it or face a crippling financial hardship.

Deep cuts, if made, would mean a dreary existence for many present and future Social Security and Medicare recipients, and would create a terrible hardship on their children and grandchildren who will somehow have to support retired family members.

But must we break our solemn commitments to those who worked so hard and paid their fair share into Social Security and Medicare?

(next page please)

(3)

No, it need not happen, not if you join with me, and millions of other Americans — right now.

Many politicians and bureaucrats are saying that we can't afford Social Security and Medicare. Recently, the powerful Federal Reserve Chairman, Alan Greenspan, called for cuts in both. And it's no secret that the recently-formed National Economic Commission will recommend cuts or taxation of Social Security benefits early next year.

Well, we've got to show them. We must take action by mounting a mass Petition drive and forming a huge organization to protect Social Security and Medicare. Leaders like Congressman Claude Pepper and others are doing their part. Now we must do ours.

It is my goal to deliver 5,000,000 Petitions to the Congress of the United States this year alone.

These Petitions demand the preservation and improvement of Social Security and Medicare by keeping the solemn commitment they represent for our people.

Over 50 years ago, I was working for my father in the White House as Secretary to the President.

Then I served for 11 years as a Member of the United States Congress.

So I know, as well as anyone, how powerful is our Constitutional right "to Petition the government for a redress of grievances."

So please, right now, sign and mail me your Petition. It has never been so necessary, so urgent, that you take action. It's addressed to your U.S. Senators and Congressman:

At the same time, please consider joining your National Committee to Preserve Social Security and Medicare.

The National Committee is a nonprofit, tax-exempt organization, comprised solely of concerned Americans, like you, who have invested a small amount to help block those who would destroy Social Security and Medicare. We have no source of income other than the Membership Dues and voluntary contributions of ordinary Americans who want our nation to keep its commitment to the Social Security and Medicare programs.

As a Member, your Annual Dues are only $10. If at any time during the course of your Membership you become unhappy with the National Committee, your Membership Dues will be refunded to you immediately — no questions asked.

And as a Member, you will receive a personal, gold-embossed plastic Membership Card and our regular newspaper, "Saving Social Security," which includes vital information on how your Senators and Congressman vote on Social Security and Medicare issues and on government actions, such as the proposals to hide the budget deficit through cuts in the COLA, or the fights to win fair protection of older Americans against the financial ruin of catastrophic illness.

Your "Saving Social Security" newspaper carries stories about Social Security, Medicare and other benefits for which you may qualify — such as the hospice and home health care benefits.

In addition, as a Member, you will be enrolled in our Legislative Alert Service which will immediately advise you of fast-breaking developments in Washington involv-

(over please)

(4)

ing Social Security and Medicare benefits. And our Legislative Alert Service works! We've already helped defeat numerous attempts to cut Social Security and Medicare benefits by flooding Congress with letters, post cards, mailgrams and phone calls.

And, most importantly, you will be helping to make it possible to continue our work here in the Capital with many leaders in Congress to protect, defend and improve the Social Security and Medicare programs.

Remember, my father founded Social Security 53 years ago. Now I need your help to protect Social Security and Medicare.

So, please act today. Sign and return to me your Petition to your U.S. Senators and your Congressman. These legislators may or may not agree with our program — so we must let them know where you stand:

SENATOR LAWTON MAINOR CHILES JR.
SENATOR BOB GRAHAM
CONGRESSMAN LAWRENCE J. SMITH

And please join your National Committee to Preserve Social Security and Medicare at the same time — but in any case, please act today. I have enclosed a special return envelope to speed your reply.

Urgently awaiting your reply, I am,

Most sincerely yours,

James Roosevelt

James Roosevelt
United States Congressman, (Retired)
Chairman, National Committee
to Preserve Social Security
and Medicare

P.S. CONCERNED AMERICAN: THOUSANDS OF ORDINARY AMERICANS, PEOPLE LIKE YOU, HAVE INVESTED $10 OF THEIR HARD-EARNED MONEY TO SEND YOU THE ENCLOSED PETITION. NATURALLY, THEY HOPE YOU WILL ALSO JOIN THEM AS A MEMBER IN THE MOVEMENT TO PROTECT SOCIAL SECURITY AND MEDICARE. SO PLEASE RETURN YOUR MEMBERSHIP APPLICATION TO ME. IF YOURS IS AMONG THE FIRST 50 APPLICATIONS RECEIVED FROM FLORIDA, YOU WILL RECEIVE FREE THE SLIM, DESKTOP CALCULATOR PICTURED ON THE FLAP OF THE ENCLOSED RETURN ENVELOPE.

IF YOU FAIL TO AT LEAST RETURN YOUR PETITION, THE INVESTMENT OF SO MANY AMERICANS WILL GO TO WASTE. AT THE SAME TIME, I WILL BE VERY DISAPPOINTED IF YOU DON'T JOIN, BECAUSE WE MUST CONTINUE TO COLLECT PETITIONS AND FUND OUR WORK WITH CONGRESS. SO PLEASE, JOIN YOUR FELLOW AMERICANS, AS A MEMBER, IF YOU POSSIBLY CAN.

Thank you, Jim

Prepared and mailed by the National Committee to Preserve Social Security, a nonprofit, tax-exempt organization, 2000 K St., N.W. Washington, D.C. 20006.

The National Committee is totally independent of Congress, every government agency, and all political parties.

Contributions to the National Committee are not tax-deductible, and you need make no special contributions other than annual dues.

The National Committee spends its budget in approximately the following way: legislative advocacy 43%, educational activities 22%, fund raising 15%, administration 17%, surplus 3%. Detailed financial reports are available from the National Committee and the charitable solicitations department of most states.

Exhibit 9-2: National Committee to Preserve Social Security and Medicare

Comment:

The name Roosevelt holds magic for the over-55s.

"Certified Petition Number 13352288 M-9959089" is an annoyance because of the length of the number. Does this technique personalize or *de*personalize? In my opinion the attempt to look "official" produces mixed results.

Opening copy is superb: "My father started Social Security. Now, we must act to protect Social Security and Medicare!" The word "act" can be dangerous in fund raising copy, but its use here is logical.

The letter is loaded with specific threats the reader is to help counteract. On page three the writer introduces personal history, a reminder that he is not only a Roosevelt but an involved Roosevelt. This gives the "we" additional power.

Part of a relatively expensive oversize mailing, the letter asks for $10 dues. Introduction of a desktop calculator "if yours is among the first 50 applications received" is totally out of key and in my opinion damages the image of the organization.

The all-caps p.s. is too long. It would be too long even if it were set in caps and lower case, but as typeset it's hard reading. Tone changes here. Phrases such as "If you fail to..." abandon the paternal flavor. But for some readers, this quick kick may be the response-generator.

THE HARVEST INGATHERING APPEAL
Meals on Wheels for the Aged
AUTHORITY FUND-RAISING/NO 07-700063-0001 (W.O.)

CENTRAL CO-ORDINATING OFFICE	REGIONAL OFFICES:
PO BOX 57497	TRANSVAAL (0151) 4118
SPRINGFIELD	OFS/NATAL (0331) 94-9241
2137	CAPE (824) 26610

Dear Mr Cowden

Sincere greetings!

Mr T. is now 84 years old. He's lonely and penniless. His son, an only child, was killed in a motor accident two years ago. Like so many other Senior Citizens he has had to sell his valuables in order to survive. Last month he managed to get a few Rand for his war medals.

"All that I now have left is my bed and a few changes of clothing. I never dreamt it would come to this. I can live with my aching joints; I can bear the loneliness; but the poverty and the hunger . . . , I just feel like weeping."

Today thousands of lonely Senior Citizens are experiencing similar nightmares. For them it is a desperate struggle just to stay alive. Please join hands with us this Christmas in bringing a little light into the lives of our down-trodden elderly folk.

I invite you to sponsor a number of Senior Citizens at the Meals on Wheels Christmas Functions for the Aged. The invitations that our volunteer helpers will be handing to them are enclosed with this letter. Instructions will be found at the foot of the Invitations.

You will never know what your kindness means to them.

Thank you.

Yours sincerely

F. Campbell
FRANCIS CAMPBELL
DIRECTOR

- -

MEALS ON WHEELS FOR THE AGED
CHRISTMAS DINNER SPONSORSHIP
P.O. Box 57497, Springfield, 2137

T 0829537CO: Please tick the number of Christmas dinners you would like to sponsor and detach this slip from the above. Enclose the invitations, together with this slip and your cheque/postal order (made payable to Meals on Wheels for the Aged) in the Freepost envelope provided. Please note any change of address alongside.

Mr B Cowden
20 Leighton Park
Alexander Ave
Fourways
2055

Yes! I am/we are happy to sponsor :-

☐	50 CHRISTMAS DINNERS FOR THE AGED = R400
☐	25 CHRISTMAS DINNERS FOR THE AGED = R200
☐	10 CHRISTMAS DINNERS FOR THE AGED = R 80
☐	4 CHRISTMAS DINNERS FOR THE AGED = R 32
☐	3 CHRISTMAS DINNERS FOR THE AGED = R 24
☐	2 CHRISTMAS DINNERS FOR THE AGED = R 16
☐	1 CHRISTMAS DINNER FOR THE AGED = R 8

(I understand that contributions are redistributed for use in the provinces where donors reside. Should surplus funds become available please use them in your other services for the needy aged.)

THE HARVEST INGATHERING APPEAL
Meals on Wheels for the Aged

CENTRAL CO-ORDINATING OFFICE	REGIONAL OFFICES:
PO BOX 57497	TRANSVAAL (0151) 4118
SPRINGFIELD	OFS/NATAL (0331) 94-9241
2137 AUTHORITY FUND RAISING No. 07-700063-0001 (W.O.)	CAPE (824) 26610

Dear Mr Cowden   17th July

Warm greetings to you. I trust that you and your loved ones are in good health and in good spirits.

Grandma found life somewhat different to what she expected after Granddad passed away. 'It's the little things,' she said, 'that really hurt.'

The heart-breaking moments deciding what to do with his clothing. The strange sensation when you habitually make two cups of tea instead of one. The feeling of unbelief as you find yourself absent-mindedly moving toward the bedroom to ask his advice on something or other. The sadness as you see the flowers that he planted in spring begin to whither under the blight of winter. Then there are the letters addressed to 'Mr & Mrs' . . .

Broken hearts need good friends. Meals on Wheels is so much more than just a Meal Delivery Service for the elderly. With every meal there comes a friend. A friend who really cares. The meal she brings is a token of love from another friend who cares - from someone like you.

Once again I invite you to join hands with Meals on Wheels for the Aged by 'Hosting a Granny'. You and Meals on Wheels make a wonderful team in bringing joy and hope into the lives of our struggling and lonely Aged.

Thank you. I wish you every success for the remainder of the year.

Yours sincerely

F. Campbell
FRANCIS CAMPBELL - DIRECTOR

✂ -

MEALS ON WHEELS FOR THE AGED
PO BOX 57497, SPRINGFIELD, 2137

Mr B Cowden
20 Leighton Park
Alexander Ave
Fourways
2055

"HOST A GRANNY" CAMPAIGN

PLAN A MEALS PER ANNUM		PLAN B MEALS PER MONTH	
365 MEALS =	R 912,50	40 MEALS =	R 100,00
200 MEALS =	R 500,00	20 MEALS =	R 50,00
100 MEALS =	R 250,00	16 MEALS =	R 40,00
50 MEALS =	R 125,00	12 MEALS =	R 30,00
30 MEALS =	R 75,00	8 MEALS =	R 20,00
20 MEALS =	R 50,00	4 MEALS =	R 10,00
15 MEALS =	R 37,50	3 MEALS =	R 7,50
10 MEALS =	R 25,00	2 MEALS =	R 5,00
8 MEALS =	R 20,00	1 MEAL =	R 2,50
MEALS =	R		

HG7SW 8858323CO

PLEASE SEE REVERSE SIDE

85

Exhibit 9-3: Meals on Wheels for the Aged

Comment:

Here we have two letters of parallel length, for the same organization.

The "Grandma" letter does induce a little sympathy—a little. Grandma doesn't seem to be *in extremis*. She's widowed, which in this age bracket isn't extraordinary.

The "Mr. T." letter has many times the impact of the "Grandma" letter. Mr. T. has genuine problems. This line has tremendous wallop:

"All that I now have left is my bed and a few changes of clothing. I never dreamt it would come to this."

We have the image of an old man, hopes and dreams shattered, facing no future, lacking every comfort, without friends or help.

Head-to-head, my opinion is the Mr. T. letter outpulled the Grandma letter by a wide margin. (Obviously this is a guess, because I have no access to actual results of these mailings.)

I haven't included insurance mailings from the American Association of Retired Persons, because these mailings are commercial rather than fund raising. In a later chapter, we'll look at Consumer Reports mailings; although they have commercial overtones, they don't take a commodity-sale posture.

CHAPTER *10*

"Humanitarian" Letters

erosion, and restore nitrogen and other
nutrients.

I'm proud to tell you that <u>60 percent</u>
of all trees planted in Guatemala today
<u>originated in a CARE forestry project</u>!

<u>But perhaps most important is that
farmers are learning that planting trees
will increase the amount of food they grow.</u>

This year alone, over 250,000 farmers
around the world will participate in CARE's
community nursery program -- producing nearly
20 million seedlings.

Half of the trees will eventually be used for firewood
as well as the prevention of erosion. Nearly 500,000
seedlings are fruit trees which will produce food and income.
Many of the remaining seedlings are nitrogen-fixing species,
used to improve the nutrient content of the soil, thus making
the land more productive for farming food.

As you can see, programs like these are having an
<u>immediate and dramatic effect</u> in the lives of the families
they touch.

But we cannot rest on the success of our efforts to
date. Many more projects are being planned right now,
projects that will help farmers turn wasteland into
productive farmland so they can provide food for their
families. <u>But we need your help</u>.

With your gift of $100, $250, $500 or more today, you
can plant a seed of hope in the hearts of farmers struggling
to provide for their families. Whatever you can send will
mean <u>so</u> <u>very</u> <u>much</u>. Please be generous. Thank you.

Sincerely,

Dr. Philip Johnston
Executive Director

P.S. Every dollar you send to CARE is matched by at least $9,
totalling $10 in goods and services. This is made
possible by grants from the U.S. Government and other
agencies cooperating with CARE.

So your gift of $100 actually provides $1,000 worth of
food, technical assistance, health services and training
to people in need.

(CARE is a major mailer. The seven examples shown here cover a period of about five months.)

Exhibit 10-1: CARE

Comment:

A rule I implement whenever I can:

> *The writer always has a stronger way to begin a message than "There is . . ." or "There are . . ."*

It's a minor point, but opening this letter with "There's a new symbol of hope..." presents the information in a lower key than this request for "$100, $250, $500 or more" should have.

Planting trees is a long-range solution to erosion, and even though this letter quotes a Nigerian farmer and adds a specific from Guatemala, reader-involvement is nominal. The p.s. has considerable strength, although it's too long; but by p.s. time the reader may (quietly) wander off.

660 First Avenue • New York, NY 10016 • (212) 686-3110 • Cable: PARCELUS NY

Philip Johnston, Ph.D., *Executive Director*

May 31, 19(

Ms. Margo E Lewis
PO Box 15725
9748 Cedar Villas B
Ft Lauderdale, FL 33324

Dear Ms. Lewis:

Thank you for your generous gift of $100.00.

At CARE, we believe helping people help themselves is the
only way to achieve our ultimate goal: self sufficiency.
Your gifts make this a reality. They make it possible for
CARE field workers to teach farmers how to increase and
expand their harvests, which means more food for their
malnourished children.

Again, thank you for helping millions of people improve the
quality of their lives through CARE'S self-help programs.

Sincerely,

Philip Johnston
Executive Director

P.S. The enclosed brochure "Where There's a Will,"
highlights how through your will, you can help those in
need. Please complete the request form for further
information and return in the envelope provided.

Exhibit 10-2: CARE

Comment:

Have you been sending personalized "Thank you" letters?

If you haven't, you've missed out on the best combination of effective public relations and increased donations available to fund raisers.

This letter isn't a brilliant piece of prose, *nor should it be.* Brilliant prose often is at odds with sincerity.

The p.s. refers the reader to a formal enclosure which describes ways of bequeathing part of the estate to CARE....a logical suggestion to serious donors. The p.s. is too stiff for my taste, because this is an "inside the family" letter, but who can fault the technique?

Lloyd Bridges

July 14, 19__

Dear Friend,

Perhaps you know me from my roles on television, on stage and in the movies.

Like you, I enthusiastically support the important work of CARE.

When I was asked by Dr. Johnston to travel to Africa as a Special Envoy for CARE, I was honored that I was chosen to observe and to give a first-hand report on what the situation there is like.

"But what if I'm not favorably impressed by the relief work being done?" I asked Dr. Johnston.

"Just be honest" he replied, "and tell what you actually saw."

I recently returned from that trip, and I want to report to you that I was truly humbled, moved, and more convinced than ever that <u>the support you and I are offering through our gifts to CARE is</u> making a meaningful difference in the lives of needy and deserving families overseas.

I visited CARE projects in Gursum and Babile Woredas in Ethiopia, and I was utterly amazed at what CARE has been able to help the people there accomplish!

Most of the 115,000 people who live there are farmers who have barely been able to scratch a living out of the parched soil. But in a relatively short period of time, with CARE's help, these people have:

* started <u>45</u> community tree nurseries!

* dug <u>9</u> wells!

* planted <u>1.2 million</u> tree seedlings!

* built <u>4</u> school roof catchments to capture rain water!

(over, please)

-2-

* planted <u>70</u> fuelwood forests!

* constructed over <u>620</u> miles of hillside terraces!

* harnessed water from <u>9</u> natural springs!

* and built <u>many</u> miles of new roads!

In fact, when I visited one village in the Babile region, all the men, women and children were hard at work building a "check dam" to prevent water from running off. When the dam is finished, water will slowly filter through it leaving behind layers of silt. In this way the people are reclaiming land destroyed by erosion.

And when I visited a village in the Grawa area, teenage boys were busy digging holes in the ground with tools provided by CARE, while the young girls were fetching seedlings from a nearby truck for planting.

Everywhere I went I saw real, hard evidence of CARE programs at work, <u>programs</u> I <u>know are made possible because of your support and mine</u>.

And throughout my trip I was impressed with the way CARE keeps track of everything -- how a CARE worker checks off an inventory sheet as bags of grain and other supplies are unloaded from a railway car and piled high into a CARE truck for delivery. Yes, I can assure you that your donations are actually reaching the African people.

That's why CARE's record for food delivery is impeccable...and why CARE was given the World Without Hunger Award by President Reagan.

At the village level too, everything is monitored, every child is weighed and measured, and the neediest get the largest rations.

And, every dollar you send to CARE is matched by at least $9 in goods and services. This is made possible by grants from the U.S. Government and other agencies cooperating with CARE.

But I must admit, the one thing that impressed

(next page, please)

and touched me the most was the quiet strength, the determination, the unyielding hope reflected in the eyes of the people I met, people who have endured so much unrelenting hardship and grief.

I'll never forget one young woman I met at a feeding center in the Hararghe province of Ethiopia. She was in line, holding a child to her breast, waiting for a ration of food.

As I spoke with her through an interpreter, she told me of how she had lost her husband because of the drought, and now, all she had left were her children. And I could see that quiet determination in her eyes, a determination to survive, not just for herself, but especially for her children.

Unfortunately, for many Ethiopians like her, survival is still a daily struggle. You see, a devastating drought still holds East Africa in a deadly grip, a drought even more severe than the one we all read about and saw on our television screens in 1985.

In fact, more than 5 million Ethiopians, and millions of subsistence farmers in other African countries, are facing the prospect of hunger and even starvation because of disastrous crop losses.

Many of these people are being helped by CARE and other organizations which have enabled them to remain in their villages. Although this had not gathered as much media attention as the long lines of hungry people in camps did three years ago, there is a severe food shortage and many people who still need our help.

We're helping these determined people survive another crisis by teaching them to:

* Use high yield seed to increase their harvests

* Capture rain water to use for irrigating fields

* Provide more nutritious food and better sanitation for their children

(over, please)

---

* Start nurseries to grow seedlings which become the trees that shelter fields from wind erosion and provide firewood for cooking.

In fact, I've been told -- and I firmly believe it -- that the reason feeding centers and refugee camps are not overflowing with starving people is in a large part because of the ongoing programs you are supporting through CARE.

You should feel a deep sense of satisfaction, as I do, knowing your support of CARE is truly making a life-or-death difference for families overseas who have literally nowhere to turn to but to you and me.

But CARE cannot continue to carry out these lifesaving programs -- and continue to keep the potential disaster in Africa under control -- unless you continue your generous support.

Please, reach out to those who need your help so much, by sending the most generous gift that you can to CARE right now -- $100, $250, $500 or more if that's possible.

Thank you for reading my letter.

Sincerely,

Lloyd Bridges

P.S.   I only wish you could have been with me to witness how your support of CARE is being translated into concrete programs that are helping struggling families not only survive -- but begin to thrive!

And so I've enclosed a brief trip journal which I know cannot substitute for seeing something firsthand, but I hope it will give you some idea of what your generous support of CARE is accomplishing.

```
Dear Friend of CARE,

     A short while ago I had the opportunity to ask one
of our supporters, Mr. Lloyd Bridges, if he would act
as a Special Envoy for CARE.

     I made this request because the situation in
Ethiopia, and other areas of East Africa, has been
rapidly worsening for many months.

     Mr. Bridges agreed, and traveled to Africa to see
what the situation was like there, and how CARE
programs were touching the lives of the people in
that harsh region of the world.

     He recently returned, and I have asked him to
report on his trip to you and our other friends and
supporters.  I urge you to read his letter and his
trip journal, which I've enclosed.

     I'm convinced that once you do, you will feel an
even greater sense of accomplishment as one of CARE's
special friends.

     And I know you will want to continue to generously
support the vital work being carried out around the
world by CARE with your gifts.

                         Sincerely,

                         Dr. Philip Johnston
                         Executive Director
```

Exhibit 10-3: CARE

Comment:

This mailing had two letters—one from actor Lloyd Bridges and one from the executive director.

Another enclosure was an "African Trip Journal," with handwritten commentary and six photographs.

A celebrity-struck society that regularly discards fund raising letters may read the same letter signed by Lloyd Bridges. Properly, this letter is "I" to "You." The premise—CARE asked him to travel as Special Envoy and report what he actually saw, favorable or not—is close to outlandish, but the reader who accepts the narrative does so because of the Celebrity Syndrome.

The letter takes too long to get into gear, and some of the statistics aren't particularly favorable, even though they're punctuated by exclamation points. For example, 115,000 people dug nine wells. Is that good? They built four school roof catchments to capture rain water. Is that good?

Many fund raisers believe the hook should be dangled early. This letter makes no reference to the reason for writing until page four.

The p.s. is too long. It might have had greater effect if the writer eliminated the first paragraph and started with, "I've enclosed...."

The lift letter, from Dr. Philip Johnston, again fails to explain why the organization chose Lloyd Bridges to be Special Envoy. At best, this enclosure can be described as neutral.

(A parenthetical note: The "African Trip Journal" enclosure has a photograph on its cover: residents of Grawa-Hararghe Province, Ethiopia. Verisimilitude would have been greater if the photograph on the back, Lloyd Bridges with an Ethiopian mother and child, had appeared on the front. And *none* of the photographs of smiling, reasonably well-fed people, reinforces the point, "Even the children were silent. They were too weak from hunger to play.")

> *Dire warning: photographs and*
> *word-descriptions should match.*

Dr. Philip Johnston

A *Special Invitation*

Dear Ms. Lewis,

You are receiving this Invitation because you have always shown a special feeling for the humanitarian work of CARE and a deep understanding of the plight of people in the less fortunate parts of the world.

I thought that you would want to know about and share in a unique new program that is very special in the hearts of all of us at CARE . . .

. . . a program we call CARE for the Child.

Rather than lose time -- so many children are desperately in need of this special help -- I am taking the liberty of enclosing this interim Membership Certificate in your name. It signifies your participation in CARE for the Child.

Please let me tell you why I have taken this unusual action.

As Executive Director of CARE, I have traveled to many of the most poverty-stricken areas of this world -- and in so many countries I have been especially moved by the young children who are suffering so much through no fault of their own.

These are children who do not receive the nourishing food or the basic health and nutrition services that all children must have to grow up healthy and strong . . .

. . . refugee children who sleep on a damp, cold floor in a makeshift tent, without even a blanket to warm them. . .

. . . and children, 7 or 8 years old, who have never even heard of school but whose parents hope to earn enough to send them one day.

Each one of these children touches my heart deeply and I long to reach out to help them, in any way that I can.

But I cannot do it alone. I must find compassionate people like you who will stand with me and help in a very special way.

(please see over)

CARE 660 First Avenue, New York, NY 10016

And I believe because of your past support of CARE's work, you are that unique person I am looking for.

As a member of CARE for the Child, your gift of just $12 a month will help provide precious and needy children with nourishing food, primary health care, and more.

And you will be helping children in another important way -- by helping to build the wells that will give them clean, safe water to drink . . .

. . . by providing irrigation systems for families to grow enough food to provide a nutritious diet for their children. . .

. . . by initiating reforestation projects to plant trees for firewood to keep the children warm and cook their food . . .

. . . and so much more.

I know it is not possible to help every child in need in this world, but we can help so many of them -- one precious child at a time.

Won't you join CARE for the Child?

I hope you will carefully consider this invitation and that your answer will be "yes."

And I hope you will return the pledge form I've enclosed and mail it back to me today with your first gift of only $12, or more if you wish.

I will be so pleased to have you as part of our CARE for the Child team.

On their behalf, I thank you from the bottom of my heart.

Sincerely,

Philip Johnston
Executive Director

P.S. Please note on your CARE for the Child Enrollment Form if there is any change in the way you would like your Membership Certificate inscribed since we will be sending you a larger-size regular Certificate when your membership becomes effective.

95

Exhibit 10-4: CARE

Comment:

This letter, in a pocket of a heavily personalized mailing, obviously was limited to regular contributors.

Would the letter have been stronger had it begun with the fourth paragraph? I think so. "Rather than lose time" has urgency. "You are receiving this Invitation" is passive.

Within the brochure are photographs of children. A typical photo caption:

> **"Lakhu, a 5-year-old neighbor, brings 3-year-old Bikhi Kori to a CARE for the Children nutrition center in Gujerat, India. Bikhi's mother was too weak to help."**

Episode! Why not start the letter with one? Example:

> **"Bikhi Kori is three years old. He's hungry, day and night. A neighbor, Lakhu (age 5), brought him to our CARE for the Children nutrition center in Gujerat, India, so he wouldn't starve. His mother couldn't bring him. She was too weak . . . ."**

Reference to the recipient as a part of the "team" is a good motivator. The p.s. is inverted. A better p.s. opening: "We'll be sending you a larger-size regular Certificate as soon as your membership becomes effective, so . . . ."

> NOTE: When you make a positive *reference*, *write* as soon as, *not* when.

660 First Avenue, New York, NY 10016

August 15.

Dear Friend,

Because you're a close member of our CARE family, I want
to introduce you to some special members of our CARE team...

...our extended team of CARE "field workers." You can
see some of them pictured on the enclosed flyer.

These aren't field workers in the usual sense -- men and
women from the U.S. who have chosen to help people overseas.

They're actual villagers themselves -- living in places
like India, and Bangladesh and Mali. Trained by CARE as
village health workers, they give village women crucial
health information that saves lives -- especially children's.

This extended team is truly one of our most effective
weapons in the fight against childhood diseases and
malnutrition.

In fact, our health workers are especially effective
because they're respected and trusted <u>members of their
villages.</u>

Here's why their work is so important:

You see, millions of children in developing countries
die from malnutrition and disease each year. And what's most
heartbreaking is that so much of this suffering and death is
<u>unnecessary</u> -- often caused by poverty and lack of
information, so common in most parts of the world.

The problem begins before birth. When women are
malnourished during pregnancy, damage to the baby is not only
severe, it's likely to be irreparable.

Then at birth, many mothers deliver their babies without
a medical professional or a trained midwife in attendance.
And in many countries it is common to cut the umbilical cord
with an unsterilized knife, exposing the newborn child to
tetanus poisoning -- which can kill.

And, when a baby is sick with diarrhea, a mother may
stop breast-feeding, believing it is her milk that is making

the baby sick. Instead, she may give the child a bottle of
"millet water" made from crushed grain and water.

What the mother <u>doesn't realize</u> is that <u>breastmilk</u> would
be far better for her child -- it would be <u>substantially</u> more
nutritious, and would protect her child from deadly disease.
<u>On a steady diet of millet water a child will almost
certainly become malnourished -- especially during a bout of
diarrhea.</u>

And mothers allow their children to play in streams, not
knowing that in the water there are deadly parasites that can
enter their children's bodies -- parasites that can make them
terribly sick.

In developing countries, situations like these occur
countless times a day -- and as a result millions of children
become malnourished, blind, crippled <u>and even die.</u>

That's why CARE-trained village health workers are so
important. Dangerous situations like the one I've just
described to you can be <u>prevented</u> -- when health workers
convince mothers to adopt basic health and nutrition
measures.

I know because I've seen the dramatic effects of CARE
health programs myself, for example, in Cameroon, West
Africa.

If you could have been with us when we first visited
Mokolo in Cameroon, here's what you would have found:

* An <u>extremely</u> poor rural area... villagers barely
  able to subsist by farming, earning less that $65 a
  year per person.

* 30% of the children suffering from some form of
  malnutrition.

* An unclean and unreliable water supply contributing
  to waterborne diseases. Diarrhea and dysentery
  taking a toll on the weakened and malnourished
  bodies of adults and children alike.

* The diets of both infants and children seriously
  deficient in the proteins, vitamins and minerals
  required for growing children. Infants receiving
  "millet water." Older children eating only
  "bouille" (a thick porridge made from sorghum) or
  "fufu" (a grain cake, the usual family food).

* No clinic for villagers to go to, or money to pay
  for even basic medical care.

But over a 12 month period, CARE <u>dramatically</u> helped
improve the lives of the people living in northern Cameroon.

CARE-trained village health workers shared the knowledge

CARE taught them. They taught village women about Oral Rehydration Therapy (ORT), a lifesaving treatment for diarrheal dehydration; the importance of breast-feeding and of immunizing their children against diseases; and which foods are needed for proper nutrition.

CARE helped to set up <u>village health care centers</u> where mothers bring their children for regular checkups to weigh and measure children -- ensuring they are growing properly.

And 135 deep wells were dug to provide children and families with clean drinking water.

<u>If you could visit these villages today you'd be amazed at the difference!</u> You'd see healthy children and proud mothers caring for their babies.

But there are so many more villages yet to be reached -- villages where mothers and fathers struggle daily to overcome poverty and disease so their children may lead better lives.

That's why CARE must continue critical Mother/Child Health programs and launch new ones. It is imperative that we train as many village health workers as possible to reach the maximum number of children who are at risk.

But we can't do it alone. We rely on the continued support of people like you -- our generous and committed friends.

Will you help us reach mothers and children who are truly in need? Will you send a gift of $100, $250, $500 or more today?

Your gift today will:

1. Teach mothers to <u>breast-feed</u> their babies for optimal nutrition.

2. Teach villagers how to <u>collect and store</u> rainwater and how to dig wells and keep them clean.

3. Teach parents to <u>immediately</u> start ORT at the first signs of diarrhea in their child.

4. Train <u>midwives</u> in safe childbirth practices.

5. Teach women the importance of <u>proper nutrition</u> for themselves and their children.

6. <u>Immunize children</u> against deadly disease.

With this in mind, I hope you'll decide right now to send the most generous gift you can. The greater the gift, the more children will benefit.

And you'll feel good knowing that somewhere a child will

grow up healthier, with a real chance for a brighter future, thanks to you.

Thank you for reading this letter. And thank you for caring.

Sincerely,

Dr. Philip Johnston
Executive Director

P.S. The situation is <u>urgent</u>.

According to a recent UN report, <u>half</u> of all deaths in Africa are children -- <u>children under the age of 5!</u>

And right now only a meager 20 percent of the world's families know the lifesaving technique of oral rehydration therapy -- yet <u>every 10 seconds</u> a child dies from diarrheal dehydration!

As you can see, CARE's Mother/Child health programs are critical. Please support our efforts by sending the most generous gift you can today. <u>Thank you.</u>

Exhibit 10-5: CARE

Comment:

It's hard to imagine a less interesting opening.

Do you want to meet some special members of the team? I don't. Nor, for that matter, do I want to be called "Dear Friend" if I'm already a "close member of the CARE family." Reserve this opening for cold lists. "Good morning!" is both brighter and less arm's-length.

In the middle of page 1 we read, "Here's why their work is so important:" The next paragraph begins, "You see." No! Those two words sap out strength. If you claim importance, prove it, and prove it in the next ten words.

The letter is loaded with nuggets—examples, emotional motivators, heartstring-pullers. But the thin opening may keep many readers from reaching these nuggets.

The p.s. is too long. Why not condense it into a chewable single bite, such as:

> **"The situation is *urgent*. Every 10 seconds a child dies from diarrheal dehydration. Quickly—send the most generous gift you can."**

After yards of trenches were
dug...thousands of feet of pipe
were laid...and dozens of bags
of cement mixed and poured --

-- this little girl is drinking
<u>pure, clean water</u> for the very
first time in her life!

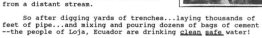

Dear Friend of CARE,

     For the very first time in her life,
this little girl, named Maria, is drinking
clean, safe water!

     And she's able to do so because <u>you,</u>
and other friends of CARE, helped her
family and their neighbors to build a
water system in their village.

     <u>This new water system means so much
to these villagers in Ecuador!</u> It means
they will no longer suffer from debilitating waterborne diseases...and they
won't have to walk miles to draw water
from a distant stream.

     So after digging yards of trenches...laying thousands of
feet of pipe...and mixing and pouring dozens of bags of cement
--the people of Loja, Ecuador are drinking <u>clean safe</u> water!

     Helping families and entire villages dig wells and create
irrigation systems is one of the most important things we do.

     And when you look at the smile on the face of this little
girl as she takes a sip of clean water, you can feel satisfaction
knowing you helped CARE make that smile possible.

     In hundreds of villages around the world, CARE water
projects have made <u>a remarkable difference</u> in the lives of
countless children like her and their families.

     That's why I'm asking you to help CARE continue to bring
water to the thirsty children and parched fields around the
world. Your gift of $100, $250, $500 or more today can help
initiate new water projects in areas where drought and unclean

CARE

water are taking a terrible toll on children and
their families.

     <u>Here's a vivid example of what your support
of CARE water projects can mean:</u>

     In the Byumba region of Rwanda, Africa, over
40,000 villagers were seeking access to clean
drinking water in August of 1985 when our fieldworkers did a needs assessment.

     <u>Rwanda</u> was chosen as a project area because
it is one of the world's poorest countries and 45%
of the rural population does not have access to
safe drinking water. As a result, <u>13%</u> of all
children born in Rwanda die before their first
birthday. Even the average man or woman in Rwanda
cannot expect to live past <u>fifty</u> years of age.

     In Rwanda, thousands of people die each year
from waterborne diseases such as typhoid, viral
hepatitis, and amoebic dysentery.

     With the help of CARE, construction on the
first of four gravity-fed water systems was begun
in April, 1987. The system would involve the
laying of <u>over 25 miles</u> of pipe by local people,
and would provide about 20,000 Rwandans with
<u>permanent access</u> to clean drinking water.

     By June of this year, two of the gravity-fed
systems had been completed, serving a total of
30,000 people, and two more are under construction.
In addition, the local people are working on
other water systems, including 12 wells, and an
entire system which will catch and store rainwater.

     An important component of this water program
is the participation of the local villagers <u>them-
selves,</u> who are not only providing much of the
labor to build the water systems, but who have
also created local Community Water Associations.
CARE fieldworkers teach the members of these
associations how to repair and maintain the water
systems so they can rely on their own resources
in the future.

     Without a doubt, this water project is a
great success. It has <u>already</u> reduced the number
of children and adults suffering from debilitating
illnesses caused by waterborne disease, and has
attracted the attention of the World Bank as a

possible model for future duplication in other parts of the country.

This is the kind of major impact CARE self-help programs can make with your support.

And right now CARE is involved in 23 major water programs in 19 different countries. But still, there are so many remote and isolated villages where lack of water for irrigation, and clean safe water for drinking are life-threatening problems:

Villages in Chad, where it hasn't rained all year...

...and areas of the Dominican Republic where 68% of the inhabitants of rural provinces cannot safely drink their water.

Your support is urgently needed if CARE is to go into these areas and initiate life-saving water programs.

Please send a generous gift today. And thank you for all you are doing to help us at CARE.

Sincerely,

Dr. Philip Johnston
Executive Director

Exhibit 10-6: CARE

Comment:

Why open a fund raising letter with, "After yards of trenches were dug..."?

How much stronger this would have been if the writer had deleted that first paragraph altogether.

The letter isn't a heartstring-tugger, as many CARE letters are; it does make its point. Is the point drowned in lyricism? Opinion: Yes. The message isn't lean enough; we have too much marbling on the meat.

Phrases such as "over 40,000 villagers were seeking access..." and "Rwanda was chosen as a project area because..." are statisticians' copy, once-removed from an emotional hook. Count the number of *passive-voice* sentences. These, too, slow down absorption.

Opinion, repeated: Three-page letters shouldn't exist. The blank fourth panel is an invitation to disregard.

DATE: 9/28/%%

TO: Ms. Margo E. Lewis
      PO Box 15725
      9748 Cedar Villas B.
      Ft Lauderdale, FL 33324

FROM: Dr. Philip Johnston
      Executive Director, CARE

RE: EMERGENCY RELIEF NEEDED IMMEDIATELY FOR FLOOD VICTIMS

Because you are one of CARE's most committed and caring
friends, I am writing to you today to ask for your special
help for the people of Bangladesh.

The heaviest monsoon rains in 70 years have devastated that
country. Millions of people have been forced to evacuate
their villages as rising flood waters cover 90% of the
country.

As many as two thousand people may have drowned and an
estimated 30 million people are homeless. The nation's main
rice crop has been destroyed. Millions of families have
been stranded on small patches of high ground, on roof tops,
or in local makeshift relief centers.

CARE's efforts by 1,400 local CARE staff to provide initial
emergency relief are nothing short of heroic. All 15 of
CARE's local missions are engaged in country-wide emergency
projects to provide one million families with one month's
supply of food.

The CARE field office in Comilla immediately began
distributing 5,000 CARE packages to the most needy. Each
package is made up of one pound of biscuits, one oral
rehydration packet, a water purification tablet, and a candle
and matches.

The CARE-Rangpur office is providing emergency supplies
consisting of rice, lentils, potatoes and water purification
tablets to 900 families stranded on two embankments, and
CARE-Barisal is distributing rice, alum, and 15,000 loaves
of bread to thousands of needy families.

Despite CARE's initial efforts to help, the situation
remains critical. Your generous support is urgently needed

---

immediately to help CARE provide:

- EMERGENCY FOOD for the hundreds of thousands of
  families who have no way to survive for the next
  several months until a new crop can be harvested.

- MEDICAL SUPPLIES to treat the recent outbreaks of
  pneumonia and eye and skin diseases, and outbreaks of
  dysentery and cholera.

- ORAL REHYDRATION SALTS to treat the hundreds of
  thousands of cases of diarrhea occurring daily and
  WATER PURIFICATION TABLETS to prevent new outbreaks.

- SEEDS for planting fast growing vegetables such as
  okra and beans.

- BUILDING MATERIALS so the people can rebuild their
  homes and reconstruct the roads, dikes, and drainage
  canals that were washed away in the flood.

An emergency gift of $32 from you today will help keep a
struggling family of 5 alive for eight weeks. $16 will help
a family for a month. Just think what a gift of $128, $256,
or even $512 will do!

Please send a generous gift today, and thank you for being
someone we can count on.

Phil Johnston

P.S. CARE's help is also urgently needed in other flood
     disaster areas...in Sudan, where over one million
     people are homeless in the worst flooding since 1946...
     in Chad where heavy rains and flooding have left 60,000
     people homeless...

     ...and in Jamaica, Mexico, Haiti and the Dominican
     Republic where hurricane Gilbert carved a wide path of
     destruction leaving hundreds dead, hundreds of
     thousands homeless, and destroying large areas of
     agricultural production.

     Your Emergency Flood Relief gift will also go to help
     these destitute victims of flood and hurricane rebuild
     their shattered lives.

Exhibit 10-7: CARE

Comment:

Printed on yellow paper, this format implicitly has verisimilitude. The danger, in using an "Urgent" approach, is letting the message lapse into less-than-urgent terminology.

This message successfully stays inside the "urgent" frame, although the similarity of paragraph-length reduces the wallop.

Bullet copy is out of place here. Why? Because bullets, even though terse, damage the effect of urgency. They're a thoughtful listing, therefore contrived. The reader's supercharged interest becomes analytical.

With this format, an organization less concerned with total image than CARE seems to me would have replaced this sentence:

"An emergency gift of $32 from you today will help keep a struggling family of 5 alive for eight weeks."

The replacement might have read:

"I need your emergency gift of $32 right now. It will help keep a discouraged, forsaken family alive for two months."

Once again the p.s. is too long. Whoever wrote this disagrees with many of us who feel the p.s. should punch, not stroke. When you write a p.s., ask yourself: Will it *increase* contributions?

Jimmy Carter
Plains, Georgia

Dear Friend,   Wednesday a.m.

As a former U.S. president, I have been asked to lend my name to the work of many fine and worthy causes.

When Rosalynn and I talked about this, we decided that we wanted to be part of something that would make a lasting difference in people's lives. Something that would mean more than just the use of our name on an organization's letterhead.

After much thought, we chose to support the work of Habitat for Humanity. And since then, I have served on Habitat's board of directors. In our book, _Everything to Gain_, we write in detail about our experiences with Habitat for Humanity, as an example of how to add excitement and challenge to one's life.

Let me tell you why I feel so strongly about the good work Habitat is doing.

As president, I had firsthand knowledge of just how serious and dehumanizing the housing problems of the poor and disadvantaged really are. And I was shocked and appalled!

Today, hundreds of thousands of families right here in America live in the most deplorable housing conditions imaginable: roach- and rat-infested ghetto flats; dilapidated rural shacks; decaying, crumbling old apartments.

One of those families was the Strongs -- Ruby, Oscar and their five children -- all struggling to get by in a cramped little shack in Sumner, Mississippi.

They had no running water, no toilet, and not much hope the day their shack was condemned and they were tossed out. In desperation, they moved into a smaller shack with grandma and 12 relatives. Then, everyone's plight worsened. And the saddest part was that they had no other choice.

But families like the Strongs are what Habitat for Humanity is all about! Under the able leadership of Millard Fuller, Habitat has made some dramatic breakthroughs by providing low-cost, affordable housing for families like the Strongs.

- With the help of caring friends like you, Habitat has set up more than 290 revolving loan funds to build housing for the poor.
- A network of more than 10,000 committed volunteer workers across this country and around the world has been developed to build and remodel modest homes.
- The good news is that this is not just a handout. Interest-free, nonprofit home loans are offered to poor people so they can pay back into the revolving loan

                                                              (over, please)

funds to help someone else in need.

As a result, low-cost, interest-free homes can be sold to disadvantaged families like the Strongs.

With that innovative approach, Habitat has already built or renovated more than 3,000 low-cost homes for the poor and is continuing to start construction on new homes at a rate of nearly six every day.

One of the new homes recently built now belongs to the Strong family!

Oh, it's not fancy, at least perhaps by the standards of most of us. But it does have bedrooms . . . and plumbing . . . and safe wiring. And for the Strong family it means a whole new life.

I know that what Habitat has done for the Strongs can be done for thousands more. In fact, we have enough land right now to build at least 5,000 more homes for needy families in the coming months.

During 1988, we need to raise more than $15 million for the construction of these houses and for all our other projects under way both here and overseas. I believe that with the help of caring people like you we can achieve our goal!

Right now we need 750,000 people who are each willing to give at least $20 to share in the life-changing accomplishments of this exciting and desperately needed work.

When I think of the dignity and self-esteem that the Strongs' new home brings them, I can't help but remember the stirring words of George Bernard Shaw:

"You see things; and you say, 'Why?' But I dream things that never were; and I say, 'Why not?'"

Through the visionary work of Habitat for Humanity, the dream of adequate low-cost housing for the disadvantaged is becoming a reality. It's happening in the spirit of Christian love, and it's not costing one red cent of taxpayers' money. To me that's one great investment!

I urge you to join Rosalynn and me in this vitally important work. Whatever you can send -- $20, $50, or more -- will make a big difference!

                                          Gratefully yours,

                                          Jimmy Carter
                                          Jimmy Carter

P.S. I know of no better investment to help restore human dignity than to help someone else like the Strong family. Please join me with your gift. Thank you.

Exhibit 10-8: Habitat for Humanity

Comment:

Does the opening give you the feeling Jimmy Carter's decision to lend his name was cold-blooded?

That was my feeling, and I wonder about the effectiveness of using the first three paragraphs as statements of personal importance rather than "join me" exhortation.

What does Habitat for Humanity do? The organization's name is ponderous, and we have no clue about its purpose until we're almost halfway through the letter.

Had the letter begun with the sixth paragraph ("Today, hundreds of thousands of families...") it might be a better "grabber"; but hundreds of thousands are too broad a base for our empathy.

The "stirring words of George Bernard Shaw" are a curious inclusion. The thought itself is too impenetrable to be stirring.

COVENANT HOUSE FLORIDA

733 BREAKERS AVE. • FT. LAUDERDALE, FL 33304 • (305) 561-5559

Friday, 11:45 PM

Dear Friend,

A lady should never get this dirty, she said.

She stood there with a quiet, proud dignity. She was incomparably dirty -- her face and hands smeared, her clothes torn and soiled. The lady was 11.

My brothers are hungry, she said. The two little boys she hugged protectively were 8 and 9. They were three of the most beautiful children I'd ever seen.

Our parents beat us a lot, she said. We had to leave. The boys nodded mutely. We had to leave, one of them echoed. The children did not cry. I struggled to manage part of a smile. It didn't come off very well. The littlest kid looked back at me, with a quick, dubious grin. I gave him a surreptitious hug. I was all choked up.

I would like to take a shower, the lady said.

Nineteen years ago, I did not know that there were thousands of runaway, abused and abandoned children like these in this country.

I learned the hard way.

One night, in the winter of 1969, six teenage runaways knocked on the door on my apartment where I was living to serve the poor of New York's Lower East Side. Their junkie pimp had burned them out of the abandoned tenement they called "home." They asked if they could sleep on my floor. I took them in. I didn't have the guts not to.

Word of mouth traveled fast. (It does among street kids.) The next day four more came. And kids have been coming ever since. It was these kids -- with no place else to go -- homeless, hungry, lacking skills, jobs, resources -- that compelled me to start Covenant House nineteen years ago. Today our crisis centers help tens of thousands of kids from all over the country -- and save them from a life of degradation and horror on the streets.

Kids like the eleven-year-old lady and her very brave little brothers. They were easy to help: to place in a foster home where beautiful kids are wanted and loved, and made more beautiful precisely because they are wanted and loved.

But sadly, not all the thousands of kids we expect to see in our Florida crisis center this year will be that lucky. These kids have very few options. Many of them will have fallen victim to the predators of the sex-for-sale and pornography "industry."

One of them put it to me very simply, and very directly:

"Bruce, I've got two choices: I can go with a john (a customer) and do what he wants, or I can rip somebody off and go to jail. I'm afraid to go to jail, Bruce. I can't get a job... I've got no skills. I've got no place to live."

This child is 16. I do not know what I would have done if I were 16 and faced with that impossible choice.

They are good kids. You shouldn't think they're not good kids. Most of them are simply trying to survive. When you are on the street, and you are cold and hungry and scared and you have nothing to sell except yourself, you sell yourself.

There was a time when I was forced to turn these kids away simply because there was no room. I can't do that anymore. I know only too well what the street holds in store for a kid all alone. That is why we run Covenant House, and that is why we keep it open 24 hours a day, seven days a week -- to give these kids an alternative, an option that leads to life and not death.

These kids come to us in need, from every kind of family background. Boys and girls. White, Black and Hispanic. Children -- sometimes with children of their own. Innocent and streetwise. They are your kids and mine. Their number is increasing at a frightening rate.

We are here for them because of you. Almost all of the money that we need to help these kids comes from people like you.

A lady should never get that dirty. And a good kid should not be allowed to fall victim to the terror of street life. As more good kids come to us, we need more help. We need yours. Won't you send whatever contribution you can in the enclosed envelope today?

Thanks for my (no, our) kids.

Peace,

Father Bruce Ritter

P.S. I'm enclosing a brochure that will tell you a little bit more about the thousands of kids who come to us each year. I hope you will read it, and give our kids whatever help you can. Thanks!

106

Exhibit 10-9: Covenant House

Comment:

This is a classic campaign which obviously works, because Covenant House has been mailing it for some years.

The opening sentence grabs and shakes the reader's interest. Phrases such as *"incomparably* dirty" show a controlled sense of humor, which the writer doesn't allow to interfere with the message.

Phrases such as "nodded mutely," "dubious grin," and "surreptitious hug" are out of key with such apt references as "street kids" and "I can go with a john (a customer) and do what he wants, or I can rip somebody off and go to jail." I have the feeling the writer is torn between gentility and shock; the result, an unhomogenized hybrid, falls short of both.

One problem may be the signature—Father Bruce Ritter. Lapsing too deeply into the vernacular would be unseemly.

Opinion: A more straightforward explanation of "Here's what we want from you" might clarify and improve response. This would be a test rather than a replacement, if only because the campaign has been in the mails for such a long time.

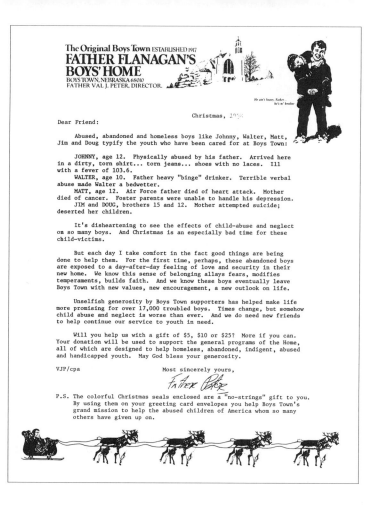

Exhibit 10-10: Father Flanagan's Boys' Home

Comment:

The illustration on the face of this letter may well be the most famous campaign in the history of direct-mail fund raising:

"He ain't heavy, Father. . .he's m'brother."

Father Flanagan's Boys' Home, originally Boys Town, has been raising funds for more than 70 years and has a history of intelligently emotionalized appeals.

This letter opens with pure examples, and each example is loaded with power. The Christmas seals, enclosed with the letter, aren't mentioned until the p.s.

Despite generalizations such as "good things are being done to help them," the letter is coherent and pointed, with no rhetorical lapses to let the reader off the hook. "May God bless your generosity" is a perfect close for "Father Peter" to use.

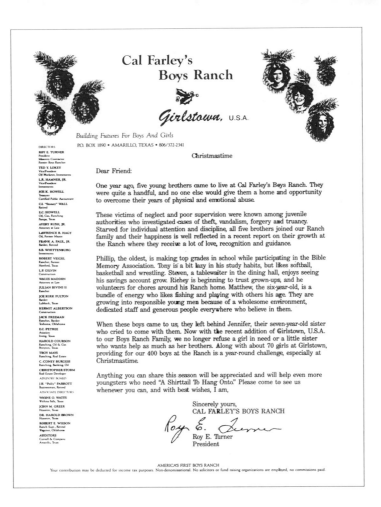

Exhibit 10-11: Cal Farley's Boys Ranch and Girlstown U.S.A.

Comment:

Cal Farley's Boys Ranch and Girlstown, U.S.A. parallel Father Flanagan's Boys' Home in type of service.

Listing the directors adds validity; but this list is too heavy in Texas/Oklahoma businesspeople. Those outside this orbit may feel they're being circularized by a cause with no ties to their own region.

Setting the letter in type formalizes it. Unindented paragraphs reinforce the formality. The reference to the boys' sister is unfinished: Is she now at Girlstown?

"A shirttail to hang onto" is an apt phrase, but why capitalize the words, which transforms the thought into a title?

Biggest problem here: The call for help is unspecific.

Monday, 19__

Dear Mr. Lewis:

Moses' little daughter Maria, pictured below, survived a disaster in Bolivia that killed almost 65% of the infants.

It was a disaster more terrible than a flood... hurricane or even an earthquake...it was infant mortality. Who in America can begin to imagine that?

Infant mortality is as regular as clockwork in the under developed nations of the world.

It's hard to imagine a place where to be thirty-seven means you're old...used up...near the end. Where diarrhea is fatal, and polio still twists and scars. Where bloated bellies and sunken cheeks from malnutrition are as common as a cold.

Yet, some are lucky. Instead of pain, they experience love -- from your Salvation Army.

But out there -- in the harsh reality of the Third World -- love is not enough. They need...

   ...solar power to keep vaccines cold;
   ...skills to get a job;
   ...farm tools, and loans for seed to bring
      about self-support and self-respect.

And, when a hurricane howls or an earthquake strikes, they need a bowl of soup, a dry shirt, a roof and a bed.

All this -- and more -- The Salvation Army can do -- <u>because you care</u>. And because caring isn't much without cash to back it up, I ask for your support. Because so many suffer. And so many can be saved.

Please, <u>touch the life of someone who needs you</u>. Send your check in the enclosed envelope today.

God bless you, Mr. Lewis,

William Crabson

Major William Crabson
Area Commander

P.S. While we continue to respond to the needs of people overseas, like little Maria, <u>we will never forget the needy in our own community</u>. Thank you for your special gift.

THANK YOU for your support of The Salvation Army through your UNITED WAY gift. This appeal provides money for special programs not supported by UNITED WAY.

Exhibit 10-12: Salvation Army

Comment:

We have the feeling we've missed something. Who is Moses? A more emotional way of opening the letter might have been:

> **"Maria (her picture is below) is alive. Two of every three children from her village in Bolivia aren't. They died in a disaster far more terrible than a flood or an earthquake."**

The wording, "Infant mortality is as regular as clockwork" is curiously dispassionate. Solar power is too advanced a concept to stir action among donors.

The Salvation Army is one of the most venerable and worthwhile eleemosynary organizations on earth, and few—including me, and, I hope, you—will question their unselfish motives. If the entire letter had the force of the fourth paragraph, it would more closely mirror the vital work The Salvation Army accomplishes.

CHAPTER *11*

Political and
Lobbying Letters

SENATOR DANIEL PATRICK MOYNIHAN

Dear Friend,

When I served as our country's permanent representative to the United Nations, I prided myself in bringing to that job the grand Irish tradition of never walking away from a fight.

And I had some good ones.

Until my arrival on the scene, our diplomats at the U.N. sat back uncomplaining while the Third World majority regularly joined forces with the Soviet bloc to bash the United States, Israel and democracy in general.

Finally, I refused to stand for any more of it.

Instead of treating irresponsible Third World governments like juvenile delinquents whose names must be kept out of the papers, I did the unthinkable. I went public.

I described the U.N. as a "Theatre of the Absurd."

I expressed openly my disdain for countries that pillory the democracies in the U.N. and then come around looking for foreign aid.

I denounced as a "terrible lie" the egregious U.N. resolution equating Zionism with racism.

But in all my time at the U.N., there was one outrage of which I was not aware.

I did not know in those days that Kurt Waldheim -- who was then U.N. Secretary General -- had for years been covering up with brazen, cynical lies his involvement in the crimes of Hitler's Reich.

And I didn't learn that in a locked archive <u>just a few blocks away from his sumptuous U.N. office was a file whose explosive contents would some day bring to light the truth about this evil man</u>.

The Waldheim file is one of 38,810 dossiers assembled between 1943 and 1948 by allied nations charged with identifying suspected Nazi war criminals. This detailed archive on the crimes and the criminals of the Third Reich was turned over in 1948 to the United Nations.

It was declared "secret." It was locked away.

And we know about it only because a researcher found in the U.S. National Archives an inventory of the names on the U.N. war crimes file and looked under "W."

And now we're beginning to learn the appalling truth about how Kurt Waldheim and thousands more like him escaped answering for their actions in the service of the Third Reich.

They escaped because we, the allies, _let_ them escape.

In some cases, most notoriously that of Klaus Barbie -- the Butcher of Lyon -- our own intelligence agencies even _helped_ them escape.

And there's more.

"Between 1950 and 1978," writes a leading expert on Nazi war criminals in America, "even an avowed Nazi could have legally entered the United States as an immigrant and become a citizen."

John Demjenjuk did just that, settling in a suburb of Cleveland, Ohio. Only decades later was he extradited to Israel to face the charge that he is, in fact, the sadistic concentration camp guard known to the victims of Treblinka as "Ivan the Terrible."

And we know of others. A top official of the Nazi puppet regime in Croatia -- a German rocket scientist accused of working slave laborers to death -- a Romanian Orthodox bishop who was once a leader of that country's Fascist Iron Guard.

How could it happen that such people were allowed to enter this country? Who was responsible?

We don't have all the answers.

But I say that we deserve to know. Indeed, I _demand_ to know.

And that's why I've taken steps to uncover the truth no matter how unsavory it may be.

I secured passage of legislation calling for "access by interested individuals and organizations to the files of the United Nations War Crimes Commission deposited in the archives of the United Nations."

And I'm pleased to say that when our government changed its long-standing position on access to the files, member nations of the U.N. War Crimes Commission agreed to go along.

By opening these archives at long last to public view, we may find information that will lead to additional war crimes prosecutions. "When we are able to combine these records with the other records we have," says the Director of the Justice Department's Office of Special Investigations, "It will be a very unique and powerful archival holding."

But, that's not the only reason I fought for public access.

Today -- at a time when anti-Semites here and in Europe are trying to convince the world that the Holocaust never happened -- we _need_ these materials.

Now, we have them.

And if I have my way, we as a nation shall also have more to say on the subject of Kurt Waldheim.

Kurt Waldheim should never have become Secretary General of the United Nations. He attained that position by deception.

And that is why I've introduced in the Senate legislation requesting the President to instruct our Ambassador to the United Nations to move to strike from the U.N. budget the $81,650 annual pension that Waldheim now collects.

It is, as they say, the _least_ we can do.

It pleases me greatly that as a Senator, I am in a position to do it.

And if you share with me the values that I have worked to promote throughout my career, I hope that I can count on you to help me retain that position -- the position of United States Senator from New York.

This year I am running for re-election. And I must confess to you that I am concerned.

I know that the Republican Senate Campaign Committee will mount a massive effort to regain a Republican majority in the Senate. My name will be at the top of their "hit list."

And I also know that Republican strategists are fully aware that there is one area in which I am very vulnerable -- and they are very strong.

What area is that?

It is money.

They have it.

I don't.

And although I do not for one moment regret my decision to make my career in non-lucrative endeavors like academics and public service, I am a realist.

_114_

4

I note that in California in 1986, Republican and Right Wing fundraisers poured millions into a losing Senate campaign. And I recall vividly that in 1984, Jesse Helms spent a record-breaking $17 million to retain his seat in North Carolina.

And so, quite frankly, I am worried.

I am convinced that in order to compete on equal terms, <u>I must now build a war chest</u>.

I must assume that I will be a prime target for the negative campaign specialists of the extreme Right Wing.

These Right Wing political activists use "independent" expenditures to launch media attacks designed to discredit candidates whose names are on their notorious "hit lists."

<u>These groups move early</u>. <u>They hit hard</u>.

And experience shows that to prevail against them, a candidate <u>must</u> be able to respond.

That is why I hope that I can count on you to become an active supporter of my campaign for re-election. I hope that I can count on you to write a check today to "Moynihan for Senate."

And I also hope that you will be generous.

If you can afford to write a check for $1,000, please do so. Or for $500, $250, $100 or even $30.

Every dollar helps. And every dollar is needed in the most urgent way.

I hope that you will stand with me.

Sincerely,

Daniel Patrick Moynihan

P.S. The Republican opposition to my re-election to the Senate is <u>very</u> powerful -- and deeply serious. We may well be facing in New York the nation's hardest fought and most expensive 1988 Senate race.

So the need is urgent. And I hope that you will honor me with your support.

Authorized and paid for by "The Moynihan Committee."

Exhibit 11-1: Senator Daniel Patrick Moynihan

Comment:

This hard-hitting letter never wavers in its *vertical* appeal to a special-interest group.

The Moynihan letter went to lists *outside* his home state. None of the recipients could vote for him. The "hook" had to be a highly emotional barb which transcends the usual geographic rationale for supporting a political candidate.

Obviously the senator couldn't send this letter to borderline conservatives. It follows the Rule of Political Agitation:

> ## When raising funds within a group united by a single interest, mirror their prejudices as strongly as possible.

If you feel the letter is too pointed and too blunt, you probably won't be able to open enough emotional stopcocks to write an effective political fund raising letter.

HANDGUN CONTROL

ONE MILLION STRONG . . . working to keep handguns out of the wrong hands.

Mr Nelson T. Shields, III
Chairman

Mrs. Sarah Brady
Vice-Chair

Mr Charles J. Orasin
President

National Committee
Mr Steve Allen
Mr Arthur Ashe
Ms. Lauren Bacall
Mrs Marjorie Benton
Mr Leonard Bernstein
Mr Lloyd Bridges
Hon. Edmund G. Brown, Sr
Ms. Ellen Burstyn
Mrs Julia Child
Mr Jackie Cooper
Mr Hume Cronyn
Hon Joseph Curran
Mr Stephen Dart
Mr William Dorman
Mr Gerald Dunfey
Mr Douglas Fairbanks, Jr
Hon. Kenneth Gibson
Rabbi Joseph B. Glaser
Ms. Betsy Gotbaum
Mr Michael Gross
Mrs. Elliot Jones Halberstam
Ms. Marette Hartley
Hon. Richard Hatcher
Hon. Janet Gray Hayes
Mr Andrew Heskell
Mr Hal Holbrook
Hon. Maynard Jackson
Mr Albert Jenner, Jr
Mrs. Shirley Knight
Ms. Patricia Kennedy Lawford
Mr Jack Lemmon
Hon. Edward Levi
Hon. John Lindsay
Ms. Marsha Mason
Ms. Jane McMichael
Dr. Karl Menninger
Mr Patrick Murphy
Mr Paul Newman
Mr George D. Newton, Jr
Mr Victor Palmieri
Mr Gregory Peck
Mr Russell Peterson
Mr Sol Price
Mr Milton Rector
Ms. Lee Remick
Mr Will Rogers, Jr
Mr James W. Rouse
Rabbi Alexander M. Schindler
Mr Neil Simon
Mr Rod Steiger
Dr. Emanuel Tanay
Ms. Jessica Tandy
Mr Eli Wallach
Ms. Ruth Warrick
Mr Francis Wheat
Mr James Whitmore
Mr Andy Williams

Dear Fellow American:

If you've ever doubted that the National Rifle Association is thumbing its nose at you just consider these frightening facts ...

FACT: As the nation mourned the senseless deaths of 43 innocent persons aboard a California airliner brought down by a madman's gun fire, the NRA was working feverishly to block all attempts to ban plastic, undetectable handguns that could easily be smuggled onto airplanes.

FACT: Right after the submachine gun massacre of 21 children and adults at a McDonald's restaurant in California, the NRA launched a massive campaign to defend the sale and distribution of "assault" weapons like the Uzi used in the San Ysidro killings.

FACT: When the nation's police asked Congress to ban the manufacture and sale of "cop killer" bullets -- ammunition that penetrates the vests worn by police -- the NRA launched a massive campaign to defend the sale of this ammunition.

THEN ... in a climate of declining handgun sales, the NRA, financed in part by the pistol makers, stepped up its campaign to legalize the mail-order sale of handguns!

NOW ... the NRA has announced that its No. 1 priority is to pass legislation that allows the sale of new machine guns!

How is that for callous disregard for the will of the people -- a will demonstrated in countless polls that prove the vast majority of Americans want some measure of reasonable handgun control!

Just think. The NRA has gotten its selfish way for years -- squashing every attempt to bring about some kind of sensible legislation to keep handguns out of the wrong hands. Enough is enough!

Must we bury another President or another 20,000 or 40,000 handgun victims before our elected legislators pass an effective national handgun law?

Just who the hell is running this country ... Congress or the National Rifle Association?

As a private citizen, and as a father whose oldest son was senselessly gunned down with a handgun, I'm fed up!

I'm fed up with the way the gun lobby has held a political pistol to the head of the Congress, threatening Senators and Representatives who dare support handgun control with political retaliation at the voting booth.

And now, the pistol lobby has pushed the McClure/Volkmer Gun Decontrol Bill through the Congress. The NRA calls this measure the first step

1400 K Street, N.W., Suite 500, Washington, D.C. 20005   (202) 898-0792

toward outright repeal of our current national gun law, the 1968 Gun Control Act, passed exactly 20 years ago after the killings of Dr. Martin Luther King, Jr., and Robert F. Kennedy.

But, fortunately, the NRA didn't get everything it wanted this time. Thanks to a powerful, new alliance forged between Handgun Control, Inc., and every major law enforcement organization -- from the Fraternal Order of Police to the International Association of Chiefs of Police -- the NRA no longer "calls all the shots" on Capitol Hill.

Seven years ago, HANDGUN CONTROL, INC., a citizens' organization formed by handgun victims, launched a program called CAMPAIGN ONE MILLION STRONG to build a force of one million Americans committed to keeping handguns out of the wrong hands. It has been a major success. We now have more than one million people signed up!

We have already proven the political power of numbers like these. It

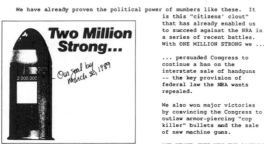

Two Million Strong...

Our goal by March 30, 1989

2,000,000

is this "citizens' clout" that has already enabled us to succeed against the NRA in a series of recent battles. With ONE MILLION STRONG we ...

... persuaded Congress to continue a ban on the interstate sale of handguns -- the key provision of federal law the NRA wants repealed.

We also won major victories by convincing the Congress to outlaw armor-piercing "cop killer" bullets and the sale of new machine guns.

AND WE'VE JUST WON TWO LANDMARK VICTORIES: ONE THAT HALTS THE SALE OF SATURDAY NIGHT SPECIALS IN THE STATE OF MARYLAND, AND ANOTHER THAT STOPS THE MANUFACTURE AND SALE OF UNDETECTABLE PLASTIC HANDGUNS THROUGHOUT THE ENTIRE NATION.

Both of these major victories came about right in the face of furious lobbying efforts by the once-invincible NRA.

Now we're ready to step up our campaign. Sarah Brady, wife of Presidential Press Secretary Jim Brady, who was wounded in John Hinckley's assassination attempt on Ronald Reagan, is traveling across America, mobilizing more people to fight for sensible handgun laws.

Richard Boyd, the former national president of the nation's largest law enforcement organization, the Fraternal Order of Police, has joined our campaign to recruit more law enforcement officials to stand up to the NRA.

And the defeat of many of the NRA's key friends on Capitol Hill in 1986 has set the stage for positive handgun control throughout the 100th Congress. Along with suffering the loss of many of its key Senators,

Representatives and challengers, the NRA has also lost its hold over the Senate Judiciary Committee, the gateway to handgun control legislation.

Handgun Control, Inc.'s allies in the Congress have pounced on this opportunity for passing stronger handgun laws by introducing a historic piece of legislation in the 100th Congress. This bill (S.466 and H.R.975) would require a seven-day waiting period to allow for a police background check for every purchaser of a handgun. This legislation already has more co-sponsors than any handgun control bill in history!

Here in the office we're calling it "The Brady Bill," in honor of Sarah Brady. And it has already been endorsed by the leading law enforcement organizations in the nation. You know how potent their lobbying can be!

It was our strong alliance with police organizations that provided the key to beating the NRA with the Saturday Night Special law in Maryland ... and then beating them again in our plastic handgun victory on Capitol Hill, where we also forged a strong bi-partisan alliance against the NRA, led by Senators Howard Metzenbaum and Strom Thurmond.

We are now lobbying for new laws that will:

** Put behind bars anyone who uses a handgun in a state crime;

** Pass national legislation to halt the national manufacture and sale of snub-nosed handguns -- often called "Saturday Night Specials" -- those favorite weapons of the criminal and the assassin;

** Register handguns so that an owner can be traced as quickly and easily as the owner of an automobile;

** Tighten control over the 200,000 handgun dealerships in America, and get pawnshops out of the handgun business.

On the face of it, you would think that the Congress would quickly pass such common sense legislation -- after all, we license drivers and register automobiles.

But our elected Representatives have been afraid to act.

Why? Because in the past they feared the National Rifle Association and not you. Make no mistake, the National Rifle Association is a mighty force to be reckoned with. Of its $70 million budget, $12 million is spent on lobbying alone. The NRA employs a full-time staff of 354, and some of its leaders believe you should be required by law to keep a gun in your home.

The NRA's self-serving actions fly in the face of poll after poll, which show that a vast majority of the American people want stricter control over handguns now.

I'm convinced that if HANDGUN CONTROL, INC., is to break the pistol lobby's grip on Congress once and for all, we must organize and mobilize that majority of concerned Americans into a powerful national political force -- so that reasonable people like you and me can finally get what we've wanted for so long: a common sense national handgun control law that

- 4 -

will lessen America's handgun violence.

Right now, the National Rifle Association has the political guns. It has an army of three million organized supporters.

Though we are now more than ONE MILLION STRONG, we must keep growing until we are as large -- or even larger than -- the NRA.

Won't you join our nation's law enforcement organizations, Sarah Brady, and over 1,000,000 other Americans who are committed to handgun control ... and help us become TWO MILLION STRONG?

With your support, we'll reach our two-million-member goal and keep surging ahead until we WIN our long, difficult fight to keep handguns out of the wrong hands.

You see, there's political power in numbers. The NRA has proved that. So we need more size and more political power to beat the handgun and ammo zealots. That's the only way we can stop the mindless handgun killings and woundings that are now as much a part of our national life as eating breakfast.

Of course, our success depends on one critical factor -- you.

The pistol lobby is nothing if not passionate. But this group is also smart enough to realize that if we, the majority of Americans, organize and act with conviction and passion too, we will have the strength to topple them from power.

I've enclosed a form to make it easy for you to sign up and make our citizens' force for handgun control grow so that we can offset -- and one day surpass -- the size and political power of the National Rifle Association. Please sign up now while this letter is before you.

Prove the NRA wrong. Prove to them that you do care about America. That you care enough to want to stop this handgun madness. That you want to keep handguns out of the wrong hands. Please act quickly -- for another one of us will be murdered by a handgun in the next 50 minutes.

Sincerely,

N. T. "Pete" Shields
Chairman

P.S.   I want the Congress to know how fast our citizens' army is growing and that "The Brady Bill" and other handgun issues must rank high on its agenda -- so be sure to fill out the coupon-sized message to Congress on the enclosed form. This will be clipped and presented to Congress by handgun victims, along with the messages of hundreds of thousands of other Americans.

P.P.S.   As a way of saying thank you, once you join HANDGUN CONTROL, INC., and become part of our CAMPAIGN TWO MILLION STRONG, I'll send you our new HANDGUN CONTROL decal.

Exhibit 11-2: Handgun Control

Comment:

Outer envelope copy is iron-fisted:

"ENCLOSED:
Your first real chance to tell the National Ri-
fle Association to go to hell! . . . "

I don't understand the final ellipsis (". . .") but so what? Can you envision *any* recipient, friend or foe, not opening this envelope?

The point of the letter is clear within the first 15 words.

The Rule of Political Agitation applies here, as it does to the Moynihan letter; and this letter, too, makes its point with power.

Part of the power comes from use of the vernacular: "thumbing its nose at you"; "Enough is enough"; "I'm fed up."

What happens if a member of the National Rifle Association gets this letter? He may put Pete Shields on a "hit" list, but from the viewpoint of fund raising logic, the writer is correct in not caring what the opposition thinks.

The double p.s. inflicts minor damage. Why? Because of my unswerving opinion based on $E^2 = 0$—the more points one emphasizes, the less emphasis pertains to any point. I see no reason *ever* to have a "P.P.S."

NATIONAL RIFLE ASSOCIATION

is pleased to extend to
MR. HERSCHELL & LEWIS
the following
SPECIAL INVITATION

*"the only rights you have are the ones you
preserve, protect and defend."*

Dear Friend and Fellow American:

What is more important to you than freedom?

Would you trade it for a life without your Constitutional rights?

The patriots who wrote the Bill of Rights...and the unselfish American heroes who have upheld your right to keep and bear arms for more than 200 years...knew then what each of us knows today: That...

The only rights you have are the ones you preserve, protect and defend.

That's why I'm writing to you now.

Now more than ever, you need to stand with nearly three million other patriotic Americans in the fight against growing numbers of anti-gunners who want to take away your 2nd Amendment right to own and use firearms.

There's only one way to keep them from succeeding.

Accept this special invitation and join the National Rifle Association.

When you join, you'll become a member of the only organization capable of protecting your firearms freedoms for yourself, your children, and for generations of Americans to come.

But when you join the NRA, you'll get more than the proud feeling that comes from protecting something that's undeniably yours.

Join NRA today and you'll receive not one, but TWO FREE GIFTS.

FIRST...You'll receive your choice of NRA's Black and Gold Insignia Shooter's Cap or the Official NRA Camouflage thermos... ABSOLUTELY FREE!

SECOND... You'll also receive FREE NRA's 1989 Sportsman's Premium Pak, full of money saving discount coupons from famous manufacturers including Omark, Federal Cartridge, Steele City Arms, Bushnell and many more.

National Rifle Association, 1600 Rhode Island Avenue, N.W.
Washington, D.C. 20036-3268

And...when you mail in your membership application, you'll be automatically entered into NRA's MILLION MEMBER CHALLENGE SWEEPSTAKES with $100,000 in prizes sure to win the heart of any gunowner, hunter or outdoor sportsman.

But that's just the beginning...

Your NRA membership gives you shooting's best value, including these exclusive NRA membership benefits:

• your choice of the American Hunter or American Rifleman magazine--- two of the world's most popular hunting and shooting magazines

• $600 gun theft insurance

• $10,000 Accidental Death and Dis-memberment insurance

• your NRA membership card and window decal...

...and access to all of NRA's hunting, shooting and safety programs.

Most important, you can rest assured we'll be working hard for you in Washington, your state capital and across America to defend your 2nd Amendment rights, to keep hunting lands open and to promote safe and responsible hunting and shooting.

I wouldn't be making such a valuable offer if I didn't think your active participation was so important right now.

So we're making it easier than ever for you to join. Make use of our convenient way to pay your dues now by credit card. Or if you prefer, you needn't send in your dues payment now. We'll bill you later and begin your membership benefits rolling as soon as we receive your prompt dues payment. Your FREE NRA GIFT, Sportsman's Premium Pak and all of NRA's great benefits are waiting for you.

If you're a gunowner and cherish your 2nd Amendment right to own and use them...

You belong in the NRA!

We believe that our gun rights, and yours are worth fighting for.

Don't delay....return your membership application today.

Sincerely,

J. Warren Cassidy
Executive Vice President

P.S. Be sure to respond before midnight, October 31st to qualify for NRA's Million Member Challenge Sweepstakes EARLYBIRD $10,000 BONUS DRAWING!

Exhibit 11-3: National Rifle Association

Comment:

Typically, organizations classified as "right wing" use patriotism as their principal weapon. The National Rifle Association is no exception.

The first sentence, "What is more important to you than freedom?" sets the tone. The letter is shot through with the word "patriot," in one form or another.

Although the format is odd—actual size of the two-sided letter is 5½" wide, 11⁹⁄₁₆" deep—the letter is both readable and coherent. The phrase "anti-gunners" is Rambo-ish, but the Rule of Political Agitation justifies such terminology.

Are "free gifts" out of key? Only a head-to-head test with the same message, *sans* gifts, would supply an answer. Except for the sweepstakes, the gifts are meaningless to those who aren't N.R.A. coreligionists, which makes me wonder about their effectiveness as incentives.

Nowhere does the letter mention a specific dollar amount. The numbers mentioned on the response device are $20 for an annual membership, $55 for a three-year membership. I'd have made the dollar-reference within the letter text, but such a reference is less mandatory in this type of mailing than in a more loosely targeted appeal.

HALT

An Organization of

AMERICANS FOR LEGAL REFORM

Dear Friend:

I'm fed up with the legal system. I want to change it, and I think you do, too.

It's too expensive, it's time-consuming, and for most of us it just doesn't work.

It's supposed to serve us. All of us.

But it doesn't.

Our legal system has been taken over by a group of people who treat the system like a private club, run for their own profit -- and at our expense.

That isn't right.

And something needs to be done about it.

That's why I want you to join me and hundreds of thousands of others to turn the legal system around. If we are to make a difference, we need you and we need you now.

Let me tell you about Natalie Genner.

When she hired a lawyer to handle her divorce, Natalie thought it was going to be a simple case. "Trust me," the lawyer said.

She let the lawyer take care of everything, as the lawyer insisted, but as the hours on the case increased, Natalie began to worry. Could she afford all this delay, she wondered. She called, but the lawyer always seemed too busy to see her.

It took two long, exhausting years to get her divorce. And when it was over the lawyer sent Natalie a bill for $23,000!

And she had no further recourse.

I wanted to share Natalie Genner's story with you not because it is a spectacular case of unfairness, but because it is typical of the thousands we hear about at HALT each year.

Here's one that angers me even more. When Eleanor Dunn, a single, childless woman of 82, was found dead in her Milwaukee

(over, please)

-2-

apartment, the court appointed a lawyer to handle her estate. The lawyer refused to let family members help with the funeral arrangements. After two months work, the lawyer billed the estate for $14,272 -- including $144.50 for attending the funeral!

When the family protested the bill and the lawyer's handling of the estate, the lawyer added on another $6,393 to his fee for the work he said he did defending his original bill.

These stories are all too typical of a civil legal system run amok.

It has become a system that rewards the legal profession first and foremost, at the expense of all of us who have no choice but to use that system or surrender our rights.

Don't get me wrong.

I don't hate lawyers.

In fact, HALT has many members who are lawyers. They, too, are trapped in a system that desperately needs reforming.

They know better than most how bar associations treat the legal system, not as a public trust but as an exclusive club.

Think about it.

The bars write the club rules, police the doors, and even protect their members from bad publicity when they go wrong.

Talk about a privileged class!

They write the laws we live by in language so difficult to understand that the average citizen needs a Latin dictionary or another lawyer to understand them.

They dominate the legislative committees that can -- and do -- stop attempts to reform those laws in ways that would make the system more humane and affordable.

They define the "practice of law," usually broadly enough to include anything they think can turn a handsome profit, then they prohibit anyone else from engaging in it.

If they catch some citizen offering routine legal services, they accuse, investigate, prosecute, convict, and

121

sentence that person to jail -- whatever it takes to be rid of the competition.

They set the price tag on their services as high as their closed market can bear, even if the "service" consists of little more than asking a secretary to fill out some standard form.

They insist on being above the law, exempt from the rules everyone else has to obey -- anti-trust law, consumer protection laws and the Federal Trade Commission's regulations governing unfair business practices.

And, when a lawyer steals from a client, fails to do his or her work, or makes a mistake, who disciplines that lawyer?

Other lawyers.

And this is almost always decided behind closed doors. Often the discipline never happens, and if it does, it usually amounts to little more than a private slap on the wrist.

HALT was founded in 1978 to change all that. We believe that the legal system is in desperate need of reform. It should belong to everyone, not only lawyers.

Probate is a perfect example of what I'm talking about.

Probate. Just the word itself seems so cloaked in mystery that understanding it must demand a high degree of technical skill and knowledge.

Don't believe it.

The fact is that probate can and should be simple enough for anyone to handle in all but the most complex and disputed cases.

It is nothing more than the processing of an inheritance, and in most countries it is fast, easy, and inexpensive. In Germany it is almost automatic, and costs very little.

But here in the United States, it can take years of frustration, and cost thousands of dollars. A very large part of what you think you are leaving to your heirs is likely to wind up in some lawyer's bank account.

Each year, lawyers in the United States collect nearly $2 billion in probate fees.

There is no reason for this. And no excuse.

Think about this: it costs 100 times as much to probate an estate here in the United States as it does in Great Britain, and it takes 17 times as long!

The plain truth is that lawyers control the probate system. And it is to their advantage to keep it looking complex. Because that seems to justify the big fees they collect for routine, mostly secretarial functions.

Hard to believe?

One of HALT's former board members knows this truth firsthand. He is a probate lawyer who not long ago probated a $120,000 estate in three hours for a fee of $210.

Under the law he could have charged $5,500 -- because in his state, as in many others, lawyers can charge not for the work done, but a percentage of the value of the inheritance being probated.

The same unnecessary, high-priced complexity is true for many other legal matters that can and should be made simple enough for the average citizen to handle alone.

To make this happen, laws MUST change, procedures MUST be made simpler, new alternatives MUST be developed, and they MUST be made available.

That is what HALT is all about.

More than 200,000 of your fellow citizens have joined HALT in the years since our founding. That is convincing evidence that the average American is as fed up as we are with the civil legal system.

Our members are like you.

They know that nothing gets changed unless people demand change.

They know that, if we can't trust our legal system, we have nowhere else to turn.

Harvard University President Derek Bok recently wrote:

> "There is far too much law for those
> who can afford it and far too little
> for those who cannot. No one can be
> satisfied with this state of affairs."

<u>We agree</u>. When law and justice go to the highest bidders, HALT is not satisfied.

When 90 percent of America's lawyers serve only 10 percent of the American people, HALT is not satisfied.

When bar associations dismiss nine of 10 <u>complaints</u> <u>against lawyers without taking any action</u>, HALT is not satisfied.

When Americans have to <u>shell out 25 billion dollars</u> a year in fees to lawyers in order to be compensated when they are injured, HALT is not satisfied.

Here is something else Harvard President Bok wrote:

> "The blunt, inexcusable fact is
> that this nation, which prides
> itself on efficiency and justice,
> has developed a legal system that
> is the most expensive in the world
> yet cannot manage to protect the
> rights of most of its citizens."

Frankly, I find this statement as believable as it is appalling. That's why I have joined HALT: to do something about it. And that's why I'm asking you to do the same.

If I can get <u>your</u> help, <u>we</u> can make a difference.

--We need to develop alternatives to the expensive,
  time-consuming lawsuits that compensate lawyers at
  the expense of victims.

--We need to throw out reams and reams of legalese which
  no one can understand, and replace it with simpler,
  shorter laws and contracts.

--We need to simplify legal procedures so Americans can
  <u>handle their own legal affairs without a lawyer</u> and
  without sacrificing the right to fair treatment.

--We need to hold unscrupulous, incompetent and lazy
  lawyers publicly accountable for their actions, like
  everyone else is.

--and more--

--We need to assure that routine legal services are open
  to competition so that their costs will again be
  within the reach of most Americans.

--We need to require that court clerks provide all
  citizens with help and simple do-it-yourself forms.

There is a lot we need to do. But what is HALT actually doing? And, why am I asking you to send me $15 to join our effort?

<u>Because HALT is the one national voice</u> that speaks out for legal reform. It is HALT's priority to make certain that reform of the civil legal system serves the public interest.

We are building a national network of state and local chapters to further our reform goals and the parallel goal of citizen education in self-help law.

We publish a series of highly-acclaimed CITIZENS LEGAL MANUALS -- simple, no-nonsense, self-help legal handbooks made available to our members. We have already distributed more than a million of them.

"Using a Lawyer...And What To Do If Things Go Wrong" is the cornerstone of HALT's library. It recognizes, as we do, that sometimes you do need a lawyer. It tells you how to shop for the best deal, what questions to ask and how to evaluate the answers you get -- and how to negotiate with the lawyer you finally choose. I'm sure you'll find this manual valuable and eye-opening, so I want to make you a special offer.

<u>I'll send you this bonus manual</u>, if you'll send me a tax-deductible contribution of $15 for your first year's membership. It will pay you back your $15 the first time you find you have to deal with a lawyer.

Our manuals tell how to buy and sell real estate with the greatest possible savings... how to build and present a case in small claims court... how to plan your estate for the <u>greatest</u> <u>savings in taxes and legal fees</u>... how to probate your inheritance quickly and inexpensively.

We have published nine titles and plan to publish more. <u>All of these manuals are available to our members</u>.

We also publish the nation's top legal reform periodical, a quarterly magazine, AMERICANS FOR LEGAL REFORM, sent free to our members.

123

It offers insightful analysis of legal reform issues and developments, tips on when and how you can help change the system, and expert reviews of self-help books and techniques.

All of these services will be made available to you if you send HALT a $15 tax-deductible contribution. But that isn't the only reason I am asking you to join.

I'm asking you because I believe you care. And because I want to add your voice to the 200,000-plus Americans who have already enrolled to speak out for true justice under the law.

When he was Chief Justice of the U.S. Supreme Court, Warren Burger warned the nation:

"We may be on our way to a society overrun by hordes of lawyers hungry as locusts."

I don't want his prediction to come true. I don't think you do, either.

Nobody says it will be easy. Our agenda is ambitious and the opposition is powerful. But the only way we can lose is if we don't try to change the system.

Join HALT now. Send in your $15 contribution today.

Sincerely,

Glenn Nishimura
Executive Director

P.S. Remember, your contribution is tax-deductible, and if you join today, I will send you a free copy of our manual, "Using a Lawyer... And What To Do If Things Go Wrong." More important, you will be joining the hundreds of thousands of others who believe that sanity needs to be restored to the legal system.

1319 F Street NW ■ Suite 300 ■ Washington D.C. 20004

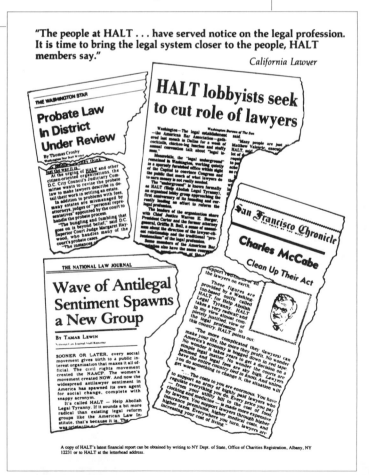

Exhibit 11-4: HALT

Comment:

"I'm fed up" seems to be a rhetorical favorite in polarized fund raising these days.

Who can quarrel with "I'm fed up"? It's as effective here as it is in the Handgun Control letter. The target of this letter is an American favorite: lawyers.

The letter is an improbable seven pages, but the eighth panel isn't wasted. It's used for reprints of press references.

The letter quickly gives the reader two episodes. Curiously, the first—about a divorce lawyer who charged $23,000—is only fractionally as interesting and motivational as the second, about a lawyer who milked an estate, including a charge of $144.50 for attending the funeral. I'd have transposed those two, or, better yet, moved the second episode up to top position in the letter.

Is the letter too long? I think so, because it sags in the middle. Maintaining pace in a seven-page letter demands copywriting beyond destructive come-to-a-stop paragraphs such as:

> "The same *unnecessary, high-priced complexity* is true for many other legal matters that can and should be made simple enough for the average citizen to handle alone.
>
> "To make this happen, laws MUST change, procedures MUST be made simpler, new alternatives MUST be developed, and they MUST be made available."

A few handwritten words might have buoyed up the "mid-letter sag." HALT is a major mailer; if the organization were my client, I'd have made two suggestions:

> 1. Test a four-page version of *this same letter* against the letter as it now stands.
> 2. Replace some of the arid portions of a letter which begins and ends with strength.

CHAPTER *12*

Religious Organization Letters

Dear Friend,

Rosh Hashanah -- a new page in the book of life ... a time of
celebration and of new beginnings ... a time when we ask for forgiveness
for our wrongdoings and shortcomings ... a time to count our blessings.

Above all, Rosh Hashanah is a time of remembrance. And, as you well
know, remembrance is the very heart of the Simon Wiesenthal Center -- not
just looking into the past, but studying it and <u>learning</u> from it, and
applying the lessons of the past to our lives today.

At this very special time of the year, I feel a sense of enormous
gratitude to you and to other friends who have honored the Simon
Wiesenthal Center with your trust and support.

I feel confident that as long as just and responsible people band
together to act as their consciences dictate, then our children and
grandchildren will live in a safer, better world. It will be a world
where "holocaust" and "genocide" are things to be remembered and
understood, but not to be feared -- because decent men and women will not
let such blights on the pages of history ever happen again.

As you well know, your support has helped us to make great strides
in our work this past year. I know you have read about them in your
copies of <u>Response</u>, so I won't enumerate them here. But please be
assured that we appreciate your concern and your generosity.

I don't know what the year ahead will bring in the way of new
challenges and confrontations. But, thanks to you, we are prepared to
face them with strength and determination. More than ever, the Simon
Wiesenthal Center stands today as a powerful force against anti-Semitism
and bigotry here in North America and around the world.

We must never rest our vigil. And we won't, as long as there are
good people like you to spur us on.

Thank you for being there for us. And, on behalf of my family and
all the staff and volunteers here at the Simon Wiesenthal Center, please
allow me to extend to you our wishes for the happiest of new years.

L'Shana Tova,

Rabbi Marvin Hier

(The Simon Wiesenthal Center is an unusually active fund raiser. The first five exhibits are letters covering a period of about four months. Not shown are newsletters with response devices mailed during that same period.)

Exhibit 12-1: Simon Wiesenthal Center

Comment:

Tying a mailing to a specific day, or time of year, enables the fund raiser to avoid the image of perpetual nag. This letter mentions Rosh Hashanah, the Jewish New Year, in each of the first two paragraphs—then, purpose served, doesn't mention it again.

Words such as *studying* and *learning* are deadly in any type of direct mail solicitation. But this letter makes no solicitation. Instead of the standard "Thank you, please" approach, it says, "Thank you"...and stops. The request for donation appears only on a separate response device.

Will this ethnically oriented greeting bring response from non-Jewish supporters of the Wiesenthal Center? I think it will, because the approach is gentle and "un-fund raiser"-like.

Simon Wiesenthal Center

<u>IT'S TIME TO RENEW YOUR 1989 MEMBERSHIP SUPPORT</u>

Dear Member,

The most important time in your relationship with the Simon Wiesenthal Center was that moment when you decided to say yes, you want to support the good work that this organization is doing.

Right now is the second most important time. Because right now, it is time for you to <u>renew</u> that support -- to say once again that you want to do what you can to help the Simon Wiesenthal Center carry on.

Stop to consider the Center's many, many activities you make possible through your membership.

We educate. We research. We mobilize public opinion. We're diplomats, investigators, watchdogs, Nazi hunters, journalists, museum directors, archivists, publishers, film producers, radio producers.

We sponsor major conferences to shed light on the spread of bigotry. We spark social action to confront it. We conduct outreach programs to high schools and colleges to teach young people the lessons of the Holocaust.

We make available a 40-panel, full-color mobile exhibit -- sent to communities throughout North America -- that dramatizes the nightmare of the Holocaust. And we distribute a poster series based upon this compelling exhibit.

We have representatives and researchers throughout the globe to report on antisemitic and terrorist activities. We expose the lies of revisionist groups who would like to convince the world that the Holocaust never happened. We meet with government leaders to discuss specific ways to quell terrorism. We press for freedom for Soviet Jews. Unlike governments, we are free of red tape and can take quicker action in fighting for human rights for the Jewish people, for all people.

We are keepers of the flame of remembrance.

And <u>you</u> are the essence of our being ...

(over please)

9760 West Pico Boulevard, Los Angeles, California 90035

Today, there are many frontiers on which we must be active. The vigil for Nazi war criminals must continue. Our estimates tell us that nearly 10,000 are still living in Western countries. The struggle for the rights of Soviet Jewry, not only the few fortunate ones that the Soviet Union has released, but the millions left behind, must be intensified.

And penetration of the Aryan Nations, other branches of the Identity network and the KKK, and our monitoring of revisionist groups ... must not only continue, but be intensified.

We need to continue enlightening world leaders about confronting antisemitic terrorism ... and educating young people about what they can do to avoid future Holocausts ... and preserving history ... and stopping the spread of antisemitic literature.

Years ago, when the Simon Wiesenthal Center was just an idea, we wondered how the public would respond to such an organization. We dreamed of being a beacon of hope in a world that needed more hope ... a force against bigotry, tyranny and terrorism. Would people care enough about our work to support it?

Yes, we learned, they would. And they did. People like you -- from more than 350,000 families -- saw the urgent need for this organization. Thanks to you, we have become the leading activist organization that fights for the rights of all people ... that protects Jewish dignity ... that speaks out against antisemitism and repression.

Help us continue. Renew your membership support. Today. Right now. Think of the future -- your future and the future of your children and grandchildren. What will their lives be like? Will terrorism continue to threaten the world? Will antisemitism thrive? Will the lessons of the Holocaust truly be learned?

You can help determine the answers to these questions by your action today -- the action of returning the enclosed form with your contribution to renew your membership in the Simon Wiesenthal Center.

Shalom,

Rabbi Marvin Hier
Dean

MH:lra

P.S. Remember, your contribution is tax-deductible. So please send as much as you can. And for whatever you send, thank you.

129

Exhibit 12-2: Simon Wiesenthal Center

Comment:

The letter is renewal-targeted, but it makes no specific dollar reference. This might be to upgrade the typical low-amount donor, because the response device lists a number of levels, from a $25 "Sponsoring Member" to a $250 "Patron."

The letter is...well, rabbi-like. For an original solicitation it may be too lyrical and self-serving, but for membership renewal it hits a quietly direct note. Had I written it, I'd have moved the section beginning, "Years ago, when the Simon Wiesenthal Center was just an idea..." to the far front. Why? Because this section has considerably more "bite" than the non-motivating first page.

SIMON WIESENTHAL CENTER

Dear Member,

A cartoon by a Pulitzer Prize-winner appears in The Los Angeles Times. It depicts a bearded Jew holding aloft a sign reading "Free Soviet Jews." His feet are planted firmly on the prostrate body of the Palestinians.

Another of our major cartoonists draws a Nazi boxcar en route to the gas chambers alongside a bus load of Palestinians headed for deportation.

Members of the Simon Wiesenthal Center from coast to coast have sent me similar unfair and grotesque articles from newspapers throughout the country.

Clearly, the recent troubling events in Israel affect each of us, whether we support Israel's actions or oppose them. To seek some perspective, I recently headed a team from the Center which visited Israel.

We were astonished to discover that a crucial dimension of this highly covered conflict has gone virtually unnoticed and unreported by the international media.

We learned it directly from the residents of Jabalya and other refugee camps. We heard in Gaza, Bethlehem and Hebron. Everywhere, young Palestinian Arabs told our video crew through our trilingual interpreter, "We want it all. Jerusalem, Tel Aviv, Haifa" ... "It's not your land. Go back to Germany." "Reagan is your friend. He will get you another country."

We met scores of young Palestinians who have become imbued with the vile Islamic Fundamentalist antisemitism which the Center has long viewed with such alarm.

We collected leaflets -- one over the signature of the PLO read: "Jewish blood is fair game." Another, in East Jerusalem, which gave instructions on how to make a homemade Molotov cocktail, stated: "You have to burn the land under the feet of the Zionists, the offspring of the culture of AIDS."

We found a new generation, fed with old antisemitic lies. Updated versions of the medieval blood libels are taking hold now in the Middle East.

As a member of the Center, you know that our mission goes well beyond perpetuating the memory and lessons of the Holocaust. We function as a global monitor, an early-warning system, dedicated to preserving the future of the world's 13 million Jews.

We do not claim to have the solution to Israel's problems, nor are we saying that all of Israel's policies are correct. There are just grievances on both sides. But the Simon Wiesenthal Center does not intend to stand by idly as insidious antisemitic manifestations increasingly become acceptable forms of protest and pass virtually unnoticed by the international community and unreported by the world press.

We must act. And with your help, we will.

The blend of Islamic Fundamentalism, mixed with antisemitism which now finds so many adherents in the Gaza Strip and the West

(over, please)

Bank, has been imported from Iran and other parts of the Islamic world. Arab newspapers in Saudi Arabia, Jordan and even Israel's lone peace partner, Egypt, are rife with classic antisemitic canards -- updated to fit contemporary events.

Clearly, the implications go far beyond the borders of the current Middle East conflict. The Center's Associate Dean just submitted his investigative field report on antisemitism in Japan -- a country with virtually no Jews. Yet during this last year alone, over two million copies of popular antisemitic books -- which blame Jews for everything from the overvalued yen to the Chernobyl nuclear disaster -- were sold in a society which boasts a 99% literacy rate.

Experts link these troubling developments to the influence of Middle East extremists, and Japan's overwhelming fear of a possible Arab oil boycott.

Recently, the Chief Judge of the United States Claims Court returned from an official speaking tour which included lectures in Pakistan and other Islamic countries. He was shocked to learn that even the most cultured, educated and enlightened people he met believed the antisemitic slurs of the best selling 1980's tracts which promote the big lie of the "Protocols of the Elders of Zion."

Whether one supports the policies of Yitzhak Shamir or Shimon Peres, we must not allow this antisemitism to go unreported and unchallenged.

The Simon Wiesenthal Center is committed to exposing these shocking developments. Here is just some of what we hope to do --

** We need your help to produce a documentary on these current developments, with a focus on our fact-finding mission to the refugee camps and Gaza. We will use our full resources so that this will be seen in communities, on cable T.V., and in meetings across the country.

** We are preparing kits for members of the U.S. Congress, Parliamentarians and other opinion makers here and abroad which will include the complete set of anti-semitic publications which the Center gathered from the Middle East, Japan, and Europe.

** We need support for our PAGE ONE Weekly national radio broadcast to bring these facts to the attention of our millions of listeners. And we will increase the flow of information to the world press and respond promptly to untruths.

The Simon Wiesenthal Center is committed to meeting this new challenge. But we must have your help.

Documentaries are very costly. The cost of our other public information programs continues to escalate. We must maintain our other ongoing activities. Finally, we dare not remain silent.

Please help by sending a special contribution as soon as possible. It is so badly needed -- and is so important to each of us. Thank you.

Sincerely,

Rabbi Marvin Hier
Dean

MH:ks

131

Exhibit 12-3: Simon Wiesenthal Center

Comment:

How close together are religion and politics? This letter shows the overlap possible when the letter-writer is confident his targets share beliefs and prejudices.

Unquestionably some recipients of this letter reject its premise. Unquestionably, too, this letter will spur other recipients, who seldom contribute to any cause, to send money.

Opinion: A hard-hitting letter such as this one should pick its most outrageous episode as its leadoff. I'd have started the letter with the gist of the *seventh* paragraph, something like this:

> **" 'Jewish blood is fair game.' That's *word for word* the message on a PLO leaflet.**
> **"Here's another: 'Go back to Germany.' "**

Curiously, this letter—in two long, legal-size pages—seems to lose its angry edge. Downshifting costs dollars, because it suggests chagrin over what's been written before. The writer of an angry letter has to keep his tone constant, not lapse into such academese as:

> **"Clearly, the implications go far beyond the borders of the current Middle East conflict."**

Writing the first sentence of an angry letter is easy. Writing a two-page angry letter isn't. If you decide to shake up your best donors, don't go out of key. You've already alienated the borderliners, so you can only gain by keeping the hard-core co-believers with you.

Simon Wiesenthal Center

9760 West Pico Boulevard   Los Angeles, California 90035

Dear Friend of the Simon Wiesenthal Center,

On March 13, I walked from my hotel to the Palais Palffy in Vienna, Austria. I was there to open our new international exhibit, "The Courage to Remember: The Holocaust 1933-1945."

The exhibit is one more way the Simon Wiesenthal Center is making sure the facts of the Holocaust <u>are</u> remembered.

Where I walked was only blocks from where uniformed storm troopers had welcomed Adolf Hitler into their city 50 years ago. It was barely a mile from the hall where, a night earlier, dignitaries and government officials had seen our award-winning film, <u>Genocide</u>.

It was not far from where, a few nights earlier, a memorial to the victims of fascism had been painted over with swastikas!

You could feel the tension all around. A people struggling with its past, the discomfort heightened by the dreadful Waldheim affair.

Our exhibit is unique. Forty dynamic display panels, each seven feet high, give a visual narrative of the Holocaust, tracing Nazi barbarism from its early crimes in 1933 until Allied soldiers opened the gates of the death camps in 1945.

I am enclosing a page of photographs for you showing just what these graphic panels look like.

In a world that wants to forget, "The Courage to Remember" reminds us of the unbelievable cruelty and terror that ended only after two of every three Jews living in Europe were systematically murdered.

But as people passed through our exhibit, a strange thing happened. Although many who came were old enough to have served

(over, please)

2.

the Nazi regime while others were too young to remember, I could see emotion in their eyes.

It was like a nation seeing its reflection in a mirror.

In some, I could see the burning resentment of a generation struggling to forget, but forced to remember. In others, I saw the pain of shame. I remembered what Simon Wiesenthal had told me years earlier:

"Never think there is a way to forgive the hate in the human heart ... or an easy way to believe that the worst has occurred and is past ... only know that hope lives when people remember."

Your support of the Simon Wiesenthal Center helps keep that hope alive.

And now we have created one of our most effective messages to date, the "Courage to Remember" exhibit.

Three years in the making, our exhibit's 40 color panels include more than 250 photographs and images, many never before seen by the public. The story of the Holocaust unfolds with individual panels devoted to such topics as:

-- Why the Jews? The Patterns of Persecution
-- Kristallnacht: The Night of Broken Glass
-- The World Turned Upside Down: The Warsaw Ghetto
-- Auschwitz-Birkenau: The Death Factory
-- Liberation: The Unmasked Horror
-- Crimes Against Humanity: Nazis on Trial
-- A Righteous Few: Survival in Hiding and Rescue
-- Remembrance and Vigilance

In a world that wants to forget, "The Courage to Remember" will be an awakening and a rebirth of the truth. As early as 1944, Simon Wiesenthal was warned by a German S.S. Officer:

"You could tell the truth about the death camps to the people in America -- and you know what would happen? They wouldn't believe you. They'd say you were crazy. They might even put you in a madhouse. How can anyone believe this terrible nightmare -- unless he has lived through it?"

(next page, please)

133

3.

And now, there are those who will tell us that the Holocaust never happened! They say it was only a myth, and the ovens of Auschwitz were used to bake bread.

They're spending hundreds of thousands of dollars to "revise" history, and it's working. Racial and religious intolerance are on the rise.

* In California, a Neo-Nazi youth group urges the "... wholesale extermination of all non-Aryans from the face of North America ..." The group has 26 chapters throughout the country, up from 15 only a year ago.

* A pamphlet circulating in Canada, "Did Six Million Really Die?", claims that few Jews perished at the hands of the Nazis, and that accounts of gas chambers are myths created by Jews to win public sympathy and German reparations.

* In France, the leader of the ultra-right National Front -- who received over 14% of the country's vote for the Presidency -- states, "I don't say the gas chambers did not exist ... but I believe it's a minor point in the history of World War II."

* In Japan, 86 antisemitic books written in the past two years are now in circulation, one of them written by Aisaburo Saito, a member of the Japanese legislature. Fewer than 1,000 Jews live in Japan.

Lies like these can do irreparable damage. We must not let them go unanswered. The truth must be told, and re-told. Young and old alike must be made to remember.

"The Courage to Remember" is a reminder that the so-called "civilized" world turned its head and allowed six million Jews to be butchered.

And now, the Simon Wiesenthal Center needs your special financial help today to take "The Courage to Remember" to people everywhere.

The exhibit is currently at the Ramstein Air Base near Frankfort, West Germany -- and will travel to Army Headquarters

(over, please)

4.

in Heidelberg. It was the centerpiece for Holocaust commemorative observances by the U.S. Military at locations where over 200,000 personnel and their families reside.

After Germany, we want to bring the exhibit back to the United States and Canada.

And in addition to this traveling exhibit, we want to distribute 1,000 poster sets of these panels throughout North America -- to universities, libraries, community centers, high schools, synagogues and churches ... to communities large and small.

The truth must reach even the most isolated communities -- especially those where antisemitism has been on the rise.

Please return your enclosed Remembrance Card today with the most generous special contribution you can afford to help the Simon Wiesenthal Center circulate the "Courage to Remember" exhibit to cities throughout North America -- and to distribute the poster series as permanent Holocaust resources.

Our children must be taught the lessons of the past. And we must tell those who continue the Nazi legacy of antisemitism and hatred that we will never stop fighting their lies.

Please help support our "Courage to Remember" exhibit by returning your special, tax-deductible contribution to me today. Thank you.

Sincerely,

Gerald Margolis
Director
Simon Wiesenthal Center

GM:ep

134

Exhibit 12-4: Simon Wiesenthal Center

Comment:

What if this four-page letter opened with the first paragraph of the third page? Mightn't the recipient be more likely to read it through?

Yet, heads unquestionably nod as the narrative proceeds, calmly and logically. Professional writing? Yes. Imperative writing? No.

Fund raising letters don't have to be imperative. But in my opinion this letter takes far too long to get to the point. Prior donors to the Simon Wiesenthal Center are totally aware of worldwide antisemitism. Novelty doesn't exist. So what does this letter want the reader to do?

The answer doesn't surface until the bottom of page three. And the cause is generalized—"We want to bring the exhibit back to the United States and Canada." A more effective technique might emphasize city-by-city, area-by-area exposure in places where domestic antisemitism is on the rise.

Donors respond to specifics far more readily than they do to generalities.

Rabbi Marvin Hier, *Dean*

Dear Member,

I have been informed by our Membership
Department that we have not yet received your
instructions for renewing your annual support.
It would help us greatly if you could let us know
why you chose not to renew at this time. Your
answer will give us a better understanding of
how our members feel about the work we do.

Would you like us to do even more? And if
so, in what area? Nazi Watch? Outreach programs
to youngsters? Conferring with world leaders
about terrorism? Public education? Please let
me know by writing your comments on the back of
this letter and returning it to me in the enclosed
reply envelope. I assure you, your views are very
important to me.

Actually, I am glad to tell you that an overwhelming majority of our members do renew their
support every year. And it occurred to me that
your not renewing was simply an oversight. So I
am also enclosing a copy of your Membership Renewal
Form so that you may still renew at this time.
Needless to say, we would welcome your continued
support.

Sincerely,

Rabbi Marvin Hier
Dean

MH:rle

Simon Wiesenthal Center 9760 West Pico Boulevard, Los Angeles, California 90035

Exhibit 12-5: Simon Wiesenthal Center

Comment:

One of the most potent resuscitators is the "How did we fail you?"
approach.

Chapter three described the five great fund raising motivators—
Fear, Exclusivity, Greed, Guilt, and Anger. All five have their place in
fund raising, but none surpasses Guilt in reviving prior donors who
haven't responded to automatic appeals.

This membership renewal letter follows that path. The close is curiously mild; "Needless to say, we would welcome your continued support" is a thin ending to a guilt-dependent letter.

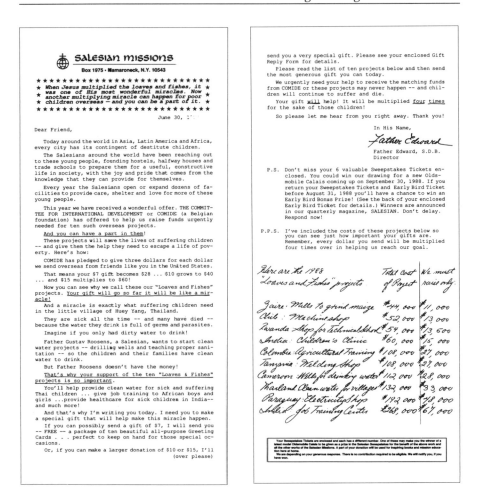

Exhibit 12-6: Salesian Missions

Comment:

The star-boxed text at the top of this letter is called a "Johnson Box."

Johnson Boxes are popular among direct response writers, many of whom feel these boxes add an extra level of interest—resulting in increased readership. I don't share that view.

I much prefer a handwritten overline to a Johnson Box, not only because handwriting is less formal but also because the very format of a Johnson Box encourages the writer to say too much too soon.

This is just such a circumstance. Nothing in the Johnson Box helps stimulate readership. In fact, having all four lines flush-right makes the box itself less readable.

As is so often true, this letter would benefit from editing. Eliminating the first three paragraphs would enable the letter to start in high gear. The "loaves and fishes" parallel then comes clear. The reader feels involvement, where the letter as written leaves the reader outside, as an observer.

Hand-underlining helps this letter, printed on both sides of a single $6'' \times 12\frac{3}{8}''$ sheet.

Two postscripts don't work. Instead, this writer should have *boxed* the second p.s., handwritten the "I've included..." copy, and typewritten the listings. If you don't agree, write it out that way and compare both verisimilitude and ease of message absorption.

Joan Rivers

Dear Friend:

Even though you may know me as a talk show hostess and comedienne, I am writing to you about something we must all take very seriously ... our common interest in the Jewish people and Israel's survival.

As an American, I believe our strategic interest in the Middle East is best served by our historic commitment to Israel's strength and security.

But not everyone agrees with me. Some of Israel's battles are often fought - and lost - 6000 miles from Jerusalem, in Washington, D.C.

For example, in 1981 some of America's most sophisticated weaponry, AWACS and F-15 enhancements, was sold to Saudi Arabia. Shocked that a threat to Israel's survival was coming from our government and knowing most Americans support Israel, I wondered why such a sale was being considered.

I discovered that individuals who profited from military sales to Arab countries, along with the petrodollar community, had lobbied Congress on behalf of the Saudi government. Together they presented a strong political challenge to America's long-standing commitment to Israel. Their challenge was aided by their political activity through PACs.

Bechtel, Mobil, Exxon and Westinghouse had PACs. Boeing and Amoco had PACs. Many other companies doing business with Saudi Arabia had PACs.

Today these companies still have PACs - political action committees. Massive contributions are being channeled to Congressional campaigns -- not directly by the corporations, which is illegal, but through their PACs.

We're lucky, for we too have a PAC - THE NATIONAL PAC.

I am a member of NatPAC. As long as PACs exist, I believe close U.S.-Israel relations should be represented. NatPAC does just that.

Unlike other fine organizations such as the UJA, the AJC, the JNF, and the American-Israel Public Affairs Committee (AIPAC), which do not contribute to candidates for Congress, The National PAC can and does.

NatPAC contributes to candidates who reject anti-Semitism, support World Jewry, and recognize Israel as a strategic asset to America and our only reliable ally in the Middle East.

Let me tell you, The National PAC makes contributions -- contributions to insure that at least one day every two years, election day, is positive for U.S.-Israel relations.

In NatPAC's founding year, The New York Times called NatPAC "the #1

contributor of all unaffiliated PACs in the country". NatPAC gave $542,000 to campaigns of candidates supportive of U.S.-Israel relations.

NatPAC has kept its #1 rating.

In 1984 NatPAC expanded to 30,000 members and gave a record $779,000 to campaigns; in 1986 NatPAC contributed $1,015,000 setting another record for bipartisan, unaffiliated PACs. The membership reached 55,000!

I cannot overstate NatPAC's good work. While other groups may lobby those already elected to Congress, NatPAC works within the American political system to elect and reelect friends of U.S.-Israel relations.

Does this help? Can we talk? Since the Senate approval of the AWACs to Saudi Arabia in 1981, Congress has prevented most major arms sales to Saudi Arabia, Jordan and other Arab states.

Why the dramatic shift in the voting behavior of the U.S. Senate? A study I saw shows that all but 2 of the Senators elected since the AWACs sale opposed a 1987 weapons sale to Saudi Arabia - this represents a switch of 19 Senate votes from "against" to "for" U.S.-Israel relations. The shift has occurred in just three elections!

THE DRAMATIC CHANGE IN SENATE VOTING CAME NOT FROM SENATORS CHANGING VOTES, BUT FROM VOTERS CHANGING SENATORS.

But all is not well. While a positive shift in support for U.S.-Israel relations in Congress is apparent, the media continues to feature anti-Israel reports on the front pages and evening news. The stories support the Arab Lobby's view that American strategic aid and support for Israel should be conditioned on Arab demands.

The information which has been promoted by the Arab Lobby, from Israel's birth through today, has recently gained wide exposure in the American press.

What the press fails to report is that the battles in the Middle East are not just for Gaza and the West Bank, but for Jerusalem, the Galilee, Jaffa, and Haifa. The battles are between Jews and Arabs for the same small piece of land -- Israel.

A further concern, anti-Semitism, has again reared its ugly head and political anti-Semitism is on the rise:

** Louis Farrakhan and his surrogates still cross America speaking to thousands of Americans, especially students, in cities including New York, Chicago and Los Angeles. Their message: the Jews are to blame for the problems at home, work, and with the order of things overseas.

139

** <u>Anti-Semitic religious leaders</u>, in the recent past, blamed
   "Jews running the banks" for the farm problems. Recently, a
   minister of a 13 million member evangelical movement stated
   that "unless (Jews) repent and get born again, they don't
   have a prayer."

** "<u>Dual-loyalty</u>" charges have again been leveled by Israel's
   opponents in an effort to undermine American support for
   close U.S.-Israel relations.

<u>This is the essence of political anti-Semitism</u>. Individuals, and
their followers, who thirst for power and abuse our great American
political system by misusing freedom of speech.

We can't underestimate the political power of anti-Semitic
leaders. They are skilled orators who have thousands of followers.
For that reason it is good to know that most leaders in America,
especially in Congress, are fighting anti-Semitism.

We are fortunate to have our leaders in America supporting the
issues we care deeply about -- close U.S.-Israel relations, opposition
to political anti-Semitism and freedom for Soviet Jewry.

With the Soviet and American governments meeting regularly to
discuss human rights, Soviet Jews are being given a reason to hope.
Their hope - and liberty - depend upon our leaders insisting to the
Soviets that Jews be freed.

We must help insure positive Members of Congress continue to be
elected. But, the rise in political anti-Semitism and Middle East
unrest makes the Arab Lobby's efforts to discredit support for Israel,
World Jewry and Congressional allies even more destructive.

What can you do?

Beyond your support for fine candidates like Senators Moynihan,
Metzenbaum, Weicker, Heinz and others, you can make a <u>national</u>
statement. You can do what I did.

You can join NatPAC. You can be a part of NatPAC's
accomplishments:

- Over $2.5 million in contributions to Senators and Representatives
  currently serving in Congress.

- 88% of the candidates NatPAC supported in the last election, many
  in tough races, won and are now in Congress.

- NatPAC is national, contributing to candidates in all 50 states --
  not just New York, California and Florida, where our community is
  strong, but also in states like South Dakota, Mississippi and
  Idaho, where our numbers are small but where support for Israel is
  just as important, if not more important.

<u>Candidates know a NatPAC contribution means support for strong U.S.-
Israel relations and World Jewry as well as opposition to anti-Semitism.</u>

I urge you to <u>make a national statement</u>. Join me in supporting
NatPAC's good work. Consider contributing $25, $50, $100, or $250
today. Whatever you can afford to invest will help elect a supportive
Congress now and through the 1990's.

I need you to help all of us at NatPAC fight the growing influence
of the Arab Lobby and their petrodollar friends. You will be helping
to fight rising political anti-Semitism in America and you will be
making a strong statement to our leaders in Washington on behalf of
Soviet Jews.

Make a positive statement. Contribute to NatPAC. For yourself,
for future generations, and for Israel.

                                    Sincerely yours,

                                    JOAN RIVERS

JR/dh

Enclosures

P.S. Enclosed is a copy of an ad NatPAC published. Inside it is a
     detailed outline of the Arab Lobby's growing political strength.
     Please examine it and act on it -- today. Thank you.

Exhibit 12-7: National PAC

Comment:

The use of celebrities as spokespeople is too well-established to warrant generalized criticism. Specific criticism is another matter.

The key question here: Why use Joan Rivers for this message? The reader finds the sophisticated informational core out of key with her reputation and background. A greater blow to verisimilitude: Terminology is totally unrelated to the way this woman communicates.

The message nucleus, in the second paragraph, is muddied by hit-and-run philosophy. What does she want us to do? The answer comes—deep in page three. By that time the impersonal, overly intellectualized message has the reader hopelessly bored.

Suggestion: Use celebrities such as Joan Rivers (who isn't universally respected nor loved) as an ancillary, the ostensible writer of a short "lift" note. Keep that note within the personality-borders of the celebrity. Credibility vanishes when the reader thinks the letter was written before the organization found a celebrity to sign it.

Beatrice Arthur

Dear Friend,

As an actress, I'm often called on to help worthy causes. I have become -- like you, I imagine -- quite selective in what I support.

I write you now about a remarkable organization doing noble work, which until recently had not been done at all. Yet, its concerns are likely to become our concerns, yours and mine, at a time of profound need.

I learned this from my own family's experience.

Two years ago, my mother died. Old and blind, she had been denied admittance to facilities for the aged to which we applied. I had to provide the care she needed. I did the best I could at the time.

Now I know how much the organization I write you about -- the National Institute for Jewish Hospice -- could have done to help my mother and me. And so I support it now, so that others may receive help when they desperately need it.

I hope that when you learn what the Institute does, you too will help. So many Jewish families, at a time of great sadness, will benefit.

You see, with each new medical advance, the likelihood of a slow decline, painful in so many ways, increases for each of us. But medicine can only do so much.

There's no medical treatment for loneliness and fear, for anguish and heartache. Doctors aren't trained to deal with such conditions. But these are human conditions.

For those beyond cure, there is still great

(over, please)

2.

need for care if a loved one's final precious days are to be worth living.

A dying person remains alive and wants to be treated with dignity as a living individual. As a "mensch." Sometimes just a loving word, a touch, an embrace, can be more potent medicine than a hundred pills.

The National Institute for Jewish Hospice provides sorely needed guidance in ways to ease the physical and emotional pain for terminally-ill Jews. Drawing on centuries of Jewish tradition and attitudes about living -- and dying -- it teaches families and professionals what isn't taught in medical school. And it teaches those left behind to deal with their grief.

I've played many roles, some of them -- like "Yenta" in the Broadway production of "Fiddler on the Roof" -- Jewish roles. In the current TV series, "Golden Girls," I play a woman who does not mince words. I call a spade a spade -- just as I did in "Maude." In that spirit, I must tell you now that the National Institute for Jewish Hospice does what needs doing. It deserves your support.

The whole idea of hospice is quite new. I recently learned that the first hospice was started by Dame Cicely Saunders in England only twenty-five years ago. Jewish hospice service is much newer. In an organized fashion, it began only two years ago, when the National Institute for Jewish Hospice was founded.

In that short time, the Institute has made impressive progress.

Through its Central Telephone Network system, volunteers provide immediate information to families about hospitals, hospice facilities, geriatric centers. About physicians, psychologists, social workers. About rabbis and synagogues.

It has established a national network of professionals experienced in hospice care ... Its publications directed to the dying

(next page, please)

142

3.

and their families are widely used ... Its
well-attended conferences broaden understanding of Jewish hospice among both Jews
and Gentiles.

Soon, its videotape cassette training
program will be available to professionals throughout the country.

I was glad to learn, though, of one thing that
the Institute does _not_ do. It doesn't spend one
penny of the money contributors entrust to it to
build offices, or costly medical centers, or buildings of any kind. I think you'll agree we have
enough buildings -- but there is a crying need for
the kind of service and solace no building can
provide.

What _is_ needed -- and believe me, it's _badly_
needed -- is the very kind of experienced, caring
counsel and direction which the Institute was set up
to provide.

When a family learns that an elder, or in some
tragic cases, a child, has been found incurably ill,
there is no more that medicine can do -- but there
is _a_ _great_ _deal_ _else_ _that_ _can_ _be_ _done_. Things that
can make the precious time left worth living.

Should the family turn to a special hospice
facility, or should it provide hospice care at
home? How can a team of physician, nurse, social
worker, and psychologist develop a "treatment
plan"? A plan which treats the dying person
humanely, Jewishly, thoughtfully -- the way you
and I would want to be treated.

A dying person remains _alive_, sometimes for a
long time. There can be therapy in just _listening_
-- to remembrances, to fervent hopes for the family,
to insights and confidences which have never before
been revealed.

Often there is a yearning to return to one's
Jewishness. What role can the rabbi and the
synagogue play? What traditions, observances and
attitudes about life and death will bring comfort?

A pious Jew can't receive spiritual nourishment

(over, please)

4.

through an IV needle. But a little bedside Seder at
Passover, the lighting of the candles at Chanukah,
can sometimes bring more peace than any tranquilizer.

These are the treatments for which the National
Institute is the "specialist," from which so many
benefit. And from which so many more _could_ benefit.

I trust by now, you realize how much the
National Institute for Jewish Hospice does. And
how much more, _with_ _your_ _support_, it can, and must
do. As a young organization it urgently _needs_ new
supporters like you, if it is to respond to the
rapidly-growing number of families turning to it
for help every day. It must not turn them away.

In a way, until now, the passage from life to
death, which each of us will someday experience, has
been an "orphan disease." None of us wants to think
about it. But the National Institute _is_ thinking
about it, and doing important work which can truly
make a difference for countless Jewish families.

Please join me in supporting the National
Institute for Jewish Hospice as generously as you
can. Your contribution is tax-deductible, of
course. But when you give -- $50, $25, $100, or
whatever you can afford -- you'll receive much more
than another tax deduction. You will know you have
performed a loving act. A true _mitzvah_.

Thank you.

Sincerely,

Beatrice Arthur

BA:sp

P.S. Please remember that -- even during times of
economic uncertainty -- this is one need which
can't be deferred.

143

Exhibit 12-8: National Institute for Jewish Hospice

Comment:

Compare this letter with the Joan Rivers letter.

Probably you'll agree the tone is warmer and more personal. Beatrice Arthur *might* have written this letter.

The letter is peppered with personal anecdotes, each of which adds credibility to the plea. The message is highly ethnicized, but this is completely logical for a letter aimed at a vertical target-group.

The p.s. is surprisingly weak. The final word, "deferred," is far too bookish to end a postscript.

October 7, 19??

Dear Friend,

IF YOU EVER FEEL LIKE THE WORLD IS PASSING YOU BY ...
... OR THAT TENSION AND WORRY ARE SHORT-CHANGING YOUR LIFE ...
... OR WONDER WHY YOU NEVER SEEM TO BE GETTING AHEAD ...

then why not _do something about it?_

Most people have feelings like these, now and then. Some drag them along into every day, living lives of drudgery with little hope or zest. _But others refuse to settle for a "half-life."_

Who are these "others"? They're the people who have dramatically changed their lives ... discovered a joy they never had before ... experienced the vitality that was lacking in their lives.

They're the people who've made an all-important decision to take the first vital step to turn their lives around.

And you can be one of them!

How do I know? Because I've seen thousands and thousands of people do it. And you, too, can do it.

You'll find the principles that make it all possible in an easy-to-read publication I send ten times a year to over 800,000 people. It's called _Plus: The Magazine of Positive Thinking._

And I want you to receive it ...

whether you can pay or not!

It costs us $8 a year to send _Plus._ If you can send $8 for it, please do. (If you can't afford $8, send what you can. Or, if funds are short right now, see the "P.S." to learn how to receive four issues of _Plus, free._)

The most important thing is to act -- now. Don't let this golden opportunity slip away. Decide right now to take that first step to vitalize your life, your outlook, your future.

Plus has the keys that can make it all happen. You've often

over, please

---

heard, "the Lord helps those that help themselves." So _help yourself!_ Make it happen. Return the enclosed card.

Do it -- for yourself!

Norman Vincent Peale

NVP:rwh

P.S. If you can't send the $8 for _Plus_, return the card anyway. I'll send four issues to you FREE because _I want you to have them._ Just check the FREE box on the card.

Exhibit 12-9: Foundation for Christian Living

Comment:

Even with Norman Vincent Peale's reputation, is a "You're a loser" opening as effective as a more universal "Positive thinking" approach?

Only those who tabulate comparative results can answer this question. As an opinion: This letter will pull better among lower income groups than among higher income groups...usually not the best anticipation in fund raising.

"I've seen thousands and thousands of people do it" has fractional energy compared with even a single example. The letter refers to a "golden opportunity." What is it? The opportunity to subscribe to a magazine?

What's lacking here is the "I-to-you" vitality one expects of a communication from Norman Vincent Peale.

The p.s. is superior, a classic example of what a p.s. should be.

CHAPTER *13*

Ecology, Environment, Wildlife Letters

WWF

World Wildlife Fund

May 23, 19⎯

Ms. Margo E. Lewis
9748 Cedar Villas
Plantation, Florida 33324

Dear Ms. Lewis,

One of the greatest pleasures I have as president of World
Wildlife Fund is acknowledging the generous support of members
like you.

And I can honestly say that your recent gift of $100.00
is truly appreciated by all of us here at WWF.

You know, with so many species facing imminent extinction,
one of WWF's greatest challenges today is the continued funding
of our many international programs.

But, I feel personally confident that we will continue to
meet this challenge with members like you who are caring and
committed to the cause of saving endangered wildlife worldwide.

And WWF is working daily to strengthen our international
conservation network. With every dollar sent, the whales, the
jaguars, and the mountain gorillas are that much safer. And
since no species exists in isolation, the protection you give
these animals also extends to countless other animals as well.

I hope you enjoy your wildlife notecards. I also hope that
every time you use one, you will be reminded of the important
role you continue to play in saving endangered animals whenever
and wherever they are threatened.

Sincerely,

William K. Reilly

1250 Twenty-Fourth Street, NW   Washington, DC 20037   USA   202/293-4800   Telex: 64505 PANDA
Affiliated with The Conservation Foundation

(World Wildlife Fund is an active and sophisticated user of the mails. The first seven exhibits in this section were sent to a $100 donor, over a period of six months. Of the seven, exhibits one through five were first class mail.)

Exhibit 13-1: World Wildlife Fund

Comment:

Why don't more organizations follow this lead, acknowledging gifts with what seems to be a personalized response?

This letter is a pure "Thank you." No "Please..." interferes with its tone. The recipient's reaction has to be 100 percent favorable—a reception-setter for the next appeal. When this letter came, I wrote the comment, "Classy acknowledgment letter," on the envelope. Re-reading it, I'd use the same words.

WWF

World Wildlife Fund

June 30, 1988

Margo E. Lewis
9748 Cedar Villas
Plantation, Florida   33324

Dear World Wildlife Member,

Do you recognize the names Ling-Ling? Hsing-Hsing? Chi-Chi?
These pandas are known and loved by millions of Americans today.

But in China, <u>poachers are slaughtering the very last giant
pandas left in the wild</u>!

Please ... we need your help to save the pandas.

When a baby panda is born, it is so tiny it can easily fit
in one of its mother's paws.

With just a thin covering of white fur -- and a voice that
sounds like a baby's cry -- the panda cuddles day and night
against its mother's large, warm body.

For months, the mother will carry her baby around with her
-- feeding her, tossing her gently between her paws to play.

Finally, when the baby is about 18 months old, it will go
off to live on its own.

But ... what will that young panda do if she is stalked by
an enemy she can never escape? What happens ... if that young
panda's fur can bring over $100,000 on the black market?

The answer is so terrible that, if you care anything at all
about saving wildlife, you <u>must</u> respond to this letter.

After you read my letter, I'm sure you will agree that we
must do everything we can to save these magnificent animals. Your
gift for $380 or whatever amount you can afford will surely help.
I have indicated an amount on your personal donation form that
would give our work to save the pandas a real boost!

(over, please)

1250 Twenty-Fourth Street, NW   Washington, DC 20037   USA   202/293-4800   Telex: 64505 PANDA

-2-

Because there <u>is</u> a way you can help save the giant panda.

As you may recall from my last letter, World Wildlife Fund
has launched a comprehensive <u>Panda Protection Program</u> to help save
these extremely rare animals.

The People's Republic of China is being tremendously helpful
in our cooperative program.

Their Ministry of Forestry is working hand-in-hand with
World Wildlife Fund to protect the panda's last remaining habitat.
They're continuing efforts with WWF to breed pandas in captivity in
Wolong Nature Reserve. And they're working to stop the poaching
that now poses such a serious threat to the panda's survival.

<u>But they have asked for much more of our help. And they
need it quickly.</u>

You see, without our help the giant panda
has almost no chance of surviving
into the 21st century!

That's no longer such a far-away time. It's only <u>12 years</u>
down the road.

Right now, fewer than 1,000 pandas are estimated to survive
in the wild. Most live in small, isolated groups of fewer than 50
individuals.

Their habitat has shrunk dramatically to six small ranges on
the eastern edge of the Tibetan Plateau.

But also reducing their numbers have been the greedy
poachers who kill pandas in their never-ending search for black
market profits.

As I told you when I last wrote, Chinese officials recently
recovered 146 panda pelts that were probably en route to Hong
Kong or Japan for sale on the black market!

With so few pandas left in the wild, <u>those 146 deaths
represent a hefty portion of the animal's small population</u>!

We now know that these pelts can fetch up to $100,000.
They're sometimes sold as prized furs or wall-hangings, sometimes
even credited with magical properties.

(next page, please)

149

China has tough animal protection laws that threaten panda poachers with imprisonment.

But even the toughest laws have not been enough to keep these poachers from killing the pandas.

Sometimes, even if pandas aren't killed intentionally for their pelts, they may be inadvertently trapped in snares set for musk-deer. This illegal musk-deer snaring is commonplace in China and even occurs inside the giant panda reserves.

<u>As a result of this double-edged threat, the panda is much closer to extinction than we've ever imagined.</u>

And it's not just poaching that's destroying the species. Logging operations and other threats to habitat are also pushing the shy animal to the point of no return.

A mass flowering of bamboo some years ago led to a heavy die-off of pandas. Scientists estimate that in some areas, this loss of the main component of their diet killed 80% of the smaller populations.

It used to be that when a species of bamboo flowered, the pandas would simply move to another valley to feed on a different species of bamboo. This is no longer possible -- since human pressures have so drastically destroyed many of the panda's former habitats.

<u>To counteract these threats, World Wildlife Fund has developed a plan to save the giant panda from extinction.</u>

I'm hoping <u>you</u> will be part of this plan.

Our program will:

1) Launch improved anti-poaching protection measures by training and equipping park wardens and patrols in China's panda reserves.

2) Plant bamboo corridors to link the panda's scattered habitats.

3) Translocate certain animals from one area of their range to another to strengthen the population.

4) Complete and analyze our giant panda survey to monitor any fluctuations in numbers or range.

5) Extend the panda reserve system.

(over, please)

You'd be surprised by how many times even the simplest measure can produce the greatest result.

For instance, to link isolated panda populations so they can breed, sometimes all that's needed is a small bridge to help the pandas cross a formerly impassable river.

<u>Your gift could help us build those bridges</u> -- and buy radio-collars to closely monitor pandas in the reserve.

<u>Your gift could help us plant "bamboo corridors"</u>, linking vital panda populations.

<u>And your gift could help us purchase radios,</u> rain gear, and tents to equip anti-poaching patrols in panda reserves.

For years, the giant panda has been recognized as a living symbol of world conservation. You as a WWF member certainly know that of all the endangered animals it was the panda that was chosen as the international symbol of World Wildlife Fund 27 years ago.

How tragic it would be for all of us if this symbol became only a relic of yet another species lost to us forever.

All of us at World Wildlife Fund are deeply worried by the discovery of those 146 panda pelts.

I think you should be worried, too.

The panda is going to become extinct ... unless you and World Wildlife Fund help to save it. Please send in your very special donation <u>today</u>.

Sincerely,

William K. Reilly
President

P.S. I've included a rather sad photo of a giant panda -- a mother who'd been nursing her new baby -- who was killed by poachers.

Take a look. Then give <u>some</u> gift, of any amount, to stop tragic panda deaths and help save these harmless and wonderful animals. I'll be waiting to hear from you.

Exhibit 13-2: World Wildlife Fund

Comment:

Specificity is one of the great keys to effective fund raising by mail.

This four-page letter attacks a single issue: poachers killing off the giant panda.

Opinion: This letter is only partially successful, because it lacks an impeller—a tie between donor and end-use.

The letter is well written, but its single failing is the first word of the comment—*specificity*. What can the recipient do? How does a donation protect the pandas? The letter says China has "tough animal protection laws." The list of five plans to save the pandas from extinction seems to have little to do with outsiders; as outlined, we seem to be meddlers in an intra-China affair.

(A private parenthetical note: We asked the World Wildlife Fund to help us gain access to the panda preserve, during a recent trip to China. Our letter went unanswered.)

What saves this mailing is a separate enclosure, a photograph of a nursing female panda killed by a poacher's snare. The p.s. refers to this picture, and unquestionably the poignancy of it brought substantial contributions.

WWF

World Wildlife Fund

September 7, 1987

Margo E. Lewis
9748 Cedar Villas
Plantation, Florida 33324

Dear World Wildlife Member:

In the next few days, a representative of World Wildlife Fund will be calling you. I'm writing today to ask a personal favor. Will you please give this phone call your undivided attention?

The call is being made at my request -- for two extremely important reasons.

<u>First</u>, to offer a heartfelt "Thank You" for all you've done to underwrite WWF's past work to protect rapidly disappearing wildlife habitats and critically endangered species.

<u>Second</u>, to ask you to join a select group of members who have undertaken a special challenge. They have agreed to pledge their personal support to an absolutely vital World Wildlife Fund initiative -- called the <u>Global Campaign to Save the Rain Forests</u>.

Saving tropical forests is the greatest conservation challenge now facing WWF. I don't know how I can emphasize that enough. How I can say it as forcefully as I believe it must be said.

Maybe I can best say it this way: In the time it takes you to read this letter more than <u>60,000</u> trees will fall in the world's rain forests. At that rate of destruction, rain forests will disappear completely in many nations by the year 2000 -- little more than a decade from now!

And when the forests disappear, up to 1/5 of all species of life on this planet will also disappear!

It's a tragically simple equation. As go the rain forests, so go the animals who depend on forest habitat for food, for shelter, for life.

I'm talking about animals like the incredibly beautiful jaguar -- threatened throughout their range and pushed to the very edge of extinction in the rain forests of Brazil. Brazil's Atlantic forest once covered an estimated 400,000 square miles. But today, fewer than 20,000 square miles remain!

And it's not just jaguars who are suffering. So are tigers, ocelots, giant river otters, spectacled bears, various species of primates (including the endangered orangutan), and thousands of exceptionally beautiful birds like the resplendent quetzal and the brilliant hyacinth macaw.

<u>Scientists have called potential loss of one-fifth of the Earth's species the most massive extinction of wildlife since the disappearance of the dinosaurs</u>. That was 60 million years ago.

And, that's not all.

The destruction of tropical forests also foretells dire, even life-threatening problems for human beings -- you and me.

Rain forests are nature's medicine chest. And as forests disappear we lose plants that provide -- or could provide -- cures to some of today's most feared diseases.

Fully 25% of all the drugs now prescribed in the United States contain plant ingredients from tropical rain forests. Drugs like vincristine, used to treat childhood leukemia and Hodgkin's disease. And reserpine, an essential drug in modern cardiology that is used to treat hypertension. And diosgenin, now administered to treat arthritis.

We call them "wonder drugs." Yet they come to us from the rosy periwinkle, the snakeroot and the yam -- all found in rain forests.

Mass destruction of the Earth's rain forests could threaten us in another way, too.

Scientists are just beginning to discover the significance of rain forests in stabilizing global climate patterns. Many are concerned that the widespread destruction of rain forests may add enough carbon dioxide to the atmosphere to increase the Earth's temperature. This <u>global warming</u> could raise the level of the oceans by several feet and turn major grain-producing regions into dustbowls.

How, exactly, are rain forests being destroyed? In several ways --

-- By massive slash-and-burn agriculture.

-- By large-scale commercial logging.

-- By badly managed cattle ranching.

(next page, please)

152

-- By ill-advised uneconomical hydroelectric projects.

-- By widespread wildlife poaching, illegal hunting, and trading, now taking place on the most massive level ever.

As you can judge for yourself, we are facing a problem of truly enormous proportions, requiring the kinds of global solutions that only an organization like World Wildlife Fund can provide.

And make no mistake. World Wildlife Fund's presence <u>is</u> felt around the globe. When other organizations simply talk about pending ecological catastrophes, WWF <u>acts</u> to prevent them.

In fact, working with our worldwide network of scientists and conservationists, we have already begun efforts to safeguard the tropical forests. At this very moment World Wildlife Fund is --

1. <u>Identifying global rain forest priority areas</u> so that we know which forests need immediate protection. High on our current list are two wildlife sanctuaries in Thailand that comprise 2,000 square miles of rain forest providing vital habitat for both Asian elephants and tigers.

2. <u>Spearheading efforts to permanently protect habitats critical to the survival of endangered species</u>. As just one example, WWF was instrumental in creating Rio Abiseo National Park in the Peruvian Andes to protect the endangered yellow-tailed woolly monkey.

3. <u>Conducting advanced ecological field research</u> in the Amazon Basin to determine exactly how much of a rain forest must be protected in order to support all the animal and plant species which live there.

4. <u>Devising innovative funding strategies</u> called "debt-for-nature" swaps, where debtor nations (often developing nations with extensive natural habitat) can convert a portion of their foreign debt burden into support for conservation.

5. <u>Clamping down on illegal wildlife trade</u> through our unique program, TRAFFIC -- a global watchdog that closely monitors wildlife trading. Many of the species threatened by international trading are denizens of the rain forest. And as forest acreage dwindles, their capture -- or killing -- is made all the easier.

Frankly, we're proud of each and every one of these innovative efforts to save the world's tropical forests.

(over, please)

<u>But</u> ... my colleagues and I are also convinced that we must do more. That we must <u>accelerate</u> these protection measures. That we must get more of our best and most loyal members involved -- people like you. Because time is running out for the tropical rain forests.

Within the next minute alone, another 50 acres will be destroyed. <u>Forever</u>. Think about it.

And remember what the destruction of forest habitat means for the future of the jaguar, the ocelot, the tiger, the spectacled bear -- the list goes on and on and could one day include an astonishing 1/5 of all life on our planet.

We must not let this tragedy happen!

That's why, when you receive your phone call from World Wildlife Fund, I urge you to make the most generous pledge you can in support of our <u>Global Campaign to Save the Rain Forests</u>.

Our goal is to raise $2.1 million by December 31st of this year.

Yes, that's an enormous amount of money. But the challenge we face is enormous, too.

And if each of us gets involved to the fullest extent we are able, we <u>will</u> have the resources we need to save the world's tropical forests.

So when your phone call comes, please support our Global Campaign to Save the Rain Forests with the most generous pledge you can make.

World Wildlife Fund's ability to pick up the pace in the battle to save our life-giving tropical rain forests depends directly upon your support of our work.

For whatever you do to help, you have my heartfelt thanks.

Sincerely yours,

William K. Reilly
President

P.S. Please know you have my word that your pledge to World Wildlife Fund's Global Campaign to Save the Rain Forests will be put to the very best use possible. And, your pledge is tax-deductible.

Exhibit 13-3: World Wildlife Fund

Comment:

Chapter three points out that *exclusivity* is the easiest to mount, of the five great motivators.

This letter presses the "exclusivity" keys: "... ask a personal favor"; "The call is being made at my request"; "...ask you to join a select group of members..."

This letter preceded a telemarketing campaign. The use is quite proper for such circumstances. Many who might resent a cold call see their objections fade when the caller asks, "Did you get Mr. Reilly's letter of September 7?" The target-individual may not remember the letter (although first class mail makes close timing feasible), but the specific question leads to acceptance.

Reaction to the letter parallels reaction to the "panda" letter: The cause is totally worthwhile, but what will the actions be? How will the organization save the rain forests and the animals in those forests?

The answers are muddy. "Identifying global rain forest priority areas" is a government committee term. "Spearheading efforts" is a generalization. "Conducting advanced ecological field research" seems to be a substitute for action, not part of it. "Devising innovative funding strategies" is what this letter represents, not a way to save the forests. "Clamping down on illegal wildlife trade" is only peripherally related to this project.

The second paragraph of page four has the meat:

"Within the next minute alone, another 50 acres will be destroyed. *Forever.* Think about it."

This at last clarifies the problem, although the means of solution remains unclear.

Unlike most Wildlife Fund letters, this one has a weak p.s., raising a question the donor may not have had before. The p.s. would be stronger had it said only, "Of course your pledge is tax-deductible."

WWF

World Wildlife Fund

William K. Reilly	H. R. H. The Prince Philip, Duke of Edinburgh
President, WWF-U.S.	*President, WWF-International*

November 9, 1988

Margo E. Lewis
9748 Cedar Villas
Plantation, Florida 33324

Dear World Wildlife Member,

While it has been only a month or so since I last wrote you, I wanted you to be among the first to know the results of the important meeting our senior program staff just held.

At that meeting, it became clear that we would have to assign far more urgent priorities than we originally thought necessary to certain of our key wildlife conservation programs.

We're accelerating our drive to save endangered wildlife from extinction and that makes it necessary for me to ask you to renew your membership with the most generous gift you have yet made to World Wildlife Fund.

While you must, of course, decide for yourself what amount to send, I am personally hoping that you will increase your generous support of our worldwide conservation efforts with a gift of $750. Your generous gift in this amount will distinguish you as a Associate Member of World Wildlife Fund.

Let me assure you, your gift right now would help with several critical programs to protect severely endangered species and habitat in three particularly remote parts of the world:

<u>Nepal:</u> Rapid deforestation and population growth along with excessive hunting and wildlife trade have pushed Nepal's snow leopard to near extinction and have threatened many other species as well, including the Gangetic dolphin, Asian elephant, tiger, musk deer, marbled cat, greater one-horned rhinoceros, and Gharial crocodile -- to name but a few.

<u>Madagascar:</u> Over five percent of the earth's plant species can be found on this "island laboratory" off the African

(next page, please)

1250 Twenty-Fourth Street, NW Washington, DC 20037 USA 202/293-4800 Telex: 64505 PANDA
Affiliated with The Conservation Foundation

- 2 -

coast. Ninety percent of its plants cannot be found anywhere else. Half of Madagascar's birds are just as rare, and most of its mammals, especially its extraordinary lemurs, do not exist in any other habitat.

But now, increased agriculture and logging pose serious threats to its remaining forests. Because more native plant species are in danger of extinction here than anywhere else on earth, Madagascar has become one of World Wildlife Fund's highest priorities.

<u>The Andes:</u> For an area of its size, the Andes region contains the greatest diversity of plants and animals on earth. Our Andean Campaign concentrates on protecting large areas of fragile montane cloud forest in five tropical countries: Bolivia, Colombia, Ecuador, Peru, and Venezuela.

Clearly, our involvement with these demanding programs means a total challenge greater than any we have previously undertaken. It is a challenge that will test the soundness of our international alliance and the dedication of our field staff -- as well as the resolve of those who, like you, must help in order for us to succeed.

Your new membership status in World Wildlife Fund will also gain you special distinction as well as other special benefits in acknowledgement of your support.

You will have the opportunity to visit actual World Wildlife Fund projects in the company of working scientists. You will also be invited to join fellow members at lectures by World Wildlife Fund staff biologists in your area, and at the informal receptions that follow such presentations.

And you will receive the yearly World Wildlife Fund calendar, with full-color wildlife photographs, taken by top international photographers; your copy of the World Wildlife Fund annual report; and frequent reports from scientists and biologists in the field.

Your past support has been more deeply appreciated than you could ever imagine, and I look forward to your continuing association. In fact, I very much hope to hear from you during the next few days.

Sincerely yours,

William K. Reilly

P.S. If you can possibly send your renewal gift in the amount I have suggested, we will also send you the exclusive WWF gold panda pin, your emblem of special support. It is fitting that this world-renowned symbol should distinguish you as someone who is dedicated to preserving the earth's wildlife.

Exhibit 13-4: World Wildlife Fund

Comment:

This is an "upgrade" letter. The fourth paragraph suggests a specific donor amount: $750. A grammatical error here: "Your generous gift in this amount will distinguish you as a [sic] Associate Member of World Wildlife Fund."

Does this mean the appellation "Dear World Wildlife Member" is wrong? Is the new title of Associate Member, *after* the $750 donation, a higher echelon than Member? The answer is unstated; when an organization delves within human ego such matters aren't inconsequential.

Associate membership has privileges—"the opportunity to visit actual World Wildlife Fund projects" is one. Which projects? Even a single specific would increase the drama of this prospective benefit considerably.

The calendar isn't a new benefit; this already comes each year. And the gold panda pin, mentioned in the excellent p.s., already sits on the dresser.

Most recipients won't overanalyze the thrust of the letter this way; if they do, they wouldn't respond anyway. To me, peripheral benefits such as these aren't highly motivational on this level. I'd prefer greater exposition of the "only you..." aspects.

Accompanying the letter was a stamped envelope, one of fund raising's most effective guilt-generators.

PARTNERS
— IN —
CONSERVATION

February 12, 19[C]

Ms. Margo E. Lewis
9748 Cedar Villas
Plantation, Florida 33324

Dear Ms. Lewis:

I am delighted to have the honor of informing you that, as one of our strongest supporters, you have been nominated to join the ranks of World Wildlife Fund's most select circle of associates, Partners in Conservation.

By accepting, you become one of a special society that has a unique leadership role in supporting the mission of World Wildlife Fund--a mission surely best described in the following observation by our international president, His Royal Highness The Prince Philip, Duke of Edinburgh:

"The World Wildlife Fund was created as a channel through which popular concern for conservation could lead to concrete action. What we cannot accomplish individually, we can achieve collectively."

As a Partner in Conservation, you will help further that collective achievement not only through your contributions of support, but through the heightened awareness you are certain to gain for our organization as one of its most notable and best-informed associates in your community.

For you will indeed be kept especially well informed about World Wildlife Fund activities. In fact, every effort will be made to ensure that your affiliation is as close as possible to that promised by the title that now awaits you--the title of <u>Partner</u> in Conservation.

You see, this select society was founded for the purpose of establishing a special bond with those supporters whose contributions and dedicated concern have made them exceptionally valued allies of World Wildlife Fund.

Now, as our organization embarks upon its second quarter-century, that bond has become more important than ever. After

A Society of World Wildlife Fund
1250 Twenty-Fourth Street, NW
Washington, DC 20037

Page Two

twenty-five years of leading the way in protecting endangered species and habitat, World Wildlife Fund has intensified its commitment to the preservation of ecosystems in their entirety. And for good reason!

Current estimates clearly indicate that without such a major, concerted effort, some 15 percent of our world's biological diversity will be lost in the next fifteen years alone, with nearly one million plant and animal species lost for all time.

Even today, the exploitation of our environment is causing the extinction of species at a rate many scientists consider to be without precedent in the history of the earth. At least one species now disappears forever every ten minutes!

Hence, World Wildlife Fund is committing its next twenty-five years to the formidable mission of stopping this alarming loss of precious life forms--a mission that will mean forging a mutually beneficial harmony between man and our planet's irreplaceable living resources.

As I indicated earlier, though, the sheer scope of this monumental task makes it among the most challenging undertakings ever assumed by our organization.

As a result, that special cadre of Americans who make up Partners in Conservation will be especially relied on in the years just ahead for the support which World Wildlife Fund staff have come to value so highly.

Surely the opportunity to play such a vital and highly valued role in so critical an undertaking will be your greatest reward as a member of this society.

Yet your membership also assures you a number of exclusive personal benefits. While these privileges are described in detail in the enclosed prospectus, there are two in particular that I want to mention here.

The first is your opportunity to join a number of your fellow associates on the annual conservation tour--typical tours have taken Partners to China and Nepal, or to Madagascar, Kenya, and Rwanda.

Nor will that be your only opportunity for such personal involvement. You will also be invited by our board of directors and national council to attend the annual World Wildlife Fund dinner, featuring the award ceremonies for the prestigious J. Paul Getty International Wildlife Prize.

157

Page Three

    As you can see, World Wildlife Fund places a very special value indeed on those who play such an exceptionally vital supporting role as Partners in Conservation.

    For that reason, it is my most earnest hope that you will now accept your formal nomination to join this select society.

    To do so requires your signature on the enclosed acceptance form and an initial annual contribution to World Wildlife Fund of one thousand dollars or more.

    As soon as your confirmation arrives, I will personally see that your name is entered on the Partners in Conservation roster and that you begin receiving all appropriate communications and materials.

    I look forward to meeting you at one of the functions now being planned for our Partners in Conservation.

Sincerely,

Russell E. Train
Russell E. Train
Chairman of the Board

Enclosures

Exhibit 13-5: World Wildlife Fund

Comment:

This communication suffers on mechanical grounds: The density of type on computer-personalized page one is noticeably lighter than page two, and page three is somewhere in between.

Exclusivity is the nucleus of this communication. The paper is textured and obviously expensive. The envelope has a first class stamp (based on three ounces, not one). The reply envelope is pre-stamped.

Amount requested to become a "Partner in Conservation"? $1,000 or more. (The letter, quite properly, spells out the amount: "one thousand dollars.")

Accompanying the letter are a printed invitation and a personalized "Partners in Conservation" reply card, plus a tasteful booklet listing the board of directors, the "National Council," and other Partners in Conservation.

Will a spectacular mailing such as this pull response justifying its extraordinary expense in postage and paper-stock? The answer lies less in the message than in the lists to which it is mailed.

World Wildlife Fund
Credit Card Services
4500 New Linden Hill Road
Wilmington, DE 19808

WILLIAM K. REILLY
PRESIDENT

Introducing the
World Wildlife Fund Visa® Card &
World Wildlife Fund MasterCard®

Dear World Wildlife Fund Member,

Now there is an easy way to <u>turn your everyday activities into support for World Wildlife Fund.</u>

You have always come through with a special effort when we've asked for your help before.

But now <u>we are not asking for a special effort.</u> Instead, we are offering you a way to support wildlife survival as a part of your everyday life - and a way to receive some extraordinary personal benefits.

Your invitation to apply for the new World Wildlife Fund MasterCard and Visa Card - issued by Mellon Bank - is enclosed.

<u>Each time you use one of these special cards, a portion of your purchase will benefit World Wildlife Fund.</u>

Just think about it. Each time you shop, each time you eat at a restaurant, each time you travel, you can be helping us save the world's endangered wildlife.

And every time you use these magnificent cards - maybe the most spectacular cards ever designed - you'll be showing your concern and appreciation for wild animals and the places where they live.

Best of all, whether you choose the Visa Card, the Master Card, or both, you'll pay <u>no annual fee for the first year</u>.

These cards go <u>beyond support for World Wildlife Fund</u>. They offer you <u>exceptional personal benefits</u> too.

Now you can <u>travel and see first-hand the rare and remarkable animals you are helping to save.</u> These <u>travel packages selected especially for World Wildlife Fund Cardmembers</u> take you on unique adventures to nature's most beautiful and amazing places.

Travel the rain forests of Peru by jungle boat. Immerse yourself in the living jungle - elusive mammals, exotic birds and rare butterflies.

(over, please)

Take an elephant safari through the forests and valleys of <u>Northern Thailand.</u> Then travel by bamboo raft to the tropical island of Koh Samui.

Visit the island nation of <u>Madagascar</u> - home to rare wildlife, including 29 species of lemur and 13 species of turtles. Float quietly down the rivers, past tall baobabs and lush orchids.

Traverse <u>Costa Rica</u> by boat, car, raft, train and plane - from the high cloud forest to the lowland rain forest. Explore over 560 species of vertebrates such as ocelots, margays, tapirs, squirrel monkeys, parrots, scarlet macaws and tucans.

Journey to the <u>Galapagos Islands</u>, the "living laboratory" whose equitorial isolation gave Charles Darwin the material for his theory of evolution. Visit 11 of these enchanted islands, with exotic species of reptiles and birds, including marine and giant land iguanas, colossal albatrosses, frigate birds and boobies.

Voyage to the islands of the remote west coast of <u>Baja California</u> - hidden shell-covered beaches and mangroves filled with tropical birds. See the migration of the magnificent gray whales as they court and breed.

These are just a few of the travel packages available with your World Wildlife Fund Visa and MasterCard. And when you choose one of these unforgettable journeys, you will be <u>guaranteed the lowest air fare</u> available as of the time of ticketing.

If you want to <u>explore the world of animal survival right in your home</u>, your World Wildlife Fund Cards will help you too. With your Card you can select from dozens of <u>wildlife videos</u> - all available, by mail or by phone, <u>at special Cardmember</u> prices. Among the VHS videos you can choose:

<u>Life on Earth</u> - David Attenborough's magnificent video encyclopedia of the marvels of nature, the secrets of evolution and the wonder of life.

<u>Search for Survival</u> - Close-up views and unusual facts about the wildlife of three continents, observed in their struggle to survive.

(next page, please)

<u>Animals Are Beautiful People</u> - The video record of four years' travel through Africa's most spectacular territories - showing wild animal behavior at its most human.

<u>Close Encounters of the Deep Kind</u> - Sail through the Pacific to solve the mysteries of the humpback whale on its annual migration to Maui for courtship and breeding.

<u>River of the Red Ape</u> - The true story of the first attempt to navigate Sumatra's Atlas River - and to penetrate to the heart of the world's last large population of orangutans.

And there are even more benefits. These cards give you <u>incomparable financial and travel privileges</u> too.

As a World Wildlife Fund Cardmember, you may qualify for a <u>credit line up to $25,000</u>. Your cards will be accepted at millions of locations worldwide.

And if you need <u>quick cash</u>, you can get it twenty-four hours a day at <u>19,000 banking machines nationwide</u> - or <u>worldwide at over 200,000 offices</u>.

Or if you prefer the convenience of checkwriting, you'll receive <u>free personalized World Wildlife Fund Checks</u>. Use these checks to access your Visa or MasterCard account - an easy way to pay bills, to get cash, or to make a donation to World Wildlife Fund.

To help you save time organizing your financial records for tax preparation, you'll receive a unique <u>year-end summary of charges</u>. This annual listing will show your World Wildlife Fund Card transactions arranged by date and by type of expense.

As a World Wildlife Fund Cardmember, you can help protect all your cards from unauthorized use with the <u>free credit card protection service</u>. Your one phone call will notify all your card companies if any of your cards are lost or stolen.

And there's more.

When you use your World Wildlife Fund Cards for travel tickets, you and your family will automatically

(over, please)

be covered by <u>$500,000 travel accident insurance.</u> (Some card companies charge $6.50 per person per trip for similar protection.)

You'll save on car rentals with your World Wildlife Fund Cards. Your Card entitles you to <u>special discount rates at Hertz, Avis and National.</u>

No one in your household needs to be left out of all these benefits. At your request, <u>free additional World Wildlife Fund Cards</u> will be provided for eligible family and household members.

A few words about how these cards came about.

We looked for a few important things when we set out to develop special cards for our members.

First, we looked for a card program that would allow you an easy way to add support to our common efforts around the world - with no additional cost. With a part of each purchase you make going to World Wildlife Fund, these cards do that.

Next we wanted a credit card program that would give something of personal value to members like you. As the long list of valuable card benefits shows, we were able to do that too.

We also wanted to create cards that showed the beauty of the wildlife you are helping to save. These spectacular cards, picturing the jaguar and the giant panda, are ones you can be proud to carry.

When you've considered it all - the benefits to World Wildlife Fund and the benefits to you - please accept this invitation and apply by returning your enclosed reply certificate today.

Sincerely,

William K. Reilly

P.S. Please remember to choose the kind of World Wildlife Fund Card you want - Visa Card, MasterCard, or both. Also remember that whichever you choose, there is no annual fee for the first year.

For the quickest possible processing of your application, please return your reply certificate before September 1, 1988.

Exhibit 13-6: World Wildlife Fund

Comment:

The first sentence misstates the proposition. This can cause confusion, and, worse, result in rejection by some who might be quite willing to use an affinity card.

A better opening—an adaptation of the third paragraph:

> **"We aren't asking for a special effort. Please read on."**

A rule of emphasis (subrule of $E^2 = 0$): Use underlining sparingly, because each underline shares emphasis with all other underlines.

Opinion: This letter has too much underlining.

Affinity cards are a painless fund raiser. Two obvious questions determine their success:

> **1. Will the member (who probably already has a Visa or MasterCard) be impelled to take the time to fill out an application for another?**
> **2. Once having the card, will the member use it?**

Opinion: This letter does a strong selling job, once it gets past its ponderous opening. Benefits are clearly stated, and the marriage of credit card and World Wildlife Fund is handled logically and thoroughly.

WWF

World Wildlife Fund

October 10, 19--

Margo E. Lewis
9748 Cedar Villas
Plantation, Florida 33324

Dear World Wildlife Member:

Did you know that gorillas are some of
the gentlest creatures on Earth?

That they're vegetarians and like to take
afternoon naps?

And that most gorillas, like most people,
are right-handed?

Those are only a few of the fascinating facts about
gorillas. One other fact is this:

Fewer than 500 mountain gorillas remain alive in the world
today!

Critically endangered, mountain gorillas may not even
survive to the year 2000. Unless you agree to help before the
year 1988 ends.

That's why I'm writing you today -- to update you on the
plight of the mountain gorilla and to ask for a gift of $380 from
you to help support one of our projects to save them!

Of those 500 remaining mountain gorillas, about 200 live
deep in East Africa in Uganda ... in a species-rich rain forest
called the Impenetrable Forest.

One group of gorillas in the Impenetrable has been closely
studied by World Wildlife Fund workers ... and is one of the most
poignant reasons I'm writing to urge you to help.

The oldest member of the family is called Zeus -- a
silverback male who leads the group by the sheer force of his
personality.

And the youngest is Zeke -- now about a year-and-a-half old
and the delight of researchers monitoring the group's activities.

(over, please)

1250 Twenty-Fourth Street, NW   Washington, DC 20037   USA
Affiliated with The Conservation Foundation

- 2 -

Like any young mountain gorilla, Zeke enjoys climbing games,
chasing the other infants, and wrestling.

Sometimes he may even tease Zeus, climbing all over him and
pulling his hair. But if Zeke goes too far, Zeus will give him a
resounding smack on the bottom to put a stop to his juvenile
antics!

Unfortunately, that's the least of the trouble Zeke will
have to face as he grows to adulthood. If he's allowed to grow
up at all.

You see, poaching and habitat destruction have already
destroyed nearly half the world's mountain gorilla population
just in the last 20 years!

Illegal lumbering ... gold-mining ... smuggling ... and
heartless poachers with machetes and snares have pushed this shy
and gentle creature right to the edge of extinction.

In the last few years, World Wildlife Fund has made a
substantial investment to save the mountain gorillas from final
destruction.

Now, we have a unique chance to protect that investment once
and for all.

The Minister of Tourism and Wildlife in
Uganda recently told WWF that if we can
commit the funds for operation, they
would declare the Impenetrable Forest a
national park!

This park would provide special protection to one of the
only two mountain gorilla populations left in the world ... as
well as other endangered species like chimpanzees, l'Hoest's
monkey, and life-giving rain forest plants.

A decision on the forest's national park status is imminent.

You can help make the Impenetrable Forest National Park a
reality.

Your past support has been especially
noteworthy and I am hoping that you will
join us in this exciting project to save
the mountain gorillas. A gift from you
now can help WWF provide the support
Uganda needs to protect the Impenetrable
Forest and the gorillas and other animals
who live there.

(next page, please)

162

Thanks to support from members just like yourself, we've already been able to stop much of the poaching that has killed so many gorillas.

But we must remain vigilant -- not only against poachers but against the many other threats that continue to hurt the gorillas and their habitat.

Gold mining in and around the forest poses a major problem. Smuggling of bamboo out of the forest eliminates some of the animals' prime habitat. And lumbering operations that use 12' pit-saws are destroying the trees of the forest and frightening the shy gorillas away.

The leader of our gorilla project in the Impenetrable Forest, Dr. Tom Butynski, recently shared with me his project proposal to help counter these threats.

First, Tom said, it's only because World Wildlife Fund has established a presence in the Impenetrable Forest that the gorillas there have been able to survive at all.

Without us, they would have no hope.

And it's only by continuing our work there -- and expanding the activities that have proved successful that we can ensure the gorillas' protection in the years ahead.

With your support WWF will help:

1. **Train new game guards in the Impenetrable Forest to keep the lid on poaching and stop other illegal activities.**

    We need to teach the guards how to apprehend poachers if they see them setting a snare ... what to do with confiscated wildlife items like skins or live animals ... and where to take the poachers once they have been apprehended.

2. **Equip the game guards.**

    The guards in the Impenetrable urgently need tents, boots, uniforms, equipment, even basic commodities like sugar and salt that the workers have a hard time getting.

(over, please)

---

3. **Continue and expand WWF conservation education programs.**

    Our conservation education program has been operating in the Impenetrable Forest for about 20 months now. Sixteen conservation education assistants regularly travel to schools, churches, market places and government offices to stress the importance of saving the trees and the wildlife found in the forest.

4. **Complete a thorough and accurate census of the mountain gorilla population.**

    Nearly 200 individual gorillas have already been identified within the forest, including the group I mentioned with our young friend Zeke and his father Zeus.

    Money is needed to assess the entire population and distribution of these animals ... and to determine carefully their future conservation needs.

The work we propose for the next three years is essential if we're to save the mountain gorilla.

And it is work we can do only with you behind us.

Please -- send as much as you possibly can, as quickly as you can.

Send your gift in for Zeke -- so this charming infant can grow into the magnificent adult gorilla nature intended him to.

Send it for the mountain gorilla species ... and send it for all life on earth.

Sincerely yours,

William K. Reilly
President

P.S.   Some time ago, we asked WWF members to write our project leader, Tom Butynski, in the Impenetrable Forest. Those special messages really gave Tom and our other workers a lift. If you'd like to send a note now, please see your Donation Card enclosed.

163

Exhibit 13-7: World Wildlife Fund

Comment:

Opening a letter with "fascinating facts" draws the reader into the letter. In this instance, the right-handed reference might have been a better opening gun to fire, because it's a genuine fact. "Did you know that gorillas are some of the gentlest creatures on Earth?" doesn't have a true factual core.

Note the exact amount of contribution: $380. Note, too, this letter doesn't wait to make its point; mention of this desired contribution is on page one.

The letter, loaded with episodes and specifics, is both entertaining and motivational. Does using boldface help or hinder? I know of no head-to-head tests, but I find boldface—a technique unknown before word processors enabled the typist to create boldface with a single keystroke—distracting.

A minirule: Distraction = thinned impact.

October 19..

Dear Digit Fund Friend:

One of Dian Fossey's last requests before her death was to Morris Animal Foundation for veterinary help to save the last few mountain gorillas. The Foundation trustees were invited by Dian to visit Karisoke in January, 1986, but as you know, her murder occurred in December, 1985. The trustees traveled to Rwanda anyway, to survey the area for a site for a veterinarian to serve. The Rwandan government selected Kinigi near park headquarters, and a brick building housing a clinic, laboratory, and residence was constructed under the direction of Dr. James Foster, Seattle, Washington.

Jim spent one and a half years in Rwanda establishing the Virunga Veterinary Center and serving as its first veterinarian. Dedication occurred in January, 1988, at which time the Rwandan government and the U. S. Embassy participated in the festivities.

Dr. David Kenny, of the Denver Zoo, followed Jim as veterinarian at the center in March and he wrote this enclosed article for the Denver Zoo Magazine. I thought you might like to have a copy. Dave's diary was filled with the health problems that developed in the gorilla population starting in February, 1988. Eight gorillas have died from a variety of causes and more than 27 gorillas have been treated by the veterinarians.

Dr. Barkley Hastings, of the London Zoo, joined Dave in July of this year and both veterinarians were extremely busy with the many sick gorillas. Barkley reports three gorillas were caught in poachers' traps this month in addition to the other illnesses. Jozi, in the research group at Karisoke, had wire embedded in her wrist and infected so seriously that no medication could revive her and a phone call reported her death on August 26, 1988. A real tragedy!

Morris Animal Foundation, however, is committed to carrying out Dian's last plea for help and with assistance from concerned friends, it may save this threatened species. The Digit Fund, now affiliated with Morris Animal Foundation, receives administrative assistance to carry on Dian's anti-poaching patrols and behavioral studies at Karisoke. Together we hope we can make the difference!

Yours truly,

Ruth

Ruth Keesling, President

Exhibit 13-8: Morris Animal Foundation

Comment:

This narrowly-targeted communication, sent only to prior contributors to the Digit Fund, is bright, clear, and easy to read.

What's lacking is a payoff. The letter seems to end because space ran out, not because the message is complete.

> *A primary rule of force-communication:*
> *Tell the reader what to do.*

Curiously, this letter and a copy of "The Zoo Review" were the only enclosures in the envelope. No request for a contribution...no response device. Opinion: Opportunity wasted.

Greenpeace

1436 U Street N.W., P.O. Box 3720, Washington, D.C. 20007

Dear Friend,

Please accept your Greenpeace Supporter decal and stamps and display them with the same sense of pride I take in presenting them to you.

Your Greenpeace decal and stamps will show your friends and neighbors that you support our fight against the slaughter of our marine life and the dumping of toxic and nuclear wastes into our seas.

The purpose of Greenpeace is to actively pursue solutions and take the risks necessary to effect change. And quite frankly, I need you to do more than display your decal.

I need you to return your enclosed Supporter's Reply Form to me today with a special contribution of $15, $25, $50 or more.

Make no mistake about it. I'm not asking you to support a bunch of wide-eyed, idealistic dreamers. Greenpeace crew members are on the front lines, risking their freedom and lives to make a difference.

Whether combatting the whale and seal hunters, the toxic polluters, or those who destroy marine habitats, our crew members directly confront the offender. In fact:

* Greenpeace activists have placed themselves between whales and explosive harpoons shot from cannons mounted on the decks of huge whaling ships in order to shield the whales from a senseless death.

* Russian soldiers have aimed their guns at our crews before arresting them for investigating a Soviet whaling station.

* Greenpeace crews have placed their bodies between harp seal pups and the swinging clubs of the seal "harvesters."

* And when we attempted to stop their dumping of toxins into the sea, polluters dropped drums of

(over, please)

Printed on recycled paper

2.

nuclear and toxic waste onto our crews and their inflatable boats.

* But the French government took the most extreme measures against us. In an attempt to stop our protest of their testing of nuclear weapons in the South Pacific, their agents blew up our ship, the "Rainbow Warrior," and killed a member of our crew.

Despite these acts against us, our actions are always nonviolent. Greenpeace maintains that we must learn to feel for all forms of life as we feel for ourselves.

Our only goal is to promote a safe and peaceful future for all of earth's creatures. We believe humankind must learn to respect all forms of life -- the whales, the seals, the forests, the seas -- as well as each other. We seek to obstruct wrongs -- without committing violence ourselves.

Ecology has taught us that humankind is not the center of life on our planet.

We must realize that once the last whale -- or any other species -- dies, all our new and expensive technology will never create another.

But we also know that identifying problems and talking about them isn't good enough. The senseless slaughter of our marine life has taught us the value of nonviolent direct confrontation.

On the high seas -- with our crews riding small inflatable boats -- we have confronted giant Soviet whaling ships.

But the risks paid off. In 1982, the International Whaling Commission voted to end all commercial killing of whales.

We've confronted the Japanese and U.S. fishing fleets to stop their killing of dolphins. And we've stood up to hunters for profit who senselessly kill seals, turtles and even kangaroos for their fur, shells and skins.

And we've challenged the commercial interests of chemical giants like Monsanto, Dow, Bayer, Occidental, Chevron, and the Swiss chemical giant Ciba-Geigy to win stricter controls on toxic air and water pollution.

In fact, in 1985, for the first time in 37 years, no radioactive waste was dumped in the world's oceans.

(next page, please)

166

3.

But these successful confrontation campaigns have had their price. Our crews have taken on the Russian Navy, the Spanish Navy, the U.S. Department of Defense, the Norwegian Coast Guard and the Royal Canadian Mounted Police.

Still Greenpeace is committed to taking on those fights the skeptics say are unwinnable. And with the support of people like you, we'll continue to beat the odds. But there is still much to be done. Because:

* Whales are still being slaughtered, now for so-called "scientific" purposes.

* Each day, the United States alone produces more than 212 million pounds of hazardous waste.

* More and more species of life are becoming extinct.

To fight back, Greenpeace has assembled a front-line force of four ships and 50 inflatable boats.

These ships and boats -- and especially our crews -- are the main defense against those who selfishly destroy our planet and kill its creatures for profit.

Whether sailing into nuclear testing zones, interfering with the slaughter of whales, blocking the driftnetting of dolphins or the dumping of toxic and nuclear wastes, our crews are ready to confront the senseless and often illegal destruction of our planet.

Greenpeace receives no government support. We depend entirely on people like you who are committed to preserving the beauty and uniqueness of our earth.

Our fight is an expensive one. Just to keep our ships and boats in port costs us more than $1.5 million a year in maintenance, and those costs are going up. Every time we confront the opposition, more money is required.

And that's why it's so important that you return your Supporter's Reply Form to me today with your contribution of $15, $25, $50 or more.

Our crew members have earned your support. They have put their lives and freedom on the line for only modest

(over, please)

4.

salaries -- or nothing at all. They face arrest and their work is often dangerous, even life-threatening. Always it is difficult.

But still they stand ready to press our fight against the killers of marine life, the dumping of toxins into our oceans and the testing of nuclear weapons.

They have already sacrificed much. But they need your support.

I urge you to do these two things today:

1. Return your Supporter's Reply Form to me today in the special postage-free envelope I've enclosed.

2. And with your Reply Form, please include your special contribution of $15, $25, $50 or more.

Too often people don't understand the consequences of their actions. But one thing should be clear. Without your support the senseless killing, destruction, and polluting will continue.

Please return your Supporter's Reply Form with your special contribution of $15, $25, $50 or more today.

Sincerely,

Steve Sawyer
Executive Director
Greenpeace USA

SS:pds

P.S. With your contribution of $15 or more, you'll receive a subscription to our news magazine, Greenpeace. But most importantly, you'll help defeat those who senselessly slaughter life and poison our planet. Please rush your Supporter's Reply Form to me today with your tax-deductible contribution of $15, $25, $50 or more.

167

Exhibit 13-9: Greenpeace

Comment:

This straightforward letter combines a no-nonsense informational core with a guilt-generating group of enclosures (decals and stamps).

Greenpeace is a high-profile, risk-taking organization whose activist approach outrages some and enthralls others. The letter is in character, pointing out the severe personal dangers Greenpeace crews undergo.

The call for a contribution appears early; the writer repeats it on page three and twice again on page four, including a strong reference in the p.s.

Opinion: For the Greenpeace type of organization, this letter has far more pulling-power than a shy, indirect approach would have.

GREENPEACE

1436 U Street N.W. • P.O. Box 3720 • Washington, DC 20007

Dear Friend,

I need you to fill out the Community Toxic Report I've enclosed and return it to me today.

Because your returned Community Toxic Report is the best way I have of knowing how _you_ and _your_ _community_ are being threatened by the production and reckless disposal of hazardous wastes.

Do you feel safe with the quality of drinking water in your community?

Do you believe state, local, and federal authorities are doing all they can to protect you and your community from hazardous wastes?

Do you agree with proposals by waste disposal "experts" to burn toxic wastes in giant incinerators in or around communities where we live, work and play?

With nearly 212 million pounds of hazardous waste produced _each_ _day_ in the U.S. alone, chances are you answered "no" to at least one of these questions. Toxic wastes — silent, pervasive, deadly — are a growing threat to the health and safety of each and every one of us.

At no other time in history has it been more important for you, for me, for all Americans to make our voices heard about this critical situation.

That's why I urge you to fill out and return your Community Toxic Report immediately.

Because while millions of our fellow citizens now agree that toxic wastes are _the_ most serious threat to public health today, rarely if ever do they get the chance to tell their government and the polluters about it.

And because they aren't being heard, many people believe that the problem of toxic wastes is just too big to do anything about.

Well, we at Greenpeace don't. _Greenpeace is one organization that is taking direct action_ against the polluters of our water, our air, and our land — fighting to cut off toxics at their source.

And with your help, we're going to do a whole lot more.

No, I'm not asking you to enlist in our front-line confrontations against the toxic polluters and waste dumpers. Our Greenpeace crew members and

(over, please)

2.

activists specially trained in nonviolent tactics will do that.

While other organizations work mainly through courts and legislatures, we sail our boats — or hike, or drive, or scuba dive — _directly to the scene_ to make a stand against the very companies that are poisoning our earth.

We confront the polluting industries in their own back yards. We demonstrate their negligence and their greed in full view of the communities where they work.

We plug the pipes of those companies who dump deadly toxic wastes into America's waterways ... we scale their smokestacks, and square off against their poison-laden ships at sea.

Greenpeace doesn't shy away from action — or mince words. We name names — _Monsanto_, a major source of PCBs and other dangerous chemicals in Boston Harbor. _Chevron_, for dumping 48 million gallons of highly toxic wastewater into San Francisco Bay each day. _Ciba-Geigy_, for spewing thousands of pounds of toxic compounds into Europe's Rhine River. And many, many more.

From the rivers and coasts of England, to Tom's River, New Jersey ... from Basel, Switzerland to the back yards of Love Canal, Greenpeace is _tackling the problem of toxic waste at its source_ — in our communities where the waste materials are generated and dumped.

And the evidence shows we are having a dramatic effect.

-- In California, where Greenpeace divers plugged Chevron's huge underwater discharge pipe in Santa Monica Bay, the Regional Water Quality Control Board fined the oil company nearly $40,000 and called for stricter pollution control standards.

-- In Maryland, American Recovery Company was fined $300,000 for pollution of Chesapeake Bay — and its facility in Baltimore was closed by the State of Maryland after a Greenpeace direct action campaign.

-- In Canada, Greenpeace activists scaled the cliffs surrounding Niagara Falls and unfurled a banner protesting chemical pollution of the Niagara River. Heeding our message, the State of New York began working with Greenpeace to produce a source reduction plan for toxic wastes in this "chemical corridor."

-- In Europe, North America and the South Pacific, ports were closed to giant incinerator ships after Greenpeace showed how burning hazardous wastes at sea spreads toxic pollution throughout the marine environment. And, the Environmental Protection Agency has been persuaded to ban ocean incineration in U.S. waters.

(next page, please)

3.

In almost all these cases, Greenpeace's direct intervention forced the issue into the public eye. And our actions against one company often put fear into others that they'll be the next to be put on public display for their wanton disregard of our planet.

And in most cases it's been enlightened citizens like yourself who sounded the alarm on toxic hazards.

That's why I am asking you to fill out your Community Toxic Report and return it to me today.

This is the best way we at Greenpeace have of measuring the level of concern about toxic wastes in your community.

In addition, I urge you to make a contribution to Greenpeace's Toxic Waste Project.

Because the distressing fact is, toxic wastes affect a whole lot more on this earth than the communities where we humans live and work.

As you know, Greenpeace is the organization that is working so hard to save the earth's endangered whale populations ... to stop the slaughter of seals, dolphins and other marine animals ... and to halt the proliferation of nuclear weapons.

All of this important work will be for naught if our rivers and lakes, our land, and the air we breathe are laden with chemical killers.

That's why this coming year, Greenpeace will pursue major anti-toxic actions and public education campaigns to drive home the need for immediate and drastic reduction of toxic wastes throughout the world:

* In Louisiana, we'll be working with local groups to oppose the construction of more than a dozen new toxic waste incinerators, land-fills, and deep-well injection facilities which poison the ground-water — facilities that will only add to the massive pollution in the region. Greenpeace's campaign will include direct actions, rallies, and promotion of improved industrial processes to reduce production of toxics at their source.

* In the Great Lakes, we're trying to stop contamination by pesticides, PCBs, dioxin and other chemicals by U.S. and Canadian corporations — poisons responsible for the deaths of scores of Beluga whales in the St. Lawrence Seaway, and tens of thousands of cases of human cancer.

* And we'll be mounting an international education campaign, to con-vince governments, industries, and the public around the world to

(over, please)

4.

prevent toxic pollution before it happens by reducing the production and use of toxic materials in the first place.

This year we'll be taking on toxic polluters in communities up and down the Atlantic seaboard, along the Mississippi and Great Lakes, in San Francisco Bay, and in Puget Sound.

You can imagine the expenses we face ensuring the success of our direct actions, and the safety of our activists — the food, the supplies, the fuel and the special equipment we need for our campaigners.

Greenpeace receives no governmental or corporate funds for our work. We depend entirely on concerned individuals like yourself for the support we need — financial and otherwise — to conduct our direct actions and educational campaigns.

That's why I need you to do two things right away:

1. Fill out and return your Community Toxic Report today. This is the most direct way for us to measure the level of concern about toxic wastes in your community and around the country.

2. With your completed Community Toxic Report, please send as generous a contribution as you can to help Greenpeace carry out our work fighting hazardous wastes wherever they occur.

We can end the threat of toxic pollution — by acting together against those who produce and dump toxic wastes. Please help by returning your Community Toxic Report today, along with a generous contribution.

Sincerely,

Steve Sawyer
Executive Director

SS:tss

P.S. Even as I write, Greenpeace activists are putting their health and safety on the line, confronting toxic polluters around the world. Please act today. Your responses provide Greenpeace valuable information. Your contribution is essential. Thank you.

Exhibit 13-10: Greenpeace

Comment:

Reading this letter back-to-back with the previous exhibit, one begins to absorb the flavor of the Greenpeace "style."

The letters are highly personal—"I" to "you." Reader-involvement is a crucial key, enhanced by this guilt-generating suggestion: "We," the organization, put human lives on the line for "you," the reader.

The letter differs from the previous exhibit in avoiding specific donation references. Instead, it asks the reader to fill out a "Community Toxic Report," a legal-size page survey enclosed. In a corner of the Report is the request for contributions. The letter says only, "Your contribution is essential." ("Essential" is an intellectualization. "Vital" or "imperative" seems more emotional.)

Working for the Nature of Tomorrow.

NATIONAL WILDLIFE FEDERATION

1412 Sixteenth Street, N.W., Washington, D.C. 20036-2266

When the Holidays are over ... your
Wildlife Christmas cards will <u>still</u> be
remembered and treasured.

Dear Friend,

This year's exciting wildlife cards are the best we've ever
offered! They're all <u>new</u> and they're all exclusive -- available
only through our catalog. You can't buy them in any store.

These are cards people love to receive ... cards that will
proudly be displayed on mantels, tabletops, or hung on Christmas
trees for all to admire.

The original art featured on each card was <u>selected from</u>
<u>hundreds of wildlife paintings</u>. Attention to detail, accuracy,
and overall beauty are the outstanding characteristics of these
one-of-a-kind cards.

And, sending NWF cards reflects not only your thoughtfulness
and good taste, but your interest in wildlife and the environment
as well. To enhance this special meaning and the uniqueness
of your greeting, a description of the wildlife subject on each
card is printed on the back along with this important message:

"This card represents a gift to the National Wildlife
Federation. <u>It reminds us of the need to conserve and</u>
<u>use wisely all of our natural resources</u>."

This year, you can choose from 22 traditional card styles
and two postcard sets. The wide range of designs and prices
provides the <u>perfect card for every taste and budget</u>. For
example ....

Look at "Home for Christmas," by Barbara Goss. This beautiful
and classic-style card captures both the spirit of the Christmas
season, and the beauty of wildlife. It's a wonderful selection.

And then there's the light-hearted "Santa!" You'll bring
a smile to everyone who sees this whimsical card -- with
Kris Kringle treating a few of his forest friends to an unexpected
dinner.

Or look at Ted Blaylock's "American Eagle." I doubt you've

---

ever seen a card to match this one -- it is a dramatic
Christmas greeting, and you'll appreciate the richness and
superlative quality of this hand-finished card.

And don't miss "Silent Night."

This is a particularly moving card done in subtle tones
and with just the right feelings about nature and the wonders
of the Christmas season. I know you'll love this card -- and
so will those who receive it from you.

Now, as you choose your cards for the upcoming season,
please keep two thoughts in mind ...

<u>First</u>, the cards you order will be among
the most memorable you've ever sent, not
only for their great beauty and quality,
but because of their important message.

And, <u>secondly</u>, remember that every purchase
you make, and every National Wildlife card
you send, will help us keep our vital
wildlife and conservation programs effective
and strong.

Moreover, you can take care of your Christmas <u>gift</u> shopping,
too, as you place your card order! The nature-related items in
our catalog were all carefully chosen for their quality, beauty
or educational value. Many are designed exclusively for us.
And, just as with our cards, each gift you select provides
support for NWF's much-needed conservation programs.

Thank you for placing your order with us, and I wish you
the happiest of Christmas seasons.

Sincerely,

Jay D. Hair

Jay D. Hair
President
NATIONAL WILDLIFE FEDERATION

P.S. I have enclosed a sheet of our new Christmas Wildlife Stamps
for you. <u>Please use them</u> on your cards and packages
to show your concern for wildlife. (It's only through your
support and contribution that we are able to lead the fight
for conservation. An extra $5, $7, or more as a tax-
deductible gift will <u>really make</u> a difference, and would be
greatly appreciated.)

Exhibit 13-11: National Wildlife Federation

Comment:

Christmas cards are a painless way to raise funds. The recipient gets something for his money, avoiding the "I'm being put upon" syndrome.

The first four paragraphs mention nothing but the cards. Then, after an almost peripheral reference to "your interest in wildlife and the environment," the description continues. The cause itself is relegated to second position, as an indented paragraph on page two and as the final sentence of the p.s.

Does this approach rival a "We need help" approach in effectiveness? In my opinion it should far outpull a conventional plea for dollars. Why? Because the typical reader feels more comfortable with the concept of buying something than with contributing to a cause whose name seems parallel to so many other causes.

WILDLIFE
CONSERVATION
INTERNATIONAL

A DIVISION OF
NEW YORK ZOOLOGICAL SOCIETY

BRONX, NEW YORK 10460
TELEPHONE 212 • 220 • 5155
TELEX 429270 NYZWCI

October 1988

Dear Friend of Nature,

When you hear the words "tropical forest," what comes to mind?

Fierce animals and tribal warriors? Incessant rain? Swarms of biting insects? Strangler vines? And... snakes!?

Well, I'd like you to relax and think again:

Imagine instead an emerald green glade, where warm beams of sunlight stream down through the forest canopy. Half of all species of living things on earth thrive here, a place blessed by nature with abundant natural resources... home to wonderful creatures like scarlet macaws, giant otters, spider monkeys, toucans, gorgeous fish and birds... and, yes, lots of insects.

This is the tropical rainforest, the earth's treasure house of biodiversity, our planet's most exuberant celebration of life, but these forests comprise only 6% of its landmass.

Now hear the roar of bulldozers and chainsaws, the raging fire... imagine the frightened animals fleeing as their forest home is blackened and destroyed.

In 1988, tropical forests are being destroyed at a tragic and alarming rate. <u>In the minute it takes to read this page, 50 acres of rainforest disappears</u>. If nothing is done, the earth's rainforests will be gone before the century is out.

Relentless economic pressure is the problem... and ignorance. Logging, mining, slash and burn farming and ranching are the culprits in this disaster. And the real tragedy is that in just a few years the land lies empty, useless... because the soil is quickly worn out and the natural resources used up.

Wildlife Conservation International is doing something about rainforest destruction... and you can too. You can join WCI's Tropical Forest Campaign. When you do, you'll be supporting WCI's field researchers and conservation action plans at work in 37 tropical forests around the globe.

CONSERVATION
EDUCATION
RESEARCH

Let me tell you about just one project -- the work of Dr. Charles Munn, our staff scientist in Peru's Amazon rainforest. For nine years, Dr. Munn has lived and worked in an area claimed by scientists as the most biologically diverse place on earth.

(over, please)

Munn began his work pioneering research on the endangered scarlet macaw and other parrots. But he soon found that protecting the macaw meant safeguarding its tropical rainforest home.

For Munn, that first research project has turned into a lifetime commitment. He has established his credibility not just by scientific expertise, but by giving slide lectures to schools in the Amazon region, training guards for parks and reserves, teaching natural resource values and philosophies, and networking with officials to draft protective laws and ensure enforcement.

Dr. Munn's field research has led to the discovery of tremendous untapped potential for a nature tourism industry -- uncharted, spectacular white-water rafting and virtually untouched areas of jungle wilderness. This is the type of <u>sustainable development</u> that can unlock a region's economic potential and leave the natural world intact.

That's WCI conservation in action. Dedicated, dynamic WCI field scientists, using their scientific skills to build conservation action plans, and using their leadership and "people" skills to ignite the local programs leading to long-term protection of our natural world.

WCI has the largest scientific field staff of any conservation organization in the United States, 14 full-time biologists, zoologists and ecologists. WCI is acknowledged as the front-line organization working to save wild animals and wild places. Won't you please help in this vitally important work with your gift to WCI's Tropical Forest Campaign?

<u>Every penny of your gift goes directly into tropical conservation projects</u>. That's because all WCI administrative and fund-raising costs, like this mailing packet, are underwritten by the New York Zoological Society, WCI's parent organization. Your gift is a sure way to support tropical rainforest protection.

I hope you will do your part, and join the campaign to save this precious and absolutely essential global resource. Thank you.

Sincerely,

George Schaller

George B. Schaller
Director for Science

P.S. For your gift of $23 or more, we will gladly send your WCI's popular WildNotes. And, for your gift of $50 or more, you will receive <u>Animal Kingdom</u> magazine, filled with spectacular color photos of wildlife. I look forward to hearing from you.

Exhibit 13-12: Wildlife Conservation International

Comment:

A donor whose name appears on many lists may become confused by the plethora of organizations which use the magic word "Wildlife" in their names.

Another letter in this chapter (Exhibit 3—World Wildlife Fund) includes a reference identical to one here:

> **"In the minute it takes to read this page, 50 acres of rainforest disappears."**

Will the reader remember the other reference? Unlikely, even if the same individual gets both letters within a short period. (This organization condenses the term into one word: "rainforest.")

Opinion: the second paragraph damages the thrust of the letter:

> **"Fierce animals and tribal warriors? Incessant rain? Swarms of biting insects? Strangler vines? And . . . snakes?"**

What does the writer gain by injecting a negative thought so early? Rain forests do have all these elements, but a direct charge into the fourth paragraph, with its poetic descriptions of the wonders of the rain forest, is more likely to generate a proper reader-attitude.

What is "biodiversity"? The writer surely has a clearer way of expressing this thought. "Networking with officials" is computer-talk.

Does a $50 gift bring a subscription to *Animal Kingdom* or a single issue? The p.s., otherwise strong, is unclear.

The handsome, full-color
1989 Sierra Club Wilderness Calendar
has been reserved for you.

Dear Nominated Member,

Quite simply, the Sierra Club Wilderness Calendar we've put aside for you is one of the most beautiful you'll ever lay eyes on.

The full-color photos magnificently reproduced in it have been painstakingly culled from a phenomenal number of submissions by nature photographers from all over the world. Month after month, you'll find all the photos in this calendar capture once-in-a-lifetime moments you'll want to look at time and time again.

And you will ... when you respond to this special opportunity to become the newest Member of the Sierra Club. Because when you do, you'll receive your copy of the 1989 Sierra Club Wilderness Calendar free. (It costs $7.95 in select bookstores.)

And that's just one of the many benefits you get as a Sierra Club Member.

I'm sure that, like most people, you've heard about the Sierra Club. But what exactly is it? A hiking club? An environmental activist group? A publishing company? The Sierra Club is ALL these things. And more.

If you feel a kinship with the outdoors -- whether you enrich your life with rugged hiking and camping, or just sitting on a hilltop and communing with nature -- your membership in the Sierra Club is bound to bring new pleasure to those memorable experiences.

As a Sierra Club Member, you belong to the only organization that combines outdoor experiences with environmental lobbying, legal action and publishing.

You also automatically become a Member of your local Sierra Club Chapter. So you'll be invited to take part in the wide variety of outings your Chapter offers every year, as well as in the Club's worldwide outings. Some may be just a short distance from your home. Others are exotic trips halfway around the world. All are led by experienced leaders and enjoyed by others who share your interests in the outdoors.

You'll also receive copies of your local Chapter's newsletter, keeping you informed about outdoor issues and grassroots activities in your area (and how you can have an impact on them).

Every other month, you'll have delivered to your home a copy of Sierra,

(over, please)

2.

the Club's informative, beautifully illustrated bimonthly magazine.

IN ADDITION ... you get a sizable discount on the Sierra Club's many publications. Beautiful nature photo books to browse through in your home. Helpful "Totebooks" to take on your outdoor trips. Books to stir your ire on major environmental matters like nuclear energy. And books to stir your love of nature.

Environmental Clout

You get the satisfaction of knowing that your membership support is one of the most effective steps you can take to create a better and safer environment. That's because the Sierra Club is the largest organization of grassroots activists working to protect the environment -- a major force in America for nearly 100 years.

Like a lot of Americans, I'm furious at what's being done to destroy the land we live in. I suspect you are, too. It's hard not to be. Irreplaceable wilderness areas and forests destroyed. Wildlife and their habitat endangered. Polluted water. Polluted air.

How much worse must it get before the people will rise up and shout, "NO MORE"?

I'm urging you to join me and the more than 425,000 other Sierra Club members who are making possible a new all-out nationwide effort to stop the marauders who would ruin forever our great natural heritage.

We're tired of empty promises and delays from government. The time has come for every man and woman concerned about mounting environmental crises to unite, to flex our muscles and to wield our full political clout.

We can wait no longer.

No, we won't stand idly by while our forests are denuded.

We won't stand idly by while government officials delay one more time confronting the grave problem of acid rain destroying our lakes, forests and wildlife.

We won't stand idly by while our coastlines and wildlife refuges are ruined by oil and gas drilling.

No, we won't stand idly by while pesticides, chemical and other deadly wastes enter our waters and the food we eat.

And yes, we will fight for our environmental rights.

I hope you share our concern ... and our dreams for an environmentally safer world. And I hope you will do one of the most important things you can

3.

to convert that concern into <u>specific action</u> to protect and preserve the environment.

<u>Join the Sierra Club</u>. We are a major force working ...

** to safeguard our remaining forests

** to get better controls over toxic air pollutants and sources of acid rain

** to save our wildlife and their habitat from needless destruction

** to get better legislation to ensure clean water

** to preserve our wild and scenic rivers and our wetlands

** to assure that the leasing of public lands for oil and gas development is more environmentally responsible

** to add new parks to our national park system

** to protect areas already preserved as national parks and wildlife refuges, especially the Arctic National Wildlife Refuge in Alaska, now threatened by oil and gas development

** to defend <u>all</u> our coastline against expanded offshore oil and gas development

It will give me great pleasure to welcome you as a new Sierra Club Member. To join, all you have to do is check your membership category on the enclosed Membership Enrollment Form. Then return the Form with your dues in the postage-free reply envelope provided for your convenience.

Sincerely,

Michael L. Fischer
Executive Director

MLF:ac

SEE THE BACK PANEL FOR MORE INFORMATION ABOUT SIERRA MAGAZINE AND THE SIERRA CLUB 1989 WILDERNESS CALENDAR THAT YOU GET AS PART OF YOUR MEMBERSHIP.

Exhibit 13-13: Sierra Club

Comment:

"Quite simply" seems a weak way of opening a letter.

Other problems here: The third paragraph offers a "special opportunity to become the newest Member." Few people want to be the newest member of any organization.

Page three has "bullet" copy, listing the organization's purposes. The second bullet:

" * **to get better controls over toxic air pollutants and sources of acid rain"**

177

More powerful wording might have been:

> **"** * * **to control toxic air pollutants and sources of acid rain"**

The third bullet:

> **"** * * **to save our wildlife and their habitat from needless destruction"**

More powerful wording, eliminating the possible thought of destruction that might *not* be needless:

> **"** * * **to protect our wildlife and their habitat from destruction"**

Is "better legislation" as specific as "enforceable legislation"? Is it actually possible "to protect areas already preserved" or is the message clearer with a single word change, to "to protect areas already designated"?

Look at the second and third paragraphs under the subhead, "Environmental Clout," on page two. These might have been a "grabber" opening for the letter. But in defense of this position, the Sierra Club may have found, as so many organizations have learned from previous result-comparisons, an offer brings better results than a plea.

JACQUES-YVES COUSTEAU

Dear Citizen of the Water Planet,

A shipwrecked sailor was struggling in the water. The shore was near, but his strength was almost spent.

Then suddenly there was a friendly presence in the water, a strong, sleek body that buoyed him up, escorted him to shallow water, saved his life.

This story, or something akin to it, has been told countless times about dolphins and porpoises. When I take it, together with what we have learned about these marvelous creatures in the past forty years, I have to give credence to at least some of these tales.

In fact, dolphins, porpoises and their larger cousins, the great toothed whales, do have a formidable intelligence. We hope some day to understand the subtleties of their brains, which rely heavily on an acoustical perception of the world around them. But the stories of rescued swimmers may find their explanation in a simpler trait, a trait that dolphins share with a majority of us animals, a trait which may be more important than any amount of brain power.

When a dolphin mother gives birth, her baby is expelled underwater. The first act following birth is critical: to lift the freshly born youngster up to the surface for its first breath. So powerful is this motherly instinct that other struggling animals have been pushed to the surface instinctively by female dolphins.

How marvelous and beautiful! The instinct to protect the next generation drives some automatic motor response in the dolphin and in many other species. To me this is marvelous because the successful replication of life is what makes our Oasis in Space such a rich biomass, fecund and prolific, forever generating and nurturing new organisms.

Surely this blessed miracle of life is the greatest treasure on earth. Yet do we earthlings cherish and guard it? On the contrary. Each month we now pour millions of tons of poisonous waste into the global water system. Many of our lakes, rivers, and coastal waters have received their mortal wound. The water is undrinkable. The fish and shellfish, if they exist at all, are contaminated.

I do not say this lightly. During the past forty years my team and I have spent thousands of hours diving with Aqua-Lungs and other underwater devices. During that time I have observed

(over, please)

The Cousteau Society   930 West 21st Street   Norfolk, Virginia 23517

---

and studied, and with my own eyes I have seen our waters sicken. Certain reefs that teemed with fish only ten years ago are now almost lifeless. The ocean bottom has been raped by trawlers. Priceless wetlands have been destroyed by landfills. And everywhere are sticky globs of oil, plastic refuse, and unseen clouds of poisonous effluents.

Is all now lost? I do not believe it. If I did, I would not be writing to you today. I passionately believe that the perceptive few who have the opportunity to see the ultimate disaster ahead must band together now to warn the slumbering many. (Is it not always thus?) Such corrective measures as exist must be put into effect immediately. Pioneering research and exploration to help us better understand the sea and its creatures must be undertaken without delay.

To this new crusade I solemnly pledge what years remain to me. I now write to you because your name has been suggested as one who might also wish to join in this supremely important undertaking.

The group to which you are invited is called The Cousteau Society. Its membership is worldwide, and one of its most important functions is to give strength and substance to my words when I take our case before governments and other great institutions.

If, instead of speaking simply as Jacques Cousteau, I can speak for hundreds of thousands of comrades, how much more closely the world will listen, how much more quickly the world will act!

A second function of The Cousteau Society is to raise funds through its membership to support the vital exploration and research projects we are even now embarking on. Your dues and any additional sum you may wish to contribute are deductible in part for U.S. federal income tax purposes. Let us return now to the oceans -- to our endangered Earth.

Often when I describe the symptoms of our environmental illness I hear remarks like, "They're only fish," or "They're only whales," or "They're only birds." I assure you that our destinies are linked with theirs in the most profound and fundamental manner. All life is interconnected and the great life-giving bank is the sea.

Our wastes cannot be "thrown away." We dump pollutants seemingly out of sight in the rivers and sea, but they eventually come back to us and our children with devastating impact -- through the food we eat, the water we drink, and the air we breathe.

If the sea continues to be used as our global sewer, and if

(next page, please)

we continue to disrupt the natural processes of our biosphere, we will undoubtedly bring upon ourselves catastrophe after catastrophe, ultimately depriving ourselves of the great resources of the sea and suffering from:

-- food contaminated beyond edibility.

-- waters ridden with disease-causing organisms.

-- the loss of vital marine products such as the marine algae extract, agar, a vital component for medical research.

-- the loss of species that may provide new sources of pharmaceuticals and other useful products.

-- shorelines and bays choked with sewage and scum, which discourage recreation and cost billions in tourism losses.

One cannot predict the exact nature of the catastrophe any more than one can describe being tossed about in an oncoming cyclone. But beyond the catastrophes above, the consequences of environmental disruption would read like a chapter out of Dante:

-- climatic changes that dramatically and dangerously alter global temperatures.

-- melting of the polar ice caps with the water levels of the oceans rising 100 feet or more.

-- population being driven inland only to meet with famine, chaos, and disease on a scale impossible to imagine.

Would the final act of global mismanagement create wretched remnants of the human race packed cheek by jowl on the remaining highlands, bewildered, starving, struggling to survive, trapped on what they would consider to be a dying planet?

One cannot say exactly, but this can be said:

Disaster in the oceans means disaster for man.

I beg you not to dismiss this possibility as science fiction. These horrors could happen. When we pollute our world there will be no place to hide.

Earth is the only planet we know of where life can exist. This is because it is that rarest of phenomena, a "water planet" -- a dynamic world water machine powered by the sun and

(over, please)

the moon, that provided the cradle in which life originated.

The ocean is life -- yet still I ask, do we earthlings cherish and guard it? Consider these deadly skirmishes in the enormous assault we have unwittingly mounted against our Water Planet ...

Killing Our Young

I implore you to understand that more than one billion children and adults do not have water safe enough to drink. That's about one-quarter of all the people in the entire world. Each year hundreds of thousands of people die from such horrors as cholera, typhoid, dysentery, hepatitis, and schistosomiasis -- die from disease because untreated municipal and human wastes are dumped directly into streams, rivers, and lakes. I can't understand. What are we doing to ourselves and to our children? Why do we let it go on?

An Ominous Warning

History is full of melancholy parables, and Easter Island is one of them -- a reminder that the resources of our island Earth are no less finite, a reminder that man's unparalleled creative gift seems fatally linked to its own self-destruct mechanism. Here, in the endless sea, a vagrant cell of human life anchored itself, created a civilization and vanished, leaving hundreds of gigantic stone statues and a handful of survivors with no conscious recollection that it had ever happened.

Yet if man is at least in part invented by himself, if living generations were born out of imaginations of people long dead, then the choices remain. Shall we -- islanders no less than they -- on island Earth -- pass on the riches of human invention and wisdom to living inheritors, or to mindless relics that mock all that was possible? Perhaps the islanders were right -- we are not victims of a god of evil; we are victims only of the evil we bring upon ourselves.

A New Look at "The Endless Bounty of the Sea"

Remember when the inexhaustible sea, so-called, was going to feed all the world's new billions? Twenty years ago I knew that the amount of life in the oceans was dwindling at a terrifying rate. Studies have shown that selected fish species are declining. Many of the most desired species of saltwater and freshwater fish

(next page, please)

- 5 -

have been over-exploited. When one species is
depleted, another becomes the focus of exploitation --
the cycle continues. Today it is not known which
species will recover.

I could add thousands more to these examples, and fill a
dozen volumes. But I hope these few will convey my distress
and concern at what is happening to our oceans, our planet, and
ourselves.

To do effective battle against such powerful forces of
destruction, our Society must be totally independent. No one
must say that The Cousteau Society was responsive to pressure
of any description. So our strength does not come from
government, institutional or selfish interests, but from
individuals like you and me.

How shall we accomplish our heavy task? We must present
the case of our Water Planet to hundreds of influential leaders
in government and industry. We must continue and dramatically
augment unconventional research into the nature and function of
the intricate elements of our fragile "water dependent"
ecosystem.

All these things are going to cost money, so I now most
earnestly and urgently implore your support.

Because the money you give now may literally help to
save the world. Save it, not only for ourselves, but
for our children and their children.

The enrollment card enclosed invites you to become a member
of The Cousteau Society at special introductory rates: $15 for
an individual membership; $25 for a family membership.

There are benefits, of course. For example, the Calypso
Log, a full-color bimonthly publication that reports on Society
expeditions, environmental issues, interviews with leading
thinkers, and much more; the Dolphin Log, a 16-page full-color
bimonthly magazine, available with family membership, filled
with facts, photos and games to interest and teach young people
about the oceans and ecology; a membership card; and an
attractive Society decal which we hope you will display
prominently and proudly.

So, please, join me as a member of The Cousteau Society ...
and stand up for life, for the future, for our Water Planet.

Gratefully,

Jacques-Yves Cousteau

Exhibit 13-14: The Cousteau Society

Comment:

This letter approaches perfection in the three decisive areas—reader attention, verisimilitude, and projection of an ominous warning.

Oddly, the letter runs five pages, with the sixth panel blank. This is the only questionable aspect of a letter whose clarity, choice of imagery, and pace exemplify the best of fund raising letter writing.

CHAPTER *14*

Miscellaneous Fund Raising Letters

CONSUMERS UNION NEWS DIGEST, P.O. BOX 2029, NORWALK, CT 06852

```
          "I spend 20 minutes with The Digest
          twice-a-month. I call it my information-
          insurance. It's easy to read and gets
          right to the point."

          A Consumers Union News Digest Subscriber

                         Tuesday 9:40 A.M.


Dear Reader:

Wouldn't it be great to discover a fast, easy way to

     track consumer news...

          keep up with trends...

               plug into new developments...

and to have the facts and information you need for your daily
decision-making.

Well, that's exactly what Consumers Union News Digest does.

          GET ALL THE IMPORTANT CONSUMER NEWS
               FROM 197 PUBLICATIONS

The Digest cuts through the information clutter for you. Our
staff digs through 197 publications to give the most important
pertinent facts and meaningful stories twice each month. Over the
course of a year that adds up to 4,937 magazines...
newsletters...trade journals...newspapers...industry and
government reports.

          CONSUMER PRODUCTS, SERVICES AND ISSUES

The Digest makes it easy to get to the heart-of-the news with 12
concise pages delivered to you twice-a-month.

If you're a consumer product manufacturer you'll find government
issues that affect your business...

If you're a consumer product marketer The Digest will help you
spot trends and consumer attitudes and opinions...

If you're in consumer services The Digest will help you find out
what's happening across-the-board -- fast and easy.

                                        (over please)
```

With The Digest, your knowledge will cover topics like these:

1.	Advertising	19.	Finance
2.	Agriculture	20.	Food & Nutrition
3.	Alcoholic Beverages	21.	Government
4.	Appliances	22.	Health & Medicine
5.	Automotive	23.	Insurance
6.	Business & Industry	24.	Legal Services
7.	Clothing & Textiles	25.	Media
8.	Computers	26.	New Products
9.	Consumer Affairs	27.	Retail Trade
10.	Consumer Research	28.	Safety
11.	Cosmetics & Toiletries	29.	Smoking
12.	Crime	30.	Taxes
13.	Children	31	Technology
14.	Demographics	32.	Telecommunications
15.	Economic Conditions	33.	Transportation
16.	Employment	34.	Travel
17.	Energy	35.	Warranties
18.	Environment	36.	Women

Just skim through The Digest to find...facts about a subject you
need to <u>research</u>...a trend you want to follow...or an area you'd
like a quick <u>briefing</u> on. You'll find the stories behind these
blurbs...

Which hamburger chain was charged with portraying
their hamburgers with "phony photographic
manipulations"...

Why baby-boomers are a threat to U.S. automakers...

The bad news for business and industry as Americans
gobble up more fish...

What's behind the new buzzword "eldercare" --
and why some predict it will be the sleeper issue
of the 1980's and the 1990's for employers...

How researchers are trying to fight baldness with a new
"combo" therapy treatment...

Unexpected "electrical pollution" that's
developing as more homes tap into solar energy...

How glucose affects aging...

Why your physician may be depressed, anxious,
worried and frustrated...

Why tomatoes, beef, potatoes, oranges, lettuce,
apples, peaches, pork, wheat, soybeans, beans,
carrots, chicken, corn and grapes can be as
dangerous as asbestos...

How your nest-egg savings compares to other
Americans...

The Digest doesn't have a fancy format. No elaborate
photos or expensive type. Just 12-pages of solid
information that's been carefully condensed to give you <u>fast
insights</u>. The result: <u>you're better informed in less time.</u>

And, The Digest is published by Consumers Union -- the same
people who publish Consumer Reports. So you're guaranteed
reliability and comprehensiveness.

<u>You'll learn how the nation's top thinkers and
trendsetters are sizing-up current affairs...</u>

What the <u>New England Journal of Medicine</u> thinks about
pesticide poisoning...

What the <u>Christian Science Monitor</u> predicts about
genetic engineering...

What advice the <u>Harvard Business Review</u> has about your
taxes and more...

<u>...and what the nation's top-policy makers are planning
for your future...</u>

Like Senator Chafee's of <u>Rhode Island</u>, recommendations
to Congress about food irradiation...

Senator Metzenbaum's new law to monitor airline
arrivals, cancellations, and overbookings...

How Representative Downing of <u>New York</u> plans to
protect U.S. trade...

And, from <u>California</u>, Representative Beilenson's,
action on anti-smoking ads...

A FREE BONUS FOR
ADDED INFORMATION COVERAGE

As a subscriber, you get a free Publication Directory. It gives you the complete name and address of every publication that appears in The Digest -- so it's easy to track down a publisher for copies of articles or additional information.

Just one more reason you'll be better informed, faster with The Digest.

GET TWO FREE ISSUES

Subscribe to a full year of Consumers Union News Digest for $48. When you enclose payment with your order you'll receive two free issues -- a total of 26 issues. Or choose to be billed later and receive 24 issues. Either way, you'll get your money-back on all unmailed issues if you are dissatisfied at anytime.

CONSIDER WHAT YOU GET...

- Easy access to the important news, information and trends from 197 magazines, newsletters, trade journals, newspapers, industry and government reports each year.
- The confidence that your knowledge of consumer news is comprehensive.
- A FREE BONUS listing of the names and addresses of publishers for each follow-up.
- Two free issues when you enclose payment.
- A full money-back guarantee.

There's no better, faster way to keep up with the news you need for both your job and personal life. Subscribe to Consumers Union News Digest now -- just return the enclosed card.

Sincerely,

Norman Leonarczyk
Director, Information Services

P.S. Two free issues of Consumers Union News Digest are yours. Simply return the enclosed postage-paid envelope with your payment.

Exhibit 14-1: Consumers Union

Comment:

The quotation above the greeting is weaker than it need be. Certainly Consumers Union can generate a testimonial with at least one specific in it. "It's easy to read and gets right to the point" is meaningless rhetoric, exposed more harshly because of the dominant position of this quotation.

Lack of specifics characterizes page one. Copy on page two, beginning, "Just skim through the Digest to find . . ." and carrying through the top of page three would have been a stronger, attention-grabbing opening.

The p.s. uses the term "postage-paid." Do you agree "postage-free" would be an improvement?

WE HAVE TWO VALUABLE BUYER'S GUIDES RESERVED IN YOUR NAME. AND THEY'RE

YOURS FREE!

WITH A LOW-COST INTRODUCTORY TRIAL SUBSCRIPTION TO CONSUMER REPORTS.

Dear Reader:

<u>Color TVs</u>. When we tested 19 & 20 inch TVs, we advised making a stereo set your first choice. Stereo TVs deliver markedly better sound than monophonic sets. Our tests also showed that even unlikely candidates such as talk shows benefit from a set equipped with stereo sound features. It's a little like being in the studio with Ed and Johnny.

<u>Lipsticks</u>. Want your lipstick to last a long time? Try Revlon Moon Drops Moisture Creme ($3.72) or Coty 24 ($4.07). Want a glossy look? Avon Coordinates (full color) ($1.99) and Cover Girl Luminesse ($2.29) are two good bets. One caveat: don't expect it all -- creaminess, staying-power and color stability from your lipstick. The best you can do is decide on the factor that's most important to you and compromise on the others.

<u>Small cars</u>. The make of a car is often a good predictor of reliability. However, while the 1987 Dodge Colt earned a "much better than average" rating for reliability when

(over please)

it was surveyed, the 1987 Dodge Omni/Charger, another small car from Chrysler Corporation, was "much worse than average" in reliability.

<u>Clothes dryers</u>. When we tested electric clothes dryers, we gave the Sears 66941 our top-rating. But it <u>was</u> expensive -- the average price was $648. The Sears model 66941 included lots of features to justify its high price -- on the other hand, the alternative models also performed quite well. For $196 <u>less</u> you might consider the Whirlpool LE9800XS.

From compact cars to compact-disc players...air conditioners to hair conditioners...home computers to home insurance...baby foods to gas barbecue grills... when you're ready to make a purchase, you need more than cash.

You need clear and unbiased brand-name Ratings. Plus tips. Tactics. And protection. Protection from deceptive advertising. Deceptive packaging. Empty warranties. Protection from disappointing or dangerous products. Protection from wasting your money and time.

For <u>objective information</u> untarnished by commercial interest of any kind, you need Consumer Reports. And now, just for trying Consumer Reports, you'll also receive:

* The 1988 Buying Guide Issue -- 400 pages packed with more than 2000 Consumer Reports Ratings and recommendations (a $5.95 value) is <u>yours free</u> just for trying Consumer Reports.

* The Medicine Show -- An indispensable guide to over-the-counter drugs and health products. A $6.50 value, it is <u>yours free</u> just for trying Consumer Reports.

Consumer Reports is unlike any other magazine published today. We refuse all outside advertising. We accept no free product samples. We buy the samples we test. We accept no commercial grants.

Most important, we are totally independent. <u>Absolutely unbiased. 100% on your side.</u>

The best. And the rest.

To compare products, you have to do more than compare prices. You have to compare performance. That's why, every month, Consumer Reports brings you brand-name Ratings and recommendations based on what a product really delivers. And whether or not it is a good buy.

When we tested the widely advertised "$3990" Yugo, we found it had the worst transmission we've seen in years -- plus remarkably poor fuel economy, too. We also found that it doesn't deliver its advertised price.

When we tested peanut butter we found the best were Jif crunchy-style and Hollywood Natural Unsalted creamy-style with the richest roasted-peanut taste. Other brand name and store brands tasted a bit raw or overroasted. And, the generic No Frills peanut butter tasted a bit rancid.

When we tested full-size vacuum cleaners, the Panasonic MC 6220 (at $210) got the same top rating we gave the Kirby Heritage II. But the Kirby cost $289 more.

Issues and answers

Every issue of Consumer Reports helps take the risk out of shopping, the stress out of choosing, the gamble out of paying the bill. As a regular reader, you'll discover reports that give you answers to questions like these:

.Which credit card is better: one with a low interest rate or one with no annual fee?
.Which cars are safest in crashes?
.Which car insurance company gives you the best service after an accident?
.Are natural vitamins more effective than synthetic brands? (the answer is no!)
.How safe is Nutrasweet?
.Do people aged 65 and older need Medicare-supplement insurance? (the answer is yes!)
.Do bathroom cleansers work better on bathrooms than all-around cleaning products? (the answer is no!)
.Which low-priced stereo speakers perform just as well as costlier models?
.Which is the only oven cleaner we judged safe

and effective? (Easy Off Non-caustic Formula Aerosol)
.Who makes the best fast food, the best frozen pizza, the best door locks, loudspeakers, laundry detergents?

.Which is the best microwave oven, computer monitor, mattress, moisturizer, moving company, pain reliever?

In every issue of Consumer Reports we give you easy-to-read Ratings of scores of brands and models of products you're likely to put in your garage, your living room, your child's room, your kitchen, your medicine cabinet.

In every issue we name names. List model numbers. Print prices. Tell you how well each product performs. Whether it's convenient. Effective. Economical. Safe to use.

From jeeps to heaps...

Every year we publish a special issue devoted solely to cars. You'll get our Ratings of more than 130 models -- all prices and all types. You'll also learn the repair records of more than 250 models. Plus how to finance a car. How to choose a good used car. How to combat the games dealers play with sticker prices. How to sidestep the "option elevator" -- and still get what you want.

Hassles and hazards you can avoid

In Consumer Reports you'll learn of important government recalls, for example: A child safety seat that may shatter in a crash. And a contact lens solution that may contain mold. You'll learn about vehicles that were recalled because they rolled with the transmission in park. You'll read about tests that showed some gas barbecue grills can cause a flash of flame. Bicycles with brakes that barely work when wet.

From nutrition and health...

When we rated plain vanilla ice creams, we found that Friendly's -- which we rated third in a field of 27 on its sensory quality -- had 140 calories per half-cup serving. Frusen Gladje (which came in #6) and Haagen Dazs (our #7) -- had 290 and 265 calories per half-cup serving, respectively.

187

When we tested chicken noodle soup, Town House Chunky
(Safeway), Kroger Chunky, Campbell's Home Cookin' and
Campbell's Chunky with Mushrooms got our highest sensory
Ratings. But if you're concerned about sodium in soup,
you'd better make your own -- servings of these soups had
sodium contents from 860mg to 1030mg.

In Consumer Reports, you'll find news on health
insurance. Vitamins. Pain killers. Sweeteners. Diet
programs. Dental care. Second-hand smoke. Salt.
Fiber. Calcium supplements. Cholesterol. High blood
pressure. Heart disease. Home exercise machines.
Tanning products and equipment.

...to investments and wealth

In Consumer Reports you'll find hundreds of
tips that can save you money (hundreds or
thousands of dollars a year).

Plus you'll also find dozens of important
reports on what to do with the money you save.

You'll find how to choose the right IRA (or other
pension plan). The right money-market fund or mutual
fund. The best kind of bank account. The best kind of
mortgage. The best sources for life, home and car
insurance. The best ways to use credit cards. The best
ways to improve your odds on a tax audit. The best ways
to save on air fares. The best ways to size up a
financial planner.

How to get your two free books

* Complete the enclosed form and return it in the
postpaid envelope. You'll receive a free copy of our
1988 Buying Guide (a $5.95 value). Its 400 pages are
packed with comparative Ratings of more than 2000
products.

* You'll also receive the most recent edition of The
Medicine Show (a $6.50 value) -- absolutely free. This
remarkably thorough 255-page book is an important
reference for you and your family.

* In addition you'll receive eleven regular monthly

(over please)

issues of Consumer Reports, including our Annual Auto
Issue and our Best Buy Gifts Issue (a total newsstand value
of $25.00). That's hundreds of brand-new, brand-name
Ratings, and scores of important tips and recommendations,
every single month.

* Plus...if you decide to become a subscriber, you'll
receive the 1989 Buying Guide just as soon as it is
published -- a $5.95 retail value.

Only after you have had a chance to judge the Buyer's
Guides and the sample issue do you have to decide whether
or not you wish to subscribe.

If you don't want to subscribe, simply write "cancel" on
our bill and return it. You owe nothing. You keep the two
Guides and the sample issue of CONSUMER REPORTS.

Please note: If you decide to subscribe, your cost under
this introductory offer is only $18. Purchased separately
these publications would cost $43.40.

-- a savings of over $25.00!

And under our money-back guarantee, you can cancel
anytime and receive a full and prompt refund on all
unmailed issues, no questions asked.

Please let us hear from you now -- while this offer is
still in effect!

Sincerely,

Jim Davis
Associate Director
Consumers Union

JD:pw

P.S.   No need to send money now, unless you prefer.
We'll gladly bill you later!

188

JQ/LE01

Exhibit 14-2: Consumers Union

Comment:

Compare the specifics of this letter with the generalizations of Exhibit 1.

This letter doesn't refer to a "cream-type lipstick"; it refers to "Revlon Moon Drops Moisture Creme ($3.72)." Can you imagine any recipient not finding many areas of personal interest?

This isn't a fund raising letter as such; but Consumers Union, as a nonprofit organization, competes in this field. The value of analyzing this letter isn't recognition of *what* it sells; rather, it's recognition of *how* it sells.

It began with a jolt at 8:32 a.m., May 18, 1980...an
earthquake registering 5.0 on the Richter scale. Then
seconds later...an explosion equal to the fury of a
ten-megaton bomb....

Mount St. Helens, a gleaming white peak in the Cascades,
erupted in a blast that took the lives of more than 60
people, imperiled thousands of others, and spewed clouds
of ash across the northwestern United States.

Dear Member:

What causes such catastrophes?

Now you have the opportunity to discover how Earth's restless churning
can account for volcanoes, earthquakes, and "tidal waves"...drastic changes
in climate...the biblical plagues of Egypt...even the shape of life itself.
All in National Geographic's highly acclaimed EXPLORING OUR LIVING PLANET.

This update of the landmark volume, first published in 1983,
brings you a fascinating look at famous legends of the Earth
and the exciting discoveries that have transformed 200 years
of earth science, illustrated with spectacular photographs
and specially commissioned paintings.

EXPLORING OUR LIVING PLANET was written by Dr. Robert
Ballard, the marine geologist who is best known for
leading the 1985 Titanic expedition and who also helped
make revolutionary discoveries about the ocean floor.
Ballard's discoveries have been featured in GEOGRAPHIC
articles and the Society's public television specials.

The book features a foreword by Walter Cronkite, former
CBS News correspondent, anchorman, and originator and
commentator of the television science series, "Universe."

You won't want to miss this new edition of the entertaining and
authoritative book that sheds light on ancient mysteries...and adds important chapters to a detective story that began more than two centuries ago.

                    *   *   *

Benjamin Franklin was among those who believed that our continents
might be moving. Likewise, mapmakers and geographers of his day noticed

---

that Africa's west coast would fit neatly into the curve of South America's
east coast...and Africa's northwest shoulder against the U.S. East Coast.

Geologists and biologists also wondered about the similarity of coal
veins in North America and Europe...about the fossil record that showed
tropical ferns growing in Greenland at the same time glaciers covered part
of Brazil and what is now equatorial Africa. And something had to account
for the existence of identical plants and animals separated by huge oceans.

You'll meet a man who explains what seem to be amazing contradictions
in nature -- German meteorologist Alfred Wegener. Discover how, in 1912,
he proposed that many millions of years ago all the continents were part of
one landmass he named Pangea, surrounded by the world ocean of Panthalassa.
That this supercontinent broke into two pieces called Gondwana and Laurasia,
which continued to break apart into a giant jigsaw puzzle -- Earth's surface
today.

In EXPLORING OUR LIVING PLANET, you'll see how all this occurred over
millions of years. You'll learn how the concept of "continental drift"
gave birth to the now widely accepted theory of plate tectonics. And you'll
pick up astounding facts about what's taking shape on our globe today. For
example, did you know...

that the Himalaya are still growing? That the ground
under Los Angeles will eventually leave the West Coast and
head for Alaska? That the Red Sea is opening up...Hawaii
is growing a new island...and Africa an inland ocean?

You'll understand better how your world works, and more about its future,
as you join scientific expeditions to far-flung corners of the globe....

Embark upon an African adventure to see where the continent is actually splitting in two, creating a giant rift valley from Mozambique to
Ethiopia. Along that rift, anthropologists such as Mary and Richard Leakey
and Donald Johanson continue to discover some of humankind's earliest
ancestors in layers of volcanic ash.

In Tanzania, visit Ngorongoro Crater, an extinct volcano where zebras,
wildebeests, and other animals roam free in a natural, arena-shaped zoo.
Locate the source of the Nile, hidden by the shifting land in central
Africa. Gaze up in awe at the eight volcanoes of Zaire's towering Virunga
range -- and see one crater three-quarters of a mile wide fill the night sky
with a sullen red glow and the threat of violent eruption.

Then, follow man's first steps into the hidden part of our world, the
strange realm miles below the ocean waves -- down, down, to darkness, cold,
and incredible pressure. From the ports of deep-sea submersibles, peer
at landscapes never seen before: lava lakes, a valley deeper than the Grand
Canyon, and a 46,000-mile-long mountain range, where Earth's hot breath
feeds bizarre communities of life...

a discovery that challenges previous theories about

the beginning of life on our planet.

Visit Iceland, possibly the world's most volcanic nation, where one field
grew so hot that farmers once dug up potatoes already half baked! You'll
be intrigued by other Icelandic stories similarly strange: the mysterious
blue haze that poisoned the countryside and darkened skies in Europe...a
minister who defied an approaching lava flow by closing the doors of his
church and delivering a sermon. The town that fought a raging volcano...and
half won.

Leaving the land of ice and fire, you'll travel to the realm of the
volcano goddess Pele, who once demanded and received human sacrifices from
the Hawaiian Islanders. Learn about the birth of Loihi: Some scientists say
this new island forming off the Hawaiian coast is the result of a magma plume
poking up through the Earth's crust. Island chains could have been formed
when the ocean floor <u>moved</u> over these plumes, called "hotspots."

You may be surprised to know there's a hotspot under
the U.S. mainland. Geologists are calling Yellowstone
National Park a "volcanic time bomb" that could explode
one day with the force of thousands of Mount St. Helens!

Age-old enigmas await you in biblical lands, as you search for the
cities of Sodom and Gomorrah, which archaeologists believe may lie beneath
the waters of the Dead Sea. Discover also that the walls of Jericho came
tumbling down -- perhaps not at the sound of Joshua's trumpet -- but from
the force of a massive earthquake.

Can you feel the Earth moving under your feet? You might imagine so,
when you venture to California along the San Andreas Fault...to Loch Ness,
where North America and Europe were joined millions of years ago...to
Guatemala, India, China, and other places where two huge pieces of
Earth's surface scrape against one another, sometimes catching edges and
building up tremendous pressure. The inevitable release causes earthquakes registering high on the Richter scale.

What exactly happens when one slab of the Earth slips under another?
Take a look at the infamous "Ring of Fire," the great chain of volcanoes
that rims the Pacific Ocean. As the ocean floor slowly disappears beneath
enormous trenches, mountains such as Mount St. Helens are born in fire.
Undersea earthquakes shake the land. And <u>tsunamis</u> -- great surges of water
-- roll from Alaska to New Zealand.

You'll be fascinated by the ways our restless planet has shaped human
history: redirecting the course of the Maya civilization...burying for
centuries the Roman city of Pompeii...leaving a trail of mineral riches
that lured Europeans to the New World.

And consider the mystery of Santorini, known to Greeks as <u>Thera</u>, where
only islands remain to outline the flooded caldera of a great volcano.

Some scholars have asked whether Thera's colossal eruption in the

Bronze Age affected the collapse of the Minoan civilization.
How is it connected to the legendary continent of Atlantis?
And did it bring on the plagues of Egypt and give rise to
the story of the parting of the waters?

Thrill to the quest to unlock Earth's mysteries...from mountaintops to
ocean depths...from prehistory to yesterday...in the fascinating pages of
EXPLORING OUR LIVING PLANET!

                    *   *   *

As a member of the National Geographic Society, you have the privilege
of examining this marvelous publication in your home -- without purchase
obligation. To do so, simply mail the enclosed Reservation Card without
delay. Send no money now.

When your copy of EXPLORING OUR LIVING PLANET arrives, share it with
family and friends. Leaf through the generously illustrated pages. Marvel
at photographs taken on the scene of powerful volcanic eruptions and
earthquakes. See dramatic paintings of nature's powers at work throughout
geological time. Unfold the map of the Mid-Ocean Ridge, the world's longest
mountain range...and be amazed by landscapes that, until just a few years
ago, we never knew existed.

Measuring 8 3/4" x 11 1/8", the book includes 97 maps, paintings, and
diagrams, the foldout map of the Mid-Ocean Ridge, 177 superb photographs,
and a detailed index -- all in 366 pages.

EXPLORING OUR LIVING PLANET, available exclusively from National
Geographic, is unsurpassed by any other single volume on this important
subject. To order your own copy, mail the enclosed postage-paid Reservation
Card today.

                              Sincerely,

                              Owen R. Anderson

ORA/ab   Owen R. Anderson

P.S. If you already own a copy of EXPLORING OUR LIVING PLANET, why not
      order a second copy for a friend who'll enjoy it as much as you do?

191

Exhibit 14-3: National Geographic Society

Comment:

Read the letter through the eyes of the intended recipient, an existing member of the National Geographic Society.

The letter is loaded with specifics, "teaser" references to the book's content. For most fund raisers, who have no books to sell, the letter is only a curio; but when the opportunity exists to tie your own fund raising to a base the reader may find more exciting, this is an excellent model.

American Association of Individual Investors

625 North Michigan Avenue
Chicago, Illinois 60611
(312) 280-0170

"The American Association of Individual Investors is an independent non-profit corporation formed for the purpose of assisting individuals in becoming effective managers of their own assets through programs of education, information and research."

You are invited to join us....over 100,000 serious independent investors improving our ability to deal with the increasingly complex world of investment. This letter tells you who we are, our objectives and the benefits of membership.

Dear Investor:

If in 1925, you had invested $1,000 in the stocks in the S&P 500, you would now have about $348,000 (excluding taxes and reinvesting dividends).

But if you had invested the $1,000 in smaller companies, you would now have almost $1.2 million dollars. And the smaller companies were generally purchased by individuals, showing that the serious individual can outperform the institutions and the popular market averages.

There is substantial historic evidence that stocks of non-giant companies, stocks not pursued by institutions, and stocks not covered by a large number of analysts outperform the market.

In addition to better long-term performance, these stocks--which we call Shadow Stocks--also avoid much of the volatility caused by "program trading," option strategies and "me too" institutional approaches such as portfolio insurance.

So we believe that you, as an individual, can obtain better investment results than most professionals -- if you are willing to spend the necessary time and exert the necessary effort. And AAII will help you, to the extent that The Boston Globe has called us "...the rough equivalent of a graduate school for little capitalists."

It was the conviction that individuals wanted to make their own decisions, increase their knowledge of investment theory and practice, and get better investment results that led us to form AAII in 1979.

Since then, our members have achieved better investment results and the non-profit American Association of Individual Investors has grown to well over 100,000 members. According to The New York Times, "A different approach, and well worth considering, is the one suggested by the American Association of Individual Investors, a non-profit organization..."

While most of our members are experienced investors with substantial sums to invest, we have programs for newer investors and those who are just beginning to accumulate net worth. The Wall Street Journal aptly describes us as a non-profit, educational group for cautious and serious investors.

Our varied educational materials cover stocks, bonds, money market investments, mutual funds, real estate, options, futures, precious metals, collectibles,

(over, please)

---

as well as the related topics of taxes, estates, using computers, and the overall management of your wealth.

We don't manage your money. We help you manage it better. Our purpose is to be a "professional association for non-professionals". To accomplish this, we provide ongoing investment education through the AAII Journal, home study materials, special publications, traveling seminars, national meetings, and local chapters in major metropolitan areas.

We offer the following benefits to our members--they are provided free with membership or at special member prices...

The AAII Journal (free to members)

Published 10 times a year, the Journal provides a continuing stream of information on investment theory and practice. Topics in a typical issue might include--how holding periods affect stock risk, evaluating current tax shelters, evaluating investment newsletters, modern portfolio theory, the effect of a tax change on investment decisions. There are regular departments: "Investor Workshop" provides practical explanations of investment mathematics; "Points of View" conducts interviews with leading investment professionals.

A special section of the Journal provides the results of screens that many investors use to select stocks (P/E ratio, debt/equity, book value, earnings growth, etc.). This can save you considerable time in your search for undervalued stocks. The Journal also identifies and examines the Shadow Stocks--stocks ignored by institutions because of size but available to individuals.

The Annual "Individual Investor's Guide to No-Load Mutual Funds" (free to members)

Published and distributed to our membership each June, this book provides in-depth analysis of almost 400 funds and discusses the process of selecting the best funds for you. This widely acclaimed book with 600,000 copies in circulation sells to the general public for $19.95, but as an AAII member it is yours free. Barron's calls it "... one of the best books around on the subject."

Local Chapter Membership

There are 40 chapters now operating in metropolitan areas and more are being added. Chapters offer the opportunity to meet with fellow members and to hear experts discuss a variety of investment topics. The similarity of interests has led to close personal relationships among members and the development of many SIGS (special interest subgroups) in such areas as computers, real estate investment, mutual funds and stock screening approaches. As a new member you can participate with no additional dues.

AAII Year-End Tax Strategy Guide (free to members)

Each year at the end of November members receive an extensive guide to the tax planning aspects of investment based on the latest laws and rulings.

Investment Seminars (at reduced cost)

Over 60 seminars are conducted in cities throughout the United States each year. There is an Introductory Seminar as well as advanced seminars in Security Analysis, Real Estate, Financial Planning, Mutual Funds and our newest - Economic

193

Analysis for Investment Decision Making. We have recently put an introductory seminar on video for those who have a difficult time traveling to seminars.

Study Programs (at reduced cost)

AAII offers a wide variety of home study materials to its members. These materials are constantly being expanded and revised and are designed to take individual investors as far as they want to go--from basics to the concepts of a graduate level course in investment theory.

Computer Users Newsletter and Subgroup

Because a rapidly growing number of AAII members are using computers in their investment decision making, a special subgroup has been formed. This optional benefit includes Computerized Investing, a bimonthly newsletter evaluating investment software and hardware, which is published by AAII. In addition, there is a member software exchange program. An electronic bulletin board is up and many investment programs are available for downloading. The price of Computerized Investing, the paramount publication in this area, is $25 per year to members, $49 per year to the general public.

AND...

Substantial discounts on investment software and investment publications (i.e., Money, Investor's Daily, Financial World, Business Week, Fortune.)

Through Standard & Poor's Corporation we have arranged for members to receive S&P reports for a large number of corporations at no cost.

Members are eligible to apply for a special AAII Gold MasterCard with no initial fee and with very special privileges ($1,000,000 travel insurance--free, credit card protection--free, rental car deductibility waiver insurance--free).

Members are eligible to participate in a special AAII money market bank account. A bank money market account that guarantees a yield above the average of all money market funds and provides the FDIC insurance of a bank. The best of both worlds. This single benefit could earn you much more than membership dues.

PLUS...

Research - The Hidden Benefit

The value of the AAII Journal, our seminars and all of our materials is enhanced by the internal research of our staff. In addition, we screen current academic research (often before publication) to find insights into improving the investment performance of our members.

We do this because research of interest primarily to the individual investor often is not covered by the business press. We not only report on that research, but we sponsor much of it by awards to doctoral students and faculty.

As a result we have been able to interest more researchers in studies relating to the strategies of the individual investor. You, as a member, are the first to learn the results.

That, in a straightforward way, is who we are, what we try to do, and our

(over, please)

---

specific programs. AAII is a totally independent non-profit association. We do not even accept advertising in our Journal. Our programs are not static. They have grown and changed to meet the needs of our members and will continue to do so with, we hope, your participation and insight.

Dues are only $49 per year. A single insight gained from our Journal, a seminar or other AAII program will repay the membership cost many times over. In fact, the publication discounts and other special benefits may exceed the dues. As Forbes says "The $49 a year it costs to belong is a bargain. The AAII Journal is a thoughtful mix of investment professionals' views ..."

However, you risk nothing by joining .....

Because we cannot fully explain AAII in a letter, the Advisory Board set this policy: If you decide at any time during the year after joining that AAII is not contributing to your investment skills, we will refund your annual membership dues in full.

We offer this unusual assurance because not only do most of our members renew each year, but 20% have become lifetime members.

We are not offering any magic formulas for overnight riches. Successful management of your assets is a long-term proposition requiring self-discipline and a reasonable investment of time and effort.

But suppose that through improved decision making, you raised your average annual yield by only 3%. In 25 years, the individual earning 12% will have twice the assets of an individual earning 9%.

Perhaps you can do better. Are you ready to try?

If so, mail the Enrollment Form with your membership payment in the enclosed postage-paid envelope. You will receive a Membership Packet which will include your AAII Membership Card and information on how to take advantage of the varied AAII programs.

Enroll now! There is so much potential gain and only a few minutes risk.

Sincerely,

James B. Cloonan

James B. Cloonan
Chairman, Advisory Board

JBC:jc

P.S. If you enroll now, in addition to the other membership benefits, we will send you a free copy of the AAII booklet, "A Lifetime Strategy for Investing in Common Stocks." Many members have told us that this guide, first published as a series in the AAII Journal, has changed their entire investment outlook.

For some independent views of AAII, please see the back of the Enrollment Form.

Exhibit 14-4: American Association of Individual Investors

Comment:

Does the four-line message above the greeting help or hinder the possibility of this letter being read?

Opinion: Both. The first sentence is self-questioning. Can 100,000 investors be considered "independent"? Yes, the number of members is reassuring, but this, the only useful component of this sentence, can be incorporated into the text. The second sentence, standing alone, would be a stronger overline.

The letter opens with a "touchstone." I think it's a poor one, because it hurls down an impossible gauntlet eliminating almost every recipient:

> **"If in 1925 you had invested $1,000 . . . you would now have . . . ."**

For any reader of this letter to qualify, he or she would have had to be at least 21 years old in 1925. That would put the reader at the upper end of the octogenarian bracket, or beyond.

Some of this copy is superior. Example:

"We don't manage your money. We help you manage it better."

Suggestion: Avoid statements such as, "Because we cannot fully explain AAII in a letter . . ." This tells the reader you want him to make a decision based on partial information.

The p.s. makes an additional offer, a sound procedure. Pointing out that the booklet was "first published as a series in the *AAII Journal*" detracts from its uniqueness.

United States Olympic Committee
OLYMPIC HOUSE 1750 East Boulder Street, Colorado Springs, Colorado 80909

GAMES OF THE XXIV OLYMPIAD. Seoul. Korea. September 17-October 2, 1988

September 2, 1988

M. Lewis
P.O. Box 15725
Plantation, Florida 33318

Dear M. Lewis:

Somewhere in a lonely field in Kansas a 15-year-old boy jumps as far as he can. Is he the next Carl Lewis?

And on a dusty road in Vermont, a girl thinks of Joan Benoit Samuelson -- and runs another mile.

And in your home, you read this letter and think, "The Olympic Games? But they're here and now!"

It's not too late for you to do your part. U.S. athletes are making the final push toward Gold, working harder than ever to shave precious fractions of a second off their times, to gain a tenth of an inch in distance. And they need your help. NOW.

Your support now can make the difference. You can turn bronze into gold for one of your country's athletes. Won't you join your team now, and send $25 or even $10 for these crucial days and weeks of the 1988 Olympic Games?

Please display the decal I've enclosed to show your support. Then choose from the official 1988 Olympic awards offered exclusively to U.S. team members.

Make that extra effort with the young long jumper -- go that extra mile with the runner. It's a team effort -- and the team needs you now!

Sincerely,

Robert H. Helmick
President

P.S. If you give $25 or more, I'll send you a spectacular 20" x 36" full-color poster as a bonus award.

Exhibit 14-5: United States Olympic Committee

Comment:

The 1988 Olympiad resulted in increased public skepticism about the true nature of these games and the participating athletes.

Cash subsidies, wild endorsement contracts, and a brewing scandal over steroids have dulled some of the luster. Supporting the games no longer is automatic patriotism; it leans toward coterie-chauvinism.

This letter, mailed third class as the games were under way, may have been sent too late. The tie is tenuous:

> **"U.S. athletes are making the final push toward Gold, working harder than ever to shave precious fractions of a second off their times, to gain a tenth of an inch in distance. And they need your help. Now.**

How? Why?

If the games already were under way, what would additional money do? How would the Committee use it?

A suggestion, if you become involved in the 1992 Olympic Games, or if your cause isn't universally loved:

Wave a flag. The U.S. Olympic Committee can wave *the* flag. Suggesting lack of patriotism engenders guilt; suggesting failure to help athletes has little worth among those who haven't previously given.

Florida Special Olympics

Sponsor an Athlete

August 15, 1988

Dear Friend,

I hope you'll take a moment now to sign and return the enclosed "Winner's Medal."

To most of us it doesn't look very important but to a mentally handicapped person, this medal is something very special indeed.

You see, it's their ticket to Florida Special Olympics and chance to feel -- perhaps for the first time -- the sheer joy of competition and winning.

For a handicapped athlete, a stadium filled with runners and jumpers, wheelchair competitions, and an atmosphere of excitement, is a dream come true.

But the sad fact is that only one out of six eligible athletes can participate in Florida Special Olympics -- simply from a lack of funds.

Although it costs only $37.50 per athlete each year, we just do not have the money to train, equip, house and transport every handicapped person who wishes to compete.

This year our goal is to include hundreds, if not thousands, of the athletes we couldn't sponsor last year ...which means thousands more dollars we need to raise!

And that's why I am writing to you today.

I believe you are the kind of person who would want to

2639 North Monroe Street, Suite 151-A • Tallahasse, Florida 32303 • (904) 385-8178

offer this life changing opportunity to a deserving athlete.

Here's what you have to do to help:

First, decide that you wish to become the personal sponsor of a Florida Special Olympian by making a tax deductible gift of $37.50 today.

Second, sign the "Winner's Medal" sponsorship card I've enclosed for you. You can even write your own personal message of encouragement to your sponsored athlete.

And finally, send in your gift and your signed "Winner's Medal" using the enclosed envelope.

When we receive your "Winner's Medal," we will give it to an eager special athlete on our waiting list -- who will hang it proudly from his or her neck.

I can't stress enough how much your sponsorship gift means to these mentally retarded children and adults.

You see, our athletes are indeed very, very special.

So many of these people face challenges that seem overwhelming or impossible to overcome. But instead of letting their disability get the best of them, they run and jump and compete with all their strength.

And even if they don't come in first, or second, or even third -- these special athletes are still winners. Because they know that just doing their best is the most important thing.

Your unselfish gift will help an athlete feel the joys and triumphs that can be so rare for a mentally retarded person. Thank you so much for caring.

Sincerely,

Ken Magee
Executive Director

P.S. Remember, just $37.50 will sponsor a Florida Special Olympics athlete for an entire year!

Please help make a special athlete's dream come true by sending me your sponsorship gift today.

Congratulations!
"You're a Winner"

I want you to know...
you're a winner in life!

And this medal card is sent
with a lot of love
from

_____
(signature)

(If you'd like to write your athlete a special
message of encouragement -- just use the
space below.)

_____
_____
_____
_____
_____
_____

Exhibit 14-6: Florida Special Olympics

Comment:

The "Winner's Medal" is a separate enclosure, a personal message to an athlete competing in the Special Olympics. It stands apart from the response device, but obviously the donor is expected to return it with a contribution.

Does this enclosure, requiring the donor to write a personal message, help response? The Florida Special Olympics would know, but only if they tested the mailing with and without the Winner's Medal.

The letter bothered me on two levels: First, the girl in the photograph seems healthy and happy. We see no evidence of any handicap. Any identification would have helped. Second, the word "equip" adds a curiously professional overtone.

The closing paragraph of the letter is a quietly forceful guilt-generator, in my opinion the proper way to end this message.

The American Legion

★ NATIONAL HEADQUARTERS ★ P.O. BOX 7017 ★ INDIANAPOLIS, INDIANA 46207 ★

For God and Country

OFFICE OF THE
NATIONAL COMMANDER

SPECIAL MONEY-SAVING OFFER
FOR NEW MEMBERS ONLY!

Dear Fellow Veteran,

First, let me take this opportunity to apologize to you. For whatever reason . . . your name does not yet appear on our membership rolls . . . and that tells me . . . we may have erred. Today, I'm inviting you to join. The plain truth is . . . **THE AMERICAN LEGION NEEDS YOU!**

I know that not everyone has the time to be active in a veterans organization. Regardless, **every veteran should still belong.** To show you just how important you are to The American Legion . . . we're prepared to put our money where our mouth is . . . and make you a special one-time, money-saving membership offer.

Here's the offer. Enclose <u>only $17</u>, and we'll validate your membership through 1988 and all of 1989! You'll receive a 1989 membership card valid through December 31, 1989 . . . entitling you to all the benefits and services enjoyed by over 2.8 million members worldwide. That's almost three months of free membership benefits and privileges!

You may ask, "Why is it so important to the Legion that I join?". The answer is simple. Without the support of a continuously growing membership, the Legion's strong voice in Congress could be weakened when it is needed most. With all the current and proposed VA budget cuts, it is now more important than ever that The American Legion strengthen its stand on retaining Disability Compensation and Pensions, Veterans preference, Veterans Outreach Centers, the VA Home Loan Program, and VA Health Care for those in need.

And just as important, when you join the Legion, you get the self-satisfaction of knowing that you are helping someone less fortunate than yourself. You'll be helping the Legion combat drug and alcohol abuse among young people . . . teenage suicide . . . missing children . . . and child abuse. And that's not all.

Your dues support programs like . . . Special Olympics . . . Legion Baseball . . . Flag Education . . . Boys and Girls State . . . High School Oratorical Programs . . . and many other programs designed to strengthen the moral fiber of our youth. But being a Legion member isn't all giving . . . there's something in it for you, too.

Your Legion membership card gives you access to over 15,000 American Legion Posts throughout the free world. Whether you take a fishing trip to Alaska . . . a tropical vacation in Hawaii . . . a golf junket to England . . . or a camping trip to the Grand Canyon . . . your membership card gives you access to a Legion Post and guarantees that you'll have a friend nearby.

And there's more . . .

(over, please)

Legion membership entitles you to a subscription to The American Legion Magazine at no additional cost . . . colorful monthly issues packed full of general interest features . . . interviews with top government officials, to give you a better understanding of the operation of our federal agencies . . . debates on the "Big Issues" from both the Democratic and Republican point of view, so you can see both sides of the story . . . updates on changes in Veterans' benefits and other legislation that affects you as a Veteran . . . information on outfit reunions, to help you renew old friendships . . . and even occasional stories of days gone by (always true) . . . to jog your memory . . . and much, much more!

The list goes on, but I think you can see why your membership is so important to the Legion. So please accept this special one-time offer and join The American Legion today! You'll be helping yourself, your fellow Veterans, and the youth of our nation . . . all for just $17.

To take advantage of this special money-saving membership offer, here's all you do. Complete and sign the enclosed enrollment form and mail it along with your $17 dues in the postage-paid envelope provided.

ACT NOW AND I'LL SEND YOU INFORMATION ON <u>FREE</u>, MONEY-SAVING TRAVEL AND LODGING DISCOUNTS YOU'LL RECEIVE JUST FOR BEING A LEGION MEMBER!

Sincerely yours,

H.F. Gierke

H.F. Gierke
National Commander
The American Legion

P.S. If you have recently joined The American Legion, please pass this special membership offer on to a friend.

201

Exhibit 14-7: American Legion

Comment:

The first paragraph at once establishes a relationship from zero-ground, an excellent rhetorical ploy.

Benefits seem to abound in this 1½-page letter. The message is clear, non-pleading, and direct.

Only the p.s. seems to miss an opportunity. Instead of establishing an expiration date, it mildly suggests lack of exclusivity. A more effective p.s. might have been, "I'm holding open your membership at this special $17 rate until [DATE]." An expiration date is logical for any offer projecting reader-benefit.

CHAPTER *15*

A Few Helpful Rules for Writing Fund Raising Letters

The line between opinion and prejudice isn't always clear. One problem of being a curmudgeon is that opinions and prejudices melt into a single blob of bias.

From statements and examples in the previous chapters, I've extrapolated some rules for fund raising letter writing. These are *my* self-imposed rules, and I offer them for your evaluation, not for your blind acceptance:

—"We need your help" is a worn-out plea.

—The deadliest attitude in fund raising is, "We always do it this way."

—Testing brings accurate information. Speculation based on personal history and personal bias (even including all the rules in this chapter *except* this one) brings results whose accuracy itself is speculative.

—(The Law of Preconceived Fund Raising Mailing Opinion) Preconceived opinions mean absolutely nothing.

—The strongest word in fund raising is "you."

—If you don't see anything wrong with "Enclosed please find," take another look at your own letters for pomposity and non-communication.

—Specifics outsell generalities.

—(The Anti-Hair-Spray Rule) A neatness complex will cost you.

—Use a typewriter face for a fund raising letter.

—Emotion outpulls intellect. Typewriting is emotional. Typesetting is intellectual. Handwriting is more emotional than typewriting, but use it sparingly or impact dissipates.

—Ragged right is more readable and more personal than flush-right.

—Indent the first line of paragraphs, to enhance personalization.

—Clarity is paramount over any other ingredient of your mailing. Without clarity, you've transmitted no message. Without a message, the target-individual *can't* respond.

—Beware of acronyms, of governmentalese, of initials instead of words.

—Big words are enemies of clarity.

—Write inside the experiential background of the typical donor. Forget your own.

—No paragraphs longer than seven lines.

—Tell the reader what to do.

—The five great fund raising motivators: fear, exclusivity, greed, guilt, and anger.

—It's almost impossible to overcircularize your bank of existing contributors.

—If you want your targets to *feel* like an in-group, treat them as family. Give them certificates and membership cards (gold ones for regular donors, "Advisory Board" membership for heaviest donors). Your family deserves no less.

—Active voice outpulls passive voice.

—Stay away from promotions which give grist to *any* critic.

—A letter with a p.s. tends to outpull a letter without a p.s. But if you enclose more than one letter, put a p.s. on only one of them.

—A principal rule of letter writing: No plural targets. It's "you," not "those of you."

—"Number one" or "#1" usually has a *positive* overtone. Look for a more negative phrase when referring to a sad human condition.

—Statistics don't motivate. Examples and victims do.

—If your letter seems flat and uninspired, consider eliminating the first paragraph or two. Some letters suffer from the writer's inability to get into gear quickly enough.

—Avoid three, five, or seven page letters unless you use the extra panel for photographs, illustrations, newspaper article reprints, or some other reinforcement.

—Be certain every paragraph makes you either a hero or a martyr.

—The writer always has a stronger way to begin a message than "There is . . ." or "There are . . ."

—Photographs and word-descriptions should match.

—When you make a *positive* reference, write *as soon as,* not *when.*

—Reserve "Dear Friend" as an opening for cold lists. "Good morning!" is both brighter and less arm's-length for those who already support you, if you don't want to use "Dear Member."

—Bullets, even though terse, damage the effect of urgency. They're a thoughtful listing, therefore contrived. The reader's supercharged interest becomes analytical.

—The p.s. should punch, not stroke. When you write a p.s., ask yourself: Will it *increase* contributions?

—(The Rule of Political Agitation) When raising funds within a group united by a single interest, mirror their prejudices as strongly as possible.

—$E^2 = 0$: The more points one emphasizes, the less emphasis pertains to any point.

—Use underlining sparingly, because each underline shares emphasis with all other underlines.

—Two postscripts are invariably weaker than a single postscript.

—Tying a mailing to a specific day, or time of year, enables the fund raiser to avoid the image of perpetual nag.

—Words such as *studying* and *learning* are deadly in any type of direct mail solicitation.

—If you use anger as your motivator, stay in character. Keep the tone constant and the pace tight and fast. Downshifting costs dollars, because it suggests chagrin over what's been written before.

—A potent resuscitator of dormant contributors is the "How did we fail you?" approach.

—If you use celebrities as spokespeople, keep them in character or verisimilitude vanishes.

—A letter whose appeal is greater among lower income groups than among higher income groups is not usually the best approach in direct mail fund raising.

—Distractions such as mechanical tricks unrelated to message = thinned impact.

—"Postage-free" is superior to "postage-paid" when referring to a reply envelope enclosed with the mailing.

—Avoid statements such as, "Because we cannot fully explain this important cause in a letter . . ." This tells the reader you want him to make a decision based on partial information.

—If you claim importance, prove it.

—If your cause isn't universally loved, wave a flag.

—Episodes or victims are light-years better than percentages in their ability to motivate the reader to contribute.

—An expiration date is logical for any offer projecting reader-benefit.

—Contractions ("I've," "Let's," "You're") are more convivial than spelled-out words ("I have," "Let us," "You are"). The fund raising letter writer can use this information either way, to establish the desired tone and relationship.

—Tests and unemotional analyses are the routes to improved fund raising response. Ego-driven edicts and decisions based on a "We've always done it this way" attitude are the routes to reduced response.

Index

N

National Anti-Vivisection Society, 76
National Committee to Preserve
    Social Security, 82–84
National Council for the Deaf, 58–59
National Geographic Society,
    190–192
National Institute for Jewish
    Hospice, 142–144
National Multiple Sclerosis Society,
    49–51
National PAC, 139–141
National Rifle Association, 119–120
National Taxpayers Union, 23–36
National Wildlife Federation,
    172–173
Neatness complex, 7
North Shore Animal League, 77–78

O

Openings, 130, 132, 138, 178, 204
  effective, 80, 84, 107, 108, 119,
    164, 202
  ineffective, 43, 45, 53, 54, 68–69,
    89, 96, 99, 101, 105, 110, 135,
    146, 161, 177, 195
  positive, 50, 204
Overcirculizing, 14, 19, 204

P

Paragraphs, 12, 69, 204
Passive voice, 15, 47, 69, 96, 202,
    204
Patriotism, 120, 197, 206
Photographs, 94, 96, 151, 205
Pomposity, 6, 203
Preconceived opinions, 36, 203
Prejudices, mirroring, 116
Premiums, 18–19, 84, 108, 173
  apparent value, 19
Presentation: cost, 19, 158
  computer-personalization, 19
  hand-written, 47
  materials, 158
Providing partial information, 205

P.S., 151, 173, 185, 205
  diluting, 40, 119, 138, 204
  effective, 59, 90, 146, 156, 168,
    175, 195
  ineffective, 43, 84, 89, 94, 96, 99,
    103, 144, 154, 202
Publisher's Clearing House, 18, 78

R

Ragged right, 7, 8, 204
Response device, 3, 67, 128
Rule of Political Agitation, 115–116,
    119, 120, 205

S

St. Jude Children's Research
    Hospital, 23, 37–40
St. Louis Symphony, 45
Salesian Missions, 137–138
Salutations, 45, 47, 50, 99, 205
Salvation Army, 110–111
S.A. National Council for the Deaf,
    see National Council for the
    Deaf
Saturation factor, 14
Sierra Club, 176–178
Simon Wiesenthal Center, 127–136
SPCA, Johannesburg, 75
Specificity, 37, 78, 84, 128, 151,
    156, 164, 185, 189, 192, 204,
    205
Specifics Superiority Principle, 6
Statistics, 53, 94, 101, 204, 206
Sweepstakes, 2, 14, 18–19, 46, 61,
    78, 120
  language use, 18

T

Testimonial Copy, 53, 185
Testing, 3
  comparison, 4, 61, 146
Tests, 2–4, 19, 107, 120, 201, 203,
    206
Timing, 128, 205
Typewriter face, 7, 8, 66, 68, 109,
    138, 204